The People of
FIFE
at Home and Abroad
1800-1850

By
David Dobson

Copyright © 2022
by David Dobson
All Rights Reserved

Published for Clearfield Company by
Genealogical Publishing Company
Baltimore, Maryland
2022

ISBN: 9780806359502

Introduction

The County of Fife lies on the East Coast of Scotland; it is a peninsula bounded by the Firth of Tay to the north, the North Sea to the east, the Firth of Forth to the south, and the counties of Clackmannan, Perth and Kinross to the west. In the Dark Ages it was a distinct Pictish province, hence to name Kingdom of Fife. Scotland's King James VI described it as 'a beggar's mantle with a golden fringe' as the economy was driven by the coastal fishing villages in the East Neuk and the coal exports to the Netherlands from burghs such as Culross.

By the nineteenth century Fife had become a centre of heavy industry based on the significant coal seams of west Fife, and the county's emergence as a major producer of textiles. Since the medieval period, hand loom weaving had been the source of employment, but the rise of the factory system caused an expansion of urban centres and a decline of the old domestic textile industry. The linen industry became centred in Fife burghs, notably Dunfermline, which later specialised in the production of linoleum. The collieries were mainly located in south-west Fife, where ports to handle exports were established.

The Agricultural Revolution of the late eighteenth century resulted in a rise in the output of grain, mostly for domestic use but also for distilling and export. However, Fife's rural population declined from 31% in 1801 to 4.5% in 1901. Fishing, based in the East Neuk villages, such as Pittenweem and Anstruther, was a major employer in the early nineteenth century but has declined in recent years. St Andrews, which for nearly 700 years had been the ecclesiastical capital of Scotland and a major centre of Pilgrimage before the Reformation of 1560, remained in decline until the University of St Andrews, founded 1413, began to expand and the popularity of golf rose in the late nineteenth century gave rise to golf pilgrims bound for the 'Home of Golf'.

This book aims to identify residents and former residents of Fife during the early nineteenth century. It is largely based on primary sources especially local newspapers, gravestone inscriptions, and documents held in the National Archives of Scotland.

Among the manuscript sources I consulted were some of the burgess rolls of the period. Since the medieval period Scotland's burghs were semi-autonomous under the control of burgesses. Only burgesses could elect or form burgh councils, operate businesses, train apprentices, hold civic office, and trade within the burgh boundaries. Burgesses were a self-perpetuating oligarchy, representing the merchants and the craftsmen. To achieve economic and social success prior to the 19th-century, it was necessary to be the son of an existing burgess, marry the daughter of a burgess, serve an apprenticeship under a local burgess, purchase the right, or on occasion be honoured by the right, This system worked satisfactorily for centuries until social and economic pressures, especially the Industrial Revolution, brought it to an end--apart from as a method by which the burgh could honour individuals who brought some benefit to the community.

David Dobson
Dundee, 2022

REFERENCES

ACK Alexander Cowan, his kinsfolk and connections, [Perth, 1915]

AJ Aberdeen Journal, series

ANY St Andrew's Society of New York

AP St Andrew's Society of Philadelphia

AOSC Annals of the Original Secession Church, 1896

AR Acadian Recorder, series

ARM Madeira Regional Archives, Funchal

BM Blackwood's Magazine, series

CuBR Crail Burgess Roll

CM Caledonian Mercury, series

CP Canada and its Provinces, Toronto, 1914

DCA Dundee City Archives

DGH Dumfries and Galloway Herald, series

DJ Dunfermline Journal, series

DM Dunfermline Museum

DP Dunfermline Post, series

EA Edinburgh Advertiser, series

EC Edinburgh Courant, series

EEC Edinburgh Evening Courant, series

EFR East Fife Records, series

ERA Edinburgh Register of Apprentices

F Fasti Ecclesiae Scoticanae, [Edinburgh 1915]

FA Fife Advertiser, series

FFP Fife Free Press, series

FH Fife Herald, series

FJ Fife Journal, series

GBF Genealogy of the Blue Family

DM Dunfermline Museum

HT Halifax Times, series

Imm.NE Immigrants to New England

KBR Kirkcaldy Burgess Roll

LCL Leith Commercial Lists, series

MAGU Matriculation Albums of Glasgow University

NARA National Archives Records Administration, Washington, DC

NBC New Brunswick Courier, series

NRS National Records of Scotland, Edinburgh

PC Perth Courier, series

PJ People's Journal, series

POD Post Office Directory

RGNA Royal Gazette of North America, series

S The Scotsman, series

SBC Sexton's Book of Crail, 1794-1827, ms

SG Scottish Guardian, series

SM Scots Magazine, series

SO Stirling Observer, series

SOP Setons of Parbroath, [New York, 1890]

UPC United Presbyterian Church

W Witness, series

WS The History of the Society of Writers, [Edinburgh, 1890]

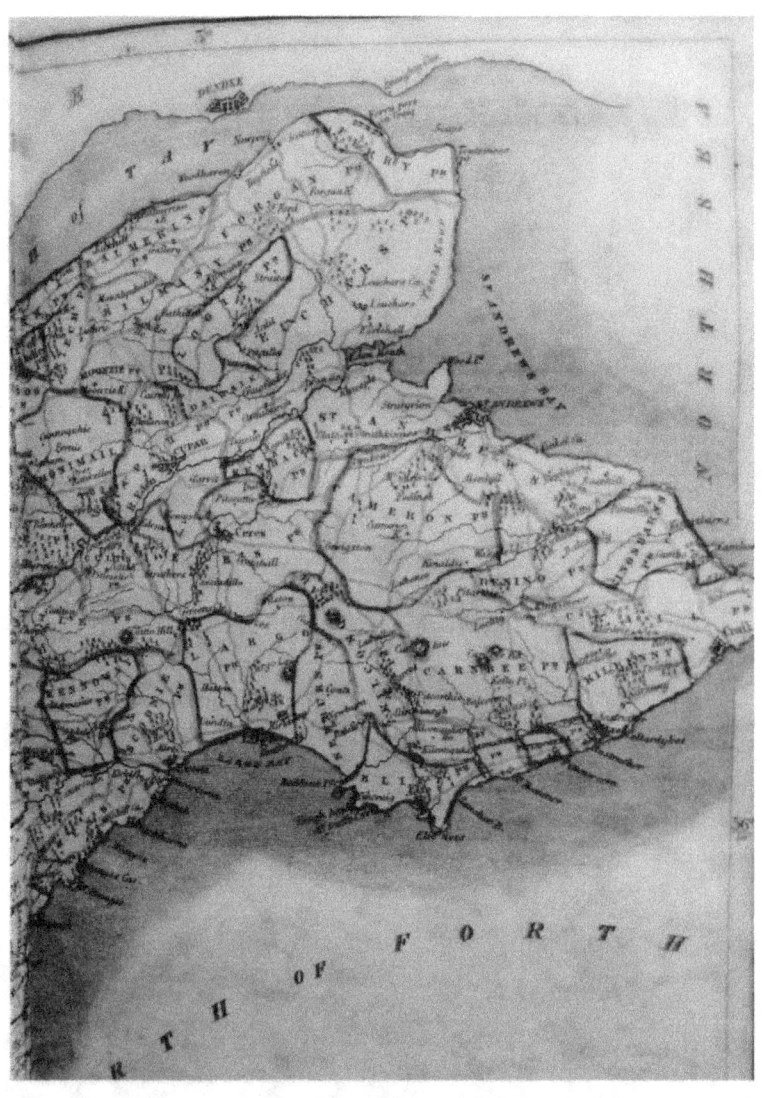

Map of Firth of Forth

Burntisland

Cupar

Dysart Tolbooth

Dysart Harbor

Falkland Palace

Falkland Palace, from the Courtyard

Kirkaldy Harbor

Kirkaldy High Street

Leven, Largo Law, and Bay

Pittenweem

St. Andres, ca. 1690

St. Momance Church

Fishermen

Coastal Scene

THE PEOPLE OF FIFE, AT HOME AND ABROAD, 1800-1850

ADAM, GEORGE, a weaver, was admitted as a burgess of Kirkcaldy, Fife, on 13 August 1791. [KBR]

ADAM, GEORGE, born 1846, son of Alexander Adam, died in Singapore on 3 June 1876. [Dunfermline gravestone, Fife]

ADAM, GRAHAM, a weaver, son of deacon John Adam, was admitted as a burgess of Kirkcaldy, Fife, on 13 May 1791. [KBR]

ADAM, JOHN, a weaver, son of William Adam, was admitted as a burgess of Kirkcaldy, Fife, on 10 September 1791. [KBR]

ADAMSON, JOHN, born 25 August 1769, a surgeon in the Royal Navy, died on 1 November 1857. [Tulliallan gravestone, Fife]

ADAMSON, JAMES, born 1825, son of Alexander Adamson and his wife Jane Hastie, died on Grouse Island, America, on 12 June 18... [St Monance gravestone, Fife]

ADAMSON, JOHN, born 1829, son of Alexander Adamson and his wife Jane Hastie, died in Calcutta, India, on 11 February 186-. [St Monance gravestone, Fife]

ADAMSON, LAWRENCE, was admitted as a burgess of Crail in 1800. [CBR]; was admitted as a burgess of Cupar, Fife, in 1807. [CuBR]

ADAMSON, ROBERT KEY, youngest son of Dr Adamson in Cupar, Fife, died in Kingston, Jamaica, in 1827. [BM.23.66]

ADIE, ALEXANDER, from Dunfermline, Fife, settled in America by 1796. [NRS.CS17.1.15/267]

ADIE, ANDREW, a writer in Dunfermline, testament, 2 November 1800, Comm. St Andrews. [NRS]

ADIE, JAMES, a weaver and merchant in Dunfermline, testament, 7 March 1800, Comm. St Andrews. [NRS]

AIKEN, DAVID, a weaver, son in law of Robert Bald a weaver burgess, was admitted as a burgess of Dunfermline, Fife, on 11 March 1808. [DM]

AIKENHEAD, JESSIE, born 1825, daughter of Reverend Robert Aikenhead in Kirkcaldy, Fife, and wife of Robert Wood, died in Newark, New Jersey, on 22 September 1871. [S.8879]

AITCHISON, WILLIAM, a mariner in Kirkcaldy, Fife, testament,1814, Comm. Edinburgh. [NRS]

AITKEN, ANDREW, born 1835, son of Thomas Aitken and his wife Mary Meldrum, died in Havanna, Cuba, on 10 September 1858. [Abercrombie gravestone, Fife]

AITKEN, ANDREW, son of John Aitken a weaver burgess, was admitted as a burgess of Dunfermline, Fife, on 5 July 1797. [DM]

AITKEN, DAVID, in Loups, son of George Aitken tenant in South Lethans, was admitted as a burgess of Dunfermline, Fife, on 1 July 1791. [DM]

AITKEN, DAVID, a butcher, son of George Aitken a butcher in Culross, was admitted as a burgess of Dunfermline, Fife, on 4 February 1791. [DM]

AITKEN, DAVID, son of David Aitken at Loups, was admitted as a burgess of Dunfermline, Fife, on 5 July 1797. [DM]

AITKEN, GEORGE, born 1801, son of George Aitken of Thornton and his wife Janet Ponton, a Captain of the 13th Light Infantry, died in Calcutta, India, in 1831. [Cupar gravestone, Fife]

AITKEN, HENRY, son of George Aitken a burgess, was admitted as a burgess of Dunfermline, Fife, on 25 March 1805. [DM]

AITKEN, JAMES, son of John Aitken a weaver burgess, was admitted as a burgess of Dunfermline, Fife, on 4 July 1797. [DM]

AITKEN, JOHN, son of George Aitken, was admitted as a burgess of Dunfermline, Fife, on 23 May 1797. [DM]

AITKEN, JOHN, the younger of Hill of Beath, son-in-la of Robert Donald, was admitted as a burgess of Dunfermline, Fife, on 4 January 1797. [DM]

AITKEN, ROBERT, son of John Aitken of Hill of Beath, was admitted as a burgess of Dunfermline, Fife, on 27 March 1810. [DM]

AITKEN, ROBERT, second son of Robert Aitken a writer in Cupar, Fife, died in Jamaica on 12 August 1841. [FJ.14.10.1841]

AITKEN, ROBERT, born 1793, a Captain of the 6th Bengal Cavalry, died on 21 December 1852. [Cupar gravestone, Fife]

ALBURN, ROBERT, of Craigfoodie, Dairsie, Fife, testament, 10 October 1796. [NRS]

ALEXANDER, DAVID, a writer, was admitted as a burgess of Kirkcaldy, Fife, on 16 May 1793. [KBR]

ALEXANDER, JAMES, a surgeon and laboratory keeper in Dunfermline, was admitted as a burgess and guilds-brother of Dunfermline, Fife, on 4 June 1796. [DM]

ALEXANDER, JAMES, a skipper in Inverkeithing, Fife, in 1798. [NRS.S/H]

ALEXANDER, JAMES, in Inverkeithing, Fife, applied to settle in Canada on 2 March 1815. [NRS.RH9]

ALEXANDER, JOHN, a skipper in Inverkeithing, Fife, testament, Comm. St Andrews, 14 April 1804, [NRS]

ALICE, JOHN, a tailor, son-in-law of Robert Drysdale, was admitted as a burgess of Dunfermline, Fife, on 14 December 1807. [DM]

ALISON, ALEXANDER, son of William Alison a stocking maker burgess, was admitted as a burgess of Dunfermline, Fife, on 5 July 1797. [DM]

ALLAN, CHRISTIAN, born 1824, wife of William Martin late of Craigrothie, Fife, died in Buffalo, New York, on 5 January 1872. [PJ]

ALLAN, DAVID, born 1837, son of Wilson Allan in Dunfermline, Fife, a mail conductor died in Montreal, Quebec, on 9 April 1854. [DJ]

ALLAN, GEORGE, a currier from Anstruther, Fife, son of George Allan a currier there, married [1] Janet Hollingworth, daughter of Charles Hollingworth in Haddington, East Lothian, in Newark, New Jersey, on

2 November 1858, she died on 6 October 1867, [2] Emma C. Price in Harlem, New York, on 5 May 1873. [EFR]

ALLAN, ISABELLA, wife of Peter Cleghorn, died in Madras, India, on 1 June 1824. [Dunino gravestone, Fife]

ALLAN, JAMES ARCHIBALD FINNIE, born 4 January 1832, son of George Allan and his wife Mary Pagan, died in Cien Fuegos, Cuba, on 3 May 1865. [Ferryport-on-Tay gravestone, Fife]

ALLAN, JOHN, a weaver, a former apprentice to Archibald Horn a weaver burgess, was admitted as a burgess of Dunfermline, Fife, on 23 August 1799. [DM]

ALLAN, JOHN, son of John Allan a weaver burgess, was admitted as a burgess of Dunfermline, Fife, on 9 September 1802. [DM]

ALLAN, JOHN, born 1827 in Townhill, Dunfermline, Fife, died in Knightsville, Indiana, on 19 November 1897. [DJ]

ALLAN, WILLIAM, born 1842 in Kilconquhar, Fife, son of George Allan a currier, a printer-compositor who emigrated to New York in 1862, married Lizzie McCaig in Bloomfield, New Jersey, on 18 February 1869, died in Brooklyn, New York, on 28 July 1910. [EFR]

ALLAN, WILSON B., born 1797 in Dunfermline, Fife, a collector, died in Montreal, Quebec, on 19 May 1872. [PJ]

ALLASTER, DAVID, son of David Allaster a weaver burgess, was admitted as a burgess of Dunfermline, Fife, on 7 August 1795. [DM]

ALLASTER, DAVID, son of John Allaster, was admitted as a burgess of Dunfermline, Fife, on 20 August 1802. [DM]

ALLASTER, HENRY, a weaver, son of William Allaster a weaver burgess, was admitted as a burgess of Dunfermline, Fife, on 4 July 1797. [DM]

ALLASTER, JAMES, son of William James a weaver burgess, was admitted as a burgess of Dunfermline, Fife, on 5 July 1797. [DM]

ALLASTER, JOHN, son of John Allaster a weaver burgess, was admitted as a burgess of Dunfermline, Fife, on 5 July 1797. [DM]

ALLASTER, WILLIAM, son of William Allaster a weaver burgess, was admitted as a burgess of Dunfermline, Fife, on 8 August 1795. [DM]

ALLASTER, WILLIAM, son of William Allaster, was admitted as a burgess of Dunfermline, Fife, on 20 August 1802. [DM]

ALLERDYCE, ARCHIBALD, born 1818, died in Sydney, New South Wales, Australia, on 24 July 1890. [Forgan gravestone, Fife]

ANDERSON, ADAM, son of Robert Anderson a weaver burgess, was admitted as a burgess of Dunfermline, Fife, on 18 August 1792. [DM]

ANDERSON, ALEXANDER, a mason, was admitted as a burgess of Kirkcaldy, Fife, on 6 September 1790. [KBR]

ANDERSON, ALEXANDER, son-in-law of George Philp a butcher burgess, was admitted as a burgess of Dunfermline, Fife, on 25 July 1810. [DM]

ANDERSON, ALEXANDER, a gas manager in West Wemyss, Fife, father of John Anderson, born 1870, a store clerk in San Barnardino, California, died there on 19 March 1893. [PJ.6.5.1893]

ANDERSON, ALEXANDER JOHN, of Montrave, Fife, a Captain in Honourable East India Company Service, died in Lucknow, India, on 9 March 1858. [St Monance gravestone, Fife]

ANDERSON, ANDREW, a weaver, son of William Anderson a smith burgess, was admitted as a burgess of Dunfermline, Fife, on 31 October 1790. [DM]

ANDERSON, ANDREW, son of William Anderson a burgess, was admitted as a burgess of Dunfermline, Fife, on 30 July 1791. [DM]

ANDERSON, ANDREW, son of Laurence Anderson a shoemaker burgess, was admitted as a burgess of Dunfermline, Fife, on 13 March 1793. [DM]

ANDERSON, ANDREW, from North Queensferry, Fife, married Miss Carstairs, in Cellardyke, Fife, on 5 December 1839. [SO]

ANDERSON, ANNIE, born 21 March 1786 in Newburgh, Fife, died at the Cape of Good Hope, South Africa, in 1813. [Abdie gravestone, Fife]

ANDERSON, ANN, born 1792, daughter of Laurence Anderson, [1761-1813], a shoemaker, and his wife Jane Watson, died in New York on 24 November 1825. [St Andrews gravestone, Fife]

ANDERSON, BALLANTYNE MITCHELL, born 1826, died in Tirhoot, India, on 25 January 1859. [Fife gravestone]

ANDERSON, CHARLES, surgeon of the Scots Brigade, was admitted as a burgess and guilds-brother of Dunfermline, Fife, on 4 June 1795. [DM]

ANDERSON, CHARLES, son of Charles Anderson a merchant in Dunfermline, was admitted as a burgess of Dunfermline, Fife, on 29 January 1796. [DM]

ANDERSON, CLEMENT, born 1850 in North Queensferry, Fife, died in New York on 30 June 1871. [S.8729]

ANDERSON, DAVID, a writer, was admitted as a burgess of Kirkcaldy, Fife, on 16 May 1793. [KBR]

ANDERSON, DAVID, son of Michael Anderson a weaver burgess, was admitted as a burgess of Dunfermline, Fife, on 23 September 1796. [DM]

ANDERSON, DAVID, son of David Anderson a weaver burgess, was admitted as a burgess of Dunfermline, Fife, on 13 August 1796. [DM]

ANDERSON, DAVID, son-in-law of George Robertson a weaver burgess, was admitted as a burgess of Dunfermline, Fife, on 14 September 1804. [DM]

ANDERSON, DAVID, son of William Anderson, was admitted as a burgess of Dunfermline, Fife, on 24 September 1807. [DM]

ANDERSON, DAVID, from Lochgelly, was sentenced to transportation to the colonies for 7 years on 15 September 1809. [SM.71.954]

ANDERSON, EBENEZER, minister of the Original Secession Church in Cupar from 1819 to 1835, emigrated to America. [AOSC.492]

ANDERSON, GEORGE, son of George Anderson a weaver burgess, was admitted as a burgess of Dunfermline, Fife, on 16 September 1796. [DM]

ANDERSON, GEORGE, agent in Kirkcaldy for the Union Bank of Scotland in 1849. [POD]

ANDERSON, GEORGE, born 1830, son of Thomas Anderson and his wife Charlotte Nicol, an engineer who died in Amolree, India, in 1865. [Newburgh, Fife, gravestone]

ANDERSON, JAMES, born 1744, a manufacturer in Argyle, St Andrews, Fife, escaped from imprisonment there on 5 July 1794, and was thought to be bound for America or the West Indies. [EA.3189.54]

ANDERSON, JAMES, born 1765, a skipper in Cellardyke, Fife, husband of Margaret Millar, died in March 1797. [Kilrenny gravestone, Fife]

ANDERSON, JAMES, son of James Anderson a weaver burgess, was admitted as a burgess of Dunfermline, Fife, on 19 October 1796. [DM]

ANDERSON, JAMES, a butcher, was admitted as a burgess of Crail, Fife, in 1806. [CBR]

ANDERSON, JAMES, a merchant, was admitted as a burgess of Dunfermline, Fife, on 1 July 1808. [DM]

ANDERSON, JAMES, born 1797, son of Laurence Anderson, [1761-1813], a shoemaker, and his wife Jane Watson, died in Newark, New Jersey, on 12 April 1830; [St Andrews gravestone, Fife]; possibly the James Anderson, a merchant in New York, brother of Laurence Anderson, deacon of the shoemakers of St Andrews, Fife, in 1805. [NRS. B65.5.8.238/240]

ANDERSON, JAMES, born 1814, formerly parish teacher in Carnbee, Fife, died in Ontario, California, on 3 April 1899. [DJ]

ANDERSON, JOHN, a baker, was admitted as a burgess of Dunfermline, Fife, on 16 December 1808. [DM]

ANDERSON, JOHN, son of James Anderson a waulker burgess, was admitted as a burgess of Cupar, Fife, in February 1810. [CuBR]

ANDERSON, JOHN, a fisherman in Cellardyke, Fife, testament, 1811, Comm. St Andrews. [NRS]

ANDERSON, JOHN, born 1739, a mariner in Cellardyke, Fife, husband of Margaret Wood, died on 29 May 1810. [Kilrenny gravestone, Fife]; testament, 2 May 1811, Comm. St Andrews. [NRS]

ANDERSON, JOHN, a builder and quarrier n Inverkeithing, Fife, sequestration, 1822. [NRS.CS233.SEQN.A143]

ANDERSON, JOHN, born 1767 in Fife, of the Ordnance Department, settled in Halifax, Nova Scotia, in 1786, died there on 27 September 1842. [AR.1.10.1842]

ANDERSON, JOHN, born 1790, son of James Anderson, died in Halifax, Nova Scotia, on 17 July 1810. [Kilrenny gravestone, Fife]

ANDERSON, JOHN, born 2 October 1796 in Newburgh, a minister who died in Nice, France, on 16 March 1834. [Newburgh, Fife, gravestone]

ANDERSON, JOHN, a shipmaster of Kincardine, Ffe, married Mary Drysdale, in Edinburgh, 23 February 1837. [SO]

ANDERSON, JOHN, born 1819, son of Thomas Anderson and his wife Charlotte Nicoll, died in Waiwai, Auckland, New Zealand, in 1883. [Newburgh gravestone, Fife]

ANDERSON, JOHN DAVID, jr., born 1819, died in Bermuda on 31 July 1857. [Burntisland gravestone, Fife]

ANDERSON, LAURENCE, [1761-1813], a shoemaker in St Andrews, father of Ann Anderson, born 1792, died in New York on 24 November 1825. [St Andrews gravestone, Fife]

ANDERSON, MARY CATHERINE, eldest daughter of Major Anderson of Montrave, Fife, in the East India Company Service, married William Dickenson the Deputy Inspector General, in Toronto, Canada, on 5 May 1859. [CM.21740]

ANDERSON, MICHAEL, a mason, son of George Anderson, was admitted as a burgess of Kirkcaldy, Fife, on 14 September 1795. [KBR]

ANDERSON, Dr PATRICK, born 1806 in Fife, died in Trelawney, Jamaica, on 1 August 1846. [Falmouth gravestone, Jamaica]

ANDERSON, ROBERT, born 1747, a mariner in Cellardyke, Fife, husband of Margaret..., died on 7 April 1808. [Kilrenny gravestone, Fife]

ANDERSON, PETER, a saddler, son of William Anderson a brewer burgess, was admitted as a burgess of Dunfermline, Fife, on 6 August 1796. [DM]

ANDERSON, ROBERT, born 1747, a mariner in Cellardyke, Fife, husband of Margaret ...., died on 7 April 1808. [Kilrenny gravestone]

ANDERSON, ROBERT, a weaver, son of James Anderson a weaver burgess, was admitted as a burgess of Dunfermline, Fife, on 28 August 1792. [DM]

ANDERSON, ROBERT, a weaver, son of George Anderson a weaver burgess, was admitted as a burgess of Dunfermline, Fife, on 20 September 1793. [DM]

ANDERSON, ROBERT, a weaver, was admitted as a burgess of Crail, Fife, in 1792. [CBR]

ANDERSON, ROBERT, was admitted as a burgess of Crail, Fife, in 1800. [CBR]

ANDERSON, ROBERT, a land labourer, was admitted as a burgess of Crail, Fife, in 1801. [CBR]

ANDERSON, ROBERT, born 1820, son of Thomas Anderson and his wife Charlotte Nicoll, died in Darraweit Cuim, Australia, in 1885. [Newburgh, Fife, gravestone]

ANDERSON, THOMAS, a bank clerk, was admitted as a burgess of Kirkcaldy, Fife, on 20 September 1794. [KBR]

ANDERSON, THOMAS, a grocer, was admitted as a burgess of Cupar, Fife, on 10 October 1808. [CuBR]

ANDERSON, WALTER FERGUSON, born 28 January 1822, a Lieutenant Colonel of the Bombay Army, died on 1 August 1869. [Kirkcaldy gravestone, Fife]

ANDERSON, WILLIAM, son of William Anderson a weaver burgess, was admitted as a burgess of Dunfermline, Fife, on 19 September 1791. [DM]

ANDERSON, WILLIAM, son of Robert Dundas [sic] a weaver burgess, was admitted as a burgess of Dunfermline, Fife, on 31 August 1796. [DM]

ANDERSON, WILLIAM, a carpenter, was admitted as a burgess of Crail, Fife, in 1806. [CBR]

ANDERSON, WILLIAM, a wright, was admitted as a burgess of Dunfermline, Fife, on 7 March 1810. [DM]

ANDERSON, ..., agent in Newburgh, Fife, for the Commercial Bank of Scotland in 1849. [POD]

ANGUS, ANDREW, born 1771 in Dunfermline, Fife, died in Halifax, Nova Scotia, on 24 January 1834. [AR.25.1.1834]

ANGUS, ANDREW, a baker, son of Andrew Angus in Dunfermline, was admitted as a burgess of Dunfermline, Fife, on 2 December 1807 [DM]

ANGUS, GEORGE, son of George Angus a burgess, was admitted as a burgess of Dunfermline, Fife, on 4 July 1797. [DM]

ANGUS, GEORGE, born 1830, son of John Angus and his wife Mary Scott, [who died in 1873], in Cupar, died in America on 4 April 1869. [FH][Cupar gravestone, Fife]

ANGUS, JOHN, son of William Angus a farmer in North Grange and his wife Betty Gardner, died on his passage to Australia in 1853. [Abdie gravestone, Fife]

ANGUS, ROBERT, son-in-law of James Crawford, was admitted as a burgess of Dunfermline, Fife, on 15 February 1796. [DM]

ANGUS, ROBERT, born 1810, a merchant from Angus Place, Cupar, Fife, died in Hamilton, Canada, on 10 March 1885. [FH]

ANNAN, DAVID, born 1754 in Cupar, Fife, son of John Annan, husband of Mary Smith, settled in Peterbrough, New Hampshire, died in Ireland in 1802. [Imm.NE.5]

ANNAN, JOHN, born 29 April 1792, a flax-spinner at Lydox Mill, died 1 August 1869, husband of Agnes Bell, born 18 February 1791, died 13 December 1878. [Dairsie gravestone, Fife]

ANNAN, Reverend ROBERT, in Mount Pleasant, Pennsylvania, heir to his brother John Annan in Lebanon, Cupar, Fife, in 1818. [NRS.S/H]

ANNAN, THOMAS, born 1841, son of Thomas Annan and his wife Ann Sharp, an engineer who died in Calcutta, India, on 28 June 1866. [Moonzie gravestone, Fife]

ANSTRUTHER, HENRY, born 4 June 1836, a Lieutenant of the Royal Ulster Fusiliers, was killed at the Battle of Alma in Russia on 20 September 1854. [St Monance gravestone, Fife]

ARCHIBALD, ALEXANDER MURRAY, born 1829, son of John Archibald and his wife Grace Murray, died in Otago, New Zealand, on 28 May 1859. [Burntisland gravestone, Fife]

ARCHIBALD, ANNIE, born 1844, wife of Frank Davis, from Dunfermline, Fife, died in Portage, Pennsylvania, on 4 January 1907. [DJ]

ARCHIBALD, ANDREW MURRAY, born 1829, son of John Archibald and his wife Grace Murray, died in Otago, New Zealand, on 28 May 1859. [Burntisland gravestone, Fife]

ARMOUR, SAMUEL, was licensed as a minister of the Original Secession Church in Glasgow in 1811, a minister in Dunfermline, Fife, from 1811 until 1820, then emigrated to Canada. [AOSC.486]

ARMSTRONG, HENRY, quartermaster of the Dunfermline Volunteers, was admitted as a burgess and guilds-brother of Dunfermline, Fife, on 5 June 1797. [DM]

ARNOTT, EDWARD, born 1807 in Dunfermline, Fife, died at Warehouse Point, Connecticut, on 18 August 1870. [FH]

ARNOT, JOHN, was admitted as a stationer burgess and guilds-brother of Cupar, Fife, on 10 October 1808. [CuBR]

ARNOTT, JOHN, born 6 November 1845, son of Robert Arnott, died in Melbourne, Victoria, Australia, on 28 January 1877. [Anstruther Wester gravestone, Fife]

ARNOT, LAWRENCE, son of Hugh Arnot of Balcormo, Fife, of the 92nd Regiment and the 12th Portuguese Regiment, died at Vittoria, Spain, on 28 July 1813. [SM.76.78]

ARNOT, WILLIAM, son of Thomas Arnot in Fife, probate 17 November 1790, Charleston, South Carolina.

ARTHUR, ALEXANDER, a slater, was admitted as a burgess of Cupar, Fife, on 24 September 1808. [CuBR]

ATKINSON, CHARLES, from Newcastle, England, was admitted as a burgess and guilds-brother of Dunfermline, Fife, on 3 May 1791. [DM]

AUCHTERLONIE, JOHN, a mason on the Links, was admitted as a burgess of Kirkcaldy, Fife, on 17 July 1795. [KBR]

AUCHTERLONIE, WILLIAM, a weaver, was admitted as a burgess of Crail, Fife, in 1805. [CBR]

BAIN, ALEXANDER, a merchant, was admitted as a burgess of Cupar, Fife, on 24 November 1802. [CuBR]

BAIN, JOHN, agent in St Andrews, Fife, for the Bank of Scotland in 1849. [POD]

BAIRD, ALEXANDER, a merchant in Inverkeithing, Fife, sequestration, 1820. [NRS.CS233.SEQN.B162]

BAIRD, JOHN, born 1796, son of James Baird, [1772-1831], and his wife Helen Gray, [1783-1821], died on Nevis, Leeward Islands, on 5 February 1814. [Tulliallan gravestone, Fife]

BAIRNER, JOHN, was admitted as a burgess of Kirkcaldy, Fife, on 2 May 1792. [KBR]

BALCASS, JAMES, a wright, was admitted as a burgess of Kirkcaldy, Fife, on 14 February 1803. [KBR]

BALD, ALEXANDER, a Lieutenant of the Clackmannan Volunteers, was admitted as a burgess and guilds-brother of Dunfermline, Fife, on 24 February 1804. [DM]

BALD, ROBERT, from Culross, was admitted as a burgess and guilds-brother of Dunfermline, Fife, on 3 May 1791. [DM]

BALD, ROBERT, Captain of the Clackmannan Volunteers, was admitted as a burgess and guilds-brother of Dunfermline, Fife, on 22 February 1804 [DM]

BALD, WILLIAM, son of Robert Bald a weaver burgess, was admitted as a burgess of Dunfermline, Fife, on 3 July 1797. [DM]

BALEASE, ROBERT, a wright in Kirkcaldy, Fife, emigrated to America after 1823. [SG.33.2.184]

BALFOUR, ALEXANDER, a merchant, was admitted as a burgess of Kirkcaldy, Fife, on 13 September 1797. [KBR]

BALFOUR, ANN, born 1838, daughter of David Balfour and his wife Elizabeth Wallace, wife of .... Lewis, died in Hokitika, New Zealand, on 1 October 1885. [Anstruther Wester gravestone, Fife]

BALFOUR, GOURLAY, a skipper in Kinghorn Fife, son and heir of James Balfour a skipper in Kinghorn, in 1798, [NRS.S/H]; was admitted as a burgess of Kirkcaldy, Fife, on 5 December 1795. [KBR]

BALFOUR, JAMES BOWER, a Lieutenant on HMS Tartar, second son of Francis Balfour of Fernie Castle, Fife, married Martha Maria Emerson, second daughter of G. H. Emerson, Queen's Counsel, at Virginia Waters, St John's, Newfoundland, on 9 August 1859. [EEC.23414][CM21827]

BALFOUR, JAMES, born 1836, son of William Balfour and his wife Mary Duncan, died in America on 30 July 1875. [Kilrenny gravestone, Fife]

BALFOUR, JANE, daughter of Alexander Balfour in Kirkcaldy, Fife, married George Elder jr. a merchant in Montreal, Quebec, in Boston, Massachusetts, on 2 August 1845. [W.603]

BALFOUR, JOHN, in Doune, Stirlingshire, son-in-law of William Hutton, was admitted as a burgess of Dunfermline, Fife, on 24 October 1809. [DM]

BALFOUR, PETER, born 1819 in Craigrothie, Fife, settled in Hamilton, Ontario, died in January 1897. [FH.10.2.1897]

BALFOUR, THOMAS, son-in-law of Andrew Mitchell a labourer in Nethertoun, was admitted as a burgess of Dunfermline, Fife, on 28 July 1807. [DM]

BALGONIE, Lord, was admitted as a burgess and guilds-brother of Dunfermline, Fife, on 25 June 1798. [DM]

BALLINANE, DAVID, a mariner in Crail in 1799. [SBC.31]

BALLANTYNE, SUSAN STEWART, second daughter of Charles Ballantyne in Burntisland, Fife, married Reverend Arthur Buist of Charleston, South Carolina, in Edinburgh on 31 July 1820. [BM.7.583]; she died in Charleston on 19 April 1847. [EEC.21504]

BALLARDIE, THOMAS, in Anstruther Easter, Fife, a master mariner in the Royal Navy, testament, 1809, inventory 28 June 1809, Comm. St Andrews. [NRS]

BALLINGALL, CHARLOTTE, born in 1795, daughter of Alexander Ballingall in Burn Mill, Leven, Fife, widow of Alexander Sime, died in Dubuque, Iowa, on 30 November 1878. [S.11056][EFR]

BALNAVES, ALEXANDER, son of Thomas Balnaves a weaver burgess, was admitted as a burgess of Dunfermline, Fife, on 30 July 1790. [DM]

BALNAVES, DAVID, son of David Balnaves a weaver burgess, was admitted as a burgess of Dunfermline, Fife, on 18 July 1792. [DM]

BALSILLIE, ANDREW, was admitted as a burgess of Cupar, Fife, on 4 October 1814. [CuBR]

BALSILLIE, JOHN, a wright, was admitted as a burgess of Crail, Fife, in 1799. [CBR]

BALVAIRD, JOHN, a writer in Edinburgh, son of John Balvaird in Kirkland, Fife, was admitted as a Notary Public on 3 March 1792. [NRS.NP2.34.329]

BANKS, FRANCIS, a skipper in Dysart, Fife, testament, 11 November 1812, Comm. St Andrews. [NRS]

BANKS, ROBERT, from Stirling, was admitted as a burgess and guildsbrother of Dunfermline, Fife, on 3 July 1790. [DM]

BARCLAY, CHARLES, born 30 July 1790, fourth son of Reverend Dr Barclay minister at Kettle, Fife, died at Point-au-Prince, Guadaloupe, in June 1819. [S.134.19][F.5.160] [EEC.16877] [EA]

BARCLAY, ELIZABETH CLELLAND, born 12 February 1792, daughter of Reverend Dr Barclay minister at Kettle, Fife, wife of Thomas Martin a merchant in Antigua, died on 4 December 1841. [F.5.160]

BARCLAY, GEORGE, the Sheriff Clerk Depute of Dunfermline, married Louisa Anna Giles, in Surrey, England, 8 April 1852. [SO]

BARCLAY, JAMES, son-in-law of William Birrell a labourer burgess, was admitted as a burgess of Dunfermline, Fife, on 4 July 1797. [DM]

BARCLAY, JAMES ROBERTSON, was admitted as a burgess of Cupar, Fife, in 1807. [CuBR]

BARCLAY, JAMES, jr., treasurer of the burgh of Inverkeithing, a decreet, 1821. [NRS.CS40.36.72]

BARCLAY, JOHN, from Cupar, Fife, formerly in Carriacou by Grenada, returned to Cupar by 1801, testament, 26 September 1801. [NRS.SC20.33.14]

BARCLAY, Reverend JOHN, born 9 July 1795, son of Reverend Dr Barclay minister at Kettle, Fife, was educated at Edinburgh University, died in Kingston, Ontario, on 26 September 1826. [BM.21 119] [F.5.160] [AJ.4116]

BARCLAY, ROBERT, a weaver, son of John Barclay, was admitted as a burgess of Cupar, Fife, on 29 September 1795. [CuBR]

BARCLAY, ROBERT, a tailor, was admitted as a burgess of Cupar, Fife, on 28 September 1801. [CuBR]

BARDNER, ELIZABETH, second daughter of John Bardner a warehouseman in Dunfermline, Fife, married Sergeant Thomas Hart the Inspector of Musketry, in Craigton, Jamaica, on 18 January 1869. [FA]

BARNETT, ISABELLA, daughter of James Barnett, a merchant tailor in Leven, Fife, married Charles B. Owler in Andover, Massachusetts, on 10 April 1846, settled in Charlestown, Boston, Massachusetts, by 1862. [FH.28.4.1896]

BARNETT, JAMES, born 1820, son of James Barnett, a merchant tailor in Leven, Fife, died in Danvers, Massachusetts, on 30 July 1888. [FFP]

BARNETT, JOHN, son of Peter Barnett a weaver burgess, was admitted as a burgess of Dunfermline, Fife, on 7 August 1795. [DM]

BARNETT, JOHN, a trumpeter of the Royal Horse Artillery, third son of J. Barnett in Cupar, Fife, died in Agra, Calcutta, India, on 6 January 1866. [FH]

BARNETT, THOMAS, from Leven, Fife, died in Indianapolis, Indiana, on 2 September 1871. [FFP]

BARNETT, THOMAS, born 1825, youngest son of James Barnett, a merchant tailor in Leven, Fife, emigrated to the USA in 1845, died in Haverhill, Massachusetts, on 22 February 1885. [FFP]

BARNETT, WILLIAM, born 1818, a tinplate and sheet-metal worker, second son of James Barnett, a merchant tailor in Leven, Fife, emigrated to the USA in 1845, died in Andover, Massachusetts, on 9 December 1884. [FFP]

BARRIE, Reverend WILLIAM, born in Gateside, Fife, was educated at the University of St Andrews, emigrated to Canada, pastor of the Eramose congregation in Bon-Accord from 1843 until 1877, died in Guelph, Ontario, in 1879. [FA.16.8.1879] [AUPC]

BARRON, GEORGE, was admitted as a burgess of Kirkcaldy, Fife, on 2 February 1799. [KBR]

BARRON, JAMES, born 1828, son of John Barron, died at the Cook Strait, New Zealand, on 14 February 1869. [Ferryport on Craig gravestone, Fife]

BARTHOLEMEW, JOHN, in Wolridge near Dunfermline, Fife, a decreet, 1810. [NRS.CS389.1.149]

BATHGATE, SIMON, Ensign of the Loyal Stirling Volunteers, was admitted as a burgess and guilds-brother of Dunfermline, Fife, on 17 July 1804. [DM]

BAXTER, THOMAS, and his wife Janet Wilson, parents of George Baxter, born 21 January 1854, died in Silvertown, New South Wales, Australia, on 16 May 1885. [Newburgh, Fife, gravestone]

BAYNE, JAMES, born 1759, a skipper in Limekilns, Fife, died in 1814. [Rosyth gravestone, Fife]

BAYNE, JOHN, a cooper from Greenhows, Beath, Fife, was admitted as a burgess of Dunfermline, Fife, on 25 February 1790. [DM]

BAYNE, JOHN, an engineer from Edinburgh, was admitted as a burgess and guilds-brother of Dunfermline, Fife, on 6 October 1795. [DM]

BAYNE, WILLIAM, a printer from London, was admitted as a burgess of Cupar, Fife, in 1811. [CuBR]

BEANS, JOHN, a sailor in Fife, 1791. [NRS.SH]

BEATH, ANDREW, son of William Beath a baker burgess, was admitted as a burgess of Dunfermline, Fife, on 30 March 1795. [DM]

BEATH, ROBERT, son of Alexander Beath a weaver burgess, was admitted as a burgess of Dunfermline, Fife, on 4 July 1797. [DM]

BEATH, SIMEON, a merchant, was admitted as a burgess of Cupar, Fife, on 4 October 1808. [CuBR]

BEAMONT, FRANCIS, was admitted as a burgess of Dunfermline, Fife, on 16 June1796. [DM]

BELL, ANDREW, born 27 March 1753 in St Andrews, Fife, son of Alexander Bell and his wife Margaret Robertson, a graduate of the University of St Andrews, a tutor in Virginia in 1774, later a chaplain in the Service of the East India Company in Madras, India, died 27 January 1832, buried in Westminster Abbey. [Westminster Abbey gravestone]

BELL, ANDREW, bosun aboard HMS Victor son and heir of William Bell in St Andrews, Fife, in 1799. [NRS.S/H]

BELL, ANN, born in Canada, died in Kirkcaldy, Fife, on 2 March 1825. [Abbotshall gravestone, Kirkcaldy]

BELL, CATHERINE, born 1817, wife of William Roy, died in New Orleans, Louisiana, on 27 May 1858. [Cupar gravestone, Fife]

BELL, DAVID, of the 21st Fusiliers, died in Bellary, Madras, India, on 16 July 1864. [Kennoway gravestone, Fife]

BELL, JOHN, a manufacturer, was admitted as a burgess of Cupar, Fife, on 16 April 1801. [CuBR]

BELL, JOHN, a weaver in Inverkeithing, Fife, versus James Bell in Greenock, a decreet, 1822. [NRS.CS44.15.12]

BELL, JOHN, master of the Isabella Simpson of Kirkcaldy trading between Leith and Miramachi, New Brunswick, in 1829 and 1830, when sailing between Kirkcaldy, Fife, via Cromarty bound for Quebec was wrecked on Cape Chat on the St Lawrence River in 1834. [LCL][FJ][AJ]

BELL, Lieutenant ROBERT, son of Colonel George Bell, died in Madras, India, on 25 September 1835. [St Andrews gravestone, Fife]

BELL, THOMAS, master of the Traveller of Kirkcaldy from Leith to New York in 1816. [NRS.E504.22.73]

BELL, WILLIAM, a tailor, was admitted as a burgess of Kirkcaldy, Fife, on 17 July 1795. [KBR]

BELL, WILLIAM, born 1815, son of Thomas Bell and his wife Mary Tod, died on a voyage to Bermuda on 20 October 1842. [Kirkcaldy gravestone, Fife]

BENNET, ALEXANDER, a slater, son of James Bennet a slater burgess, was admitted as a burgess of Dunfermline, Fife, on 21 March 1793. [DM]

BENNET, JAMES, born 1831, died at Castle Point, Wellington, New Zealand, on 17 February 1880. [Kilconquhar gravestone, Fife]

BENNET, JOHN, a glazier, was admitted as a burgess of Kirkcaldy, Fife, on 19 December 1795. [KBR]

BERWICK, DAVID, born 1829, son of David Berwick and his wife Jean, in Chicago, Illinois, with his wife Margaret Chiene in 1876, died in Oakland, California, on 12 February 1896. [St Andrews gravestone, Fife] [NRS.S/H]

BERWICK, JAMES, born 1835, son of James Berwick and his wife Agnes Young, a banker in Hong Kong, died in St Andrews on 29 April 1881. [St Andrews gravestone, Fife]

BETHUNE, ANDREW, from Greycraig, Fife, a Lieutenant Colonel in the Service of the East India Company, died in December 1821. [NRS.PS3.16/297]

BETHUNE, Sir HENRY LINDSAY, born 12 April 1787, a Major General, died in Persia on 19 February 1851. [Kilconquhar gravestone, Fife]

BETHUNE, WILLIAM, a schoolmaster from Kennoway, Fife, later a farmer in Haldin, Canada, a deed, 1853. [NRS.SC20.34.30/24]

BETSON, Lieutenant DAVID, son of David Betson of Meikle Beath, Fife, was admitted as a burgess of Dunfermline, Fife, on 4 July 1799. [DM]

BEVERIDGE, ALEXANDER, son of William Beveridge a burgess and guilds-brother, was admitted as a burgess of Dunfermline, Fife, on 9 July 1799. [DM]

BEVERIDGE, BRUCE, a Lieutenant of the Kinross Volunteer Infantry, was admitted as a burgess and guilds-brother of Dunfermline, Fife, on 27 October 1804. [DM]

BEVERIDGE, DAVID, a baker from Irvine, Ayrshire, was admitted as a burgess of Dunfermline, Fife, on 18 May 1792. [DM]

BEVERIDGE, DAVID, a weaver, son of James Beveridge a burgess, was admitted as a burgess of Dunfermline, Fife, on 5 July 1797. [DM]

BEVERIDGE, DAVID, son of William Beveridge a manufacturer burgess, was admitted as a burgess of Dunfermline, Fife, on 5 July 1797. [DM]

BEVERIDGE, DAVID, son of David Beveridge a burgess, was admitted as a burgess of Dunfermline, Fife, on 6 October 1804. [DM]

BEVERIDGE, GEORGE, a merchant, son of Henry Beveridge, was admitted as a burgess of Kirkcaldy, Fife, on 25 September 1792. [KBR]

BEVERIDGE, GEORGE, master of the Cheerful of Kirkcaldy trading between Leith and New York in 1816, and between Greenock and Montreal in 1817. [NRS.E504.15.116; E504.22.73]

BEVERIDGE, HENRY, born 1798, son of Michael Beveridge the Controller of Customs in Kirkcaldy, Fife, died in Demerara on 17 November 1819. [BM.7.231]

BEVERIDGE, H., agent in Kirkcaldy, Fife, for the National Bank of Scotland in 1849. [POD]

BEVERIDGE, JAMES, a weaver, son of John Beveridge a burgess and guilds-brother, was admitted as a burgess of Dunfermline, Fife, on 16 August 1793. [DM]

BEVERIDGE, JAMES, son of William Beveridge, was admitted as a burgess of Dunfermline, Fife, on 5 July 1797. [DM]

BEVERIDGE, JAMES, son of James Beveridge a writer burgess, was admitted as a burgess of Dunfermline, Fife, on 11 September 1802. [DM]

BEVERIDGE, JAMES, a meal-seller, was admitted as a burgess of Dunfermline, Fife, on 29 March 1805. [DM]

BEVERIDGE, JAMES, son of James Beveridge, was admitted as a burgess of Dunfermline, Fife, on 29 March 1805. [DM]

BEVERIDGE, JOHN, a tailor, son-in-law of David Anderson a weaver burgess, was admitted as a burgess of Dunfermline, Fife, on 3 February 1790. [DM]

BEVERIDGE, JOHN, a shoemaker, son-in-law of Thomas Gibson a shoemaker burgess, was admitted as a burgess of Dunfermline, Fife, on 3 May 1790. [DM]

BEVERIDGE, JOHN, a baker, son of David Beveridge a tenant in Blairathie, and son-in-law of Robert Pearson a baker burgess, was admitted as a burgess of Dunfermline, Fife, on 19 September 1794. [DM]

BEVERIDGE, JOHN, son of John Beveridge a guilds-brother, was admitted as a burgess of Dunfermline, Fife, on 24 November 1796. [DM]

BEVERIDGE, JAMES, master of the Rose of Kirkcaldy from Dundee bound for Charleston, South Carolina, in October 1818; master of the Rose of East Wemyss, bound from Greenock to Montreal, Quebec, in 1819. [NRS.E504.11.21; E504.15.124]

BEVERIDGE, JAMES, a brewer in Albany, America, son and heir of Francis Beveridge a skipper in Kirkcaldy, Fife, 1818. [NRS.S/H]

BEVERIDGE, JOHN, a shoemaker, was admitted as a burgess of Dunfermline on 23 June 1807. [DM]

BEVERIDGE, JOHN, born 1847, son of Alexander Beveridge and his wife Isabella Pringle, died in Antwerp, Flanders, Belgium, on 6 January 1875. [Dunnikier gravestone, Fife]

BEVERIDGE, THOMAS, a writer, son of James Beveridge, was admitted as a burgess of Dunfermline on 15 August 1794. [DM]

BEVERIDGE, WILLIAM, a glover, son of Thomas Beveridge, was admitted as a burgess of Kirkcaldy, Fife, on 26 March 1793. [KBR]

BEVERIDGE, WILLIAM, son of William Beveridge, was admitted as a burgess of Dunfermline on 5 July 1797. [DM]

BEVERIDGE, WILLIAM GARDINER, born 1842, son of Alexander Beveridge, [1798-1892], a merchant in Pathhead, Kirkcaldy, Fife and his wife Isabella Pringle, formerly an engineer in the Dunnikier Foundry, died in St Thomas, Danish West Indies, on 24 August 1865. [Dunnikier gravestone, Fife] [FH]

BEVERIDGE, W., agent in Dunfermline, Fife, for the Western Bank of Scotland in 1849. [POD]

BILLERWELL, JANE, daughter of Reverend William Billerwell in Dysart, Fife, died in Hamburg, Germany, on 9 March 1852. [FH]

BIRRELL, GEORGE, son of John Birrell, a manufacturer in Kirkcaldy, Fife, and his wife Jean Wyllie, settled in Adelaide, South Australia, by 1853. [NRS.S/H]

BIRRELL, HENRY, a merchant, was admitted as a burgess of Kirkcaldy, Fife, on 1 January 1798. [KBR]

BIRRELL, HENRY, a mason, was admitted as a burgess of Dunfermline on 30 August 1797. [DM]

BISSET, ROBERT, born 1830, died in Fiji on 25 August 1884. [Dunfermline gravestone, Fife]

BISSET, THOMAS, a mason, was admitted as a burgess of Dunfermline on 26 September 1795. [DM]

BLACK, ALEXANDER, son of John Black a merchant in Anstruther, Fife, was apprenticed to William Clerihugh, a barber in Edinburgh, for six years, on 26 June 1794. [ERA]

BLACK, ALEXANDER, son of James Black, was admitted as a burgess of Dunfermline on 4 July 1797. [DM]

BLACK, ALEXANDER, born in Pittenweem, Fife, master of the <u>Crown</u> died in St John, New Brunswick, on 31 August 1842. [NBC.3.9.1842]

BLACK, ANDREW, a skipper in Pittenweem, Fife, boxmaster of the Pittenweem Sea Box Society in 1792. [NRS.B3.7.5]

BLACK, DAVID, son of John Black, was admitted as a burgess of Dunfermline on 9 April 1790. [DM]

BLACK, Reverend DAVID, of the Anti-Burgher Congregation in Dunfermline, was admitted as a burgess and guilds-brother of Dunfermline on 27 October 1790. [DM]

BLACK, DAVID, a weaver, son of David Black, was admitted as a burgess of Dunfermline on 30 July 1791. [DM]

BLACK, DAVID, a baker, son of William Black, was admitted as a burgess of Dunfermline on 5 June 1795. [DM]

BLACK, DAVID, born 1846, son of John Black and his wife Elizabeth Deas, died a Klip Drift, South Africa, on 14 January 1872. [Markinch gravestone, Fife]

BLACK, GEORGE, a sailor, son-in-law of David Beveridge, was admitted as a burgess and guilds-brother of Dunfermline on 23 June 1807. [DM]

BLACK, JAMES, a weaver from Dunning, Perthshire, was admitted as a burgess of Dunfermline on 25 June 1791. [DM]

BLACK, JAMES, a weaver, son of James Black, was admitted as a burgess of Dunfermline on 29 July 1791. [DM]

BLACK, JAMES, a tobacconist from Leith, was admitted as a burgess and guilds-brother of Dunfermline on 13 August 1793. [DM]

BLACK, JAMES, a mariner in the Royal Navy, husband of Grizel Reddie in Dysart, Fife, in 1796. [NRS.S/H]

BLACK, JAMES, son of Reverend James Black, was admitted as a burgess of Dunfermline on 21 March 1805. [DM]

BLACK, JAMES, from Sinclairtown, Kirkcaldy, Fife, later in USA, a sasine, 1819. [NRS.RS. Kirkcaldy.2/109]; died in St Joseph, Florida, in 1842. [DGH.7.6.1842]

BLACK, JAMES TAYLOR, born 1850, son of Robert Black and his wife Isabella Dow, died in Valparaiso, Chile, on 16 October 1894. [Ferry-Port-on-Craig gravestone, Fife]

BLACK, JOHN, a writer from Edinburgh, was admitted as a burgess of Dunfermline on 8 April 1791. [DM]

BLACK, JOHN, jr., a writer, son of bailie Patrick Black a baillie, was admitted as a burgess of Dunfermline on 23 July 1794. [DM]

BLACK, JOHN, from Dysart, Fife, a Lieutenant in the Royal Navy, testament, 1815, inventory 11 February 1815, Comm. St Andrews. [NRS]

BLACK, JOHN, born in Dunfermline, Fife, a Justice of the Peace in Antigua, died on 22 August 1840. [FH]

BLACK, JOHN, born 11 March 1817, late of the Hudson Bay Company, died 3 February 1879. [St Andrews gravestone, Fife]

BLACK, PETER, master of the Jean of Dysart trading between Leith and Quebec in 1817. [NRS.E504.22.77]

BLACK, RODGER, a mason in Sinclairtown, was admitted as a burgess of Kirkcaldy, Fife, on 1 January 1798. [KBR]

BLACK, WILLIAM, from Anstruther, Fife, a Lieutenant of the Royal Navy in 1809. [NRS.S/H]

BLACK, WILLIAM, born 1794 in Fife, was naturalised in South Carolina sitting on 10 October 1828. [NARA.M1183.1]

BLACK, WILLIAM, a skipper in Ferry-port on Craig, Fife, testament, 1820, Comm. St Andrews. [NS]

BLACK, WILLIAM, son of John Black in Antigua, died in Dunfermline, Fife, on 6 June 1827. [FH]

BLACK, WILLIAM, born 1837, son of William Black and his wife Christian Pyott, died in Livingstonia, Rhodesia, on 7 May 1877. [Dunbog gravestone, Fife]

BLACKWOOD, JOHN, an Ensign of the Kinross Volunteer Infantry, was admitted as a burgess and guilds-brother of Dunfermline on 27 October 1804. [DM]

BLAIK, JAMES, a tailor, son of James Blaik, was admitted as a burgess of Dunfermline on 24 July 1801. [DM]

BLAIK, JAMES, a weaver, son of William Blaik, was admitted as a burgess of Dunfermline on 20 August 1802. [DM]

BLAKE, RICHARD, born 1827 at Burn Mill, Leven, Fife, settled in Dunedin, New Zealand, died in Leven on 24 March 1877. [St Monance gravestone, Fife]

BLYTH, GEORGE, a weaver, was admitted as a burgess of Kirkcaldy, Fife, on 18 September 1802. [KBR]

BLYTH, JAMES, from Kennaway, Fife, a minister in Fala, Midlothian, from 1788 until 1793, emigrated to America. [UPC]

BOAG, DAVID, a mason, son in law of Robert Logan, was admitted as a burgess of Dunfermline on 4 July 1797. [DM]

BOGIE, ALEXANDER, a grocer, was admitted as a burgess of Kirkcaldy, Fife, on 14 June 1801. [KBR]

BONELLA, ANN, daughter of John Bonella and his wife Margaret Fernie, died in Kansas on 19 September 1859. [Leuchars gravestone, Fife]

BONES, JAMES, a merchant, was admitted as a burgess of Kirkcaldy, Fife, on 1 October 1791. [KBR]

BONNAR, ALEXANDER, a weaver, son of Alexander Bonnar, was admitted as a burgess of Dunfermline on 17 September 1802. [DM]

BONNAR, DAVID, a weaver, son of Alexander Bonnar, was admitted as a burgess of Dunfermline on 17 September 1802. [DM]

BONNAR, JOHN, a wright, son of Thomas Bonnar, was admitted as a burgess of Dunfermline on 2 August 1802. [DM]

BONTHRON, ANDREW, born 1777 in Moonzie, Fife, son of Alexander Bonthron and his wife Elspet Coit, died in New Orleans, Louisiana, on 17 August 1813. [Moonzie gravestone]

BONTHRON, HENRY, a mason, was admitted as a burgess of Kirkcaldy, Fife, on 31 May 1796. [KBR]

BONTHRON, JAMES, a fisherman in Buckhaven, Fife, inventory, 30 December 1813, Comm. St Andrews. [NRS]

BONTHRON, JOHN, born 1789 in Fife, emigrated to Philadelphia, Pennsylvania, in April 1817, naturalised on 2 June 1828 in the Circuit Court of the District of Columbia. [NARA]

BONTHRON, ROBERT, a skipper in Dubbyside, Markinch, Fife, inventory 27 November 1810; testament, 1811, Comm. St Andrews. [NRS]

BONTHRON, THOMAS, a fisherman in Buckhaven, Fife, testament, 26 July 1808, Comm. St Andrews. [NRS]

BONTHRON, WILLIAM, Deputy Collector of Customs at Inverkeithing, Fife, was admitted as a burgess and guilds-brother of Dunfermline on 16 June 1796. [DM]

BORTHWICK, AGNES JANE, wife of Reverend John Gordon late of Leslie, Fife, died in Chicago, Illinois, on 5 February 1871. [S.8611]

BORTHWICK, JOHN, a superintendent of stations in Bowen, Queensland, Australia, a sasine, 1876. [NRS.RS.Kirkcaldy 16.220]

BOSWELL, DAVID, a mason, son-in-law of James Crawford tenant in Pitbauchlie, Fife, was admitted as a burgess of Dunfermline on 8 November 1797. [DM]

BOSWELL, ELIZABETH, wife of David Reid a merchant in Jamaica, daughter and heir of David Boswell a merchant in Leven, Fife, 1797. [NRS.S/H]

BOSWELL, ROBERT, in St James, Jamaica, son and heir of David Boswell a merchant in Leven, Fife, 1797. [NRS.S/H]

BOSWELL, WILLIAM, a sign writer from Edinburgh, was admitted as a burgess of Dunfermline in 1798. [DM]

BOWER, ALEXANDER, son of Alexander and John Bower, a mariner who died in Batavia, Java, on 8 December 1830. [St Andrews gravestone, Fife]

BOWER, JOHN, son of Alexander and John Bower, a shipmaster who died in Panama on 22 April 1853. [St Andrews gravestone, Fife]

BOWES, ALEXANDER, Superintendent of Excise, also Captain of the Dunfermline Volunteers, was admitted as a burgess and guilds-brother of Dunfermline on 5 May 1797. [DM]

BOWIE, JAMES, a weaver, son of Ralph Bowie, was admitted as a burgess of Dunfermline on 4 July 1797. [DM]

BOWIE, JOHN, a weaver, son of Henry Bowie, was admitted as a burgess of Dunfermline on 4 July 1797. [DM]

BOWIE, WILLIAM, a weaver, son of Henry Bowie, was admitted as a burgess of Dunfermline on 4 July 1797. [DM]

BOWMAN, ISABELLA, in Kirkcaldy, Fife, was appointed the attorney of James Oswald Bowman in Georgetown, Maryland, on 10 May 1796. [NRS.B4.7.9]

BOWMAN, JAMES OSWALD, in Georgetown, Maryland, son and heir of David Bowman the son of David Bowman a skipper in Kirkcaldy, Fife, 1796. [NRS.S/H]

BOWMAN, JOHN, a mason, was admitted as a burgess of Crail, Fife, in 1807. [CBR]

BOWSIE, JOHN, in Kilminnin, was admitted as a burgess of Crail, Fife, in 1792. [CBR]

BOYD, JAMES, a watch and clock-maker, was admitted as a burgess of Cupar, Fife, on 3 December 1795. [CuBR]

BOYD, JOHN, 1st Lieutenant of the Royal Linlithgow Volunteers, was admitted as a burgess and guilds-brother of Dunfermline on 4 July 1797. [DM]

BRAID, GEORGE, born 1781, son of Andrew Braid a merchant in St Andrews, Fife, died in Savanna la Mar, Jamaica, on 13 July 1802. [EA.4046.02]

BRAID, NORMAN, born 1791, son of John Braid and his wife Catherine Porterfield, a surgeon who died in Borneo on 22 July 1811. [St Andrews gravestone, Fife]

BRAID, WILLIAM, a wright, was admitted as a burgess of Dunfermline on 16 September 1806. [DM]

BREMNER, JAMES, a Writer to the Signet, was admitted as a burgess of Dunfermline on 26 September 1796. [DM]

BREWSTER, GEORGE, MD, in the Royal Navy, son of Reverend George Brewster in Scoonie, Fife, died in Port Royal, Jamaica, on 5 April 1850. [W.1108]

BRIDGES, ANDREW, a mason in Leslie, Fife, son-in-law of James Jack, a wigmaker in Dunfermline, was admitted as a burgess of Dunfermline on 1 October 1788. [DM]

BRIGGS, DAVID, a merchant in Rio de Janeiro, Brazil, heir of Mary Reston, widow of John Briggs, in Kirkcaldy, Fife, 1817. [NRS.S/H]

BRIGGS, Major JAMES, died in Bergen-op-Zoom, the Netherlands, on 3 April 1855. [Largo gravestone, Fife]

BRIGGS, JOHN, late of Calcutta, India, a sasine, 1790. [NRS.RS.Fife.2614]

BRIGGS, WILLIAM, Quartermaster of the 20th Bengal Native Infantry, died in Moorshedabad, India, in 1827. [Largo gravestone, Fife]

BRODIE, JAMES, son-in-law of James Lothian, a tailor burgess, was admitted as a burgess of Dunfermline on 4 July 1797. [DM]

BRODIE, JOHN, a stay-maker, was admitted as a burgess of Kirkcaldy, Fife, on 18 January 1793. [KBR]

BRODIE, JOHN, a skipper in Dysart, Fife, in 1794. [NRS.S/H]

BRODIE, JOSEPH, born 20 August 1783, son of Reverend Alexander Brodie in Carnbee, Fife, and his wife Helen Pitcairn, a merchant in Hamburg, Germany, died on 14 March 1826. [F.V.190]

BRODIE, WILLIAM, a sloop-master, was admitted as a burgess of Crail, Fife, in 1794. [CBR]

BROTHERSTON, Reverend PETER, was admitted as a burgess of Dunfermline on 1 August 1808. [DM]

BROWN, A., agent in Newburgh, Fife, for the Central Bank of Scotland in 1849. [POD]

BROWN, AGNES, born 1841, daughter of John Brown and his wife Isabella Duncan, wife of Revered Andrew Baillie, died in Lucea, Jamaica, on 25 November 1872. [St Andrews gravestone, Fife]

BROWN, ALEXANDER, a slater, was admitted as a burgess of Kirkcaldy, Fife, on 29 January 1803. [KBR]

BROWN, ALEXANDER, born 1815, an engineer of the Netherlands Indies Company, died in Surabaya, Java, on 9 July 1863. [Balmerino gravestone, Fife]

BROWN, ANN, daughter of William Brown and his wife Janet Ogilvy, wife of Laurence Constable Browne, died in St Petersburg, Russia, on 16 June 1814. [St Andrews gravestone, Fife]

BROWN, DAVID, born 1785, son of David Brown and his wife Helen Oswald, died in Jamaica on 2 January 1830. [Kingsbarns gravestone, Fife]

BROWN, DAVID, a tailor, son-in-law of John Brown, was admitted as a burgess of Dunfermline on 10 August 1804. [DM]

BROWN, GEORGE, born 1832, son of Charles Brown and his wife Mary Kinnear, died in Brooklyn, New York, on 24 February 1874. [Ferry-Port-on-Craig gravestone, Fife]

BROWN, JAMES, born 1768 a skipper, husband of Margaret Arnot, died on 8 November 1836. [Ferry-port-on-Craig gravestone, Fife]

BROWN, JAMES, a wright, was admitted as a burgess of Crail, Fife, in 1796. [CBR]

BROWN, JAMES, a cabinet maker, was admitted as a burgess of Crail, Fife, in 1796. [CBR]

BROWN, JAMES, surgeon of the North Fencible Highlanders, was admitted as a burgess and guilds-brother of Dunfermline on 27 February 1799. [DM]

BROWN, JAMES, Captain of the Loyal Stirling Volunteers, was admitted as a burgess and guilds-brother of Dunfermline on 17 July 1804. [DM]

BROWN, JAMES, a mariner in Inverkeithing, Fife, testament, 14 October 1813, Comm. St Andrews. [NRS]

BROWN, JAMES, born 1838, son of Thomas Brown and his wife Margaret Balfour in Cellardyke, Fife, died in Antwerp, Belgium, on 9 December 1889. [Anstruther Easter gravestone, Fife]

BROWN, JANE, youngest daughter of James Brown in Kinghorn, Fife, and William Walker, son of Thomas Walker in Blebo Mains ,Fife, were married in Melbourne, Victoria, Australia, on 2 August 1856. [AJ.5686]

BROWN, JOHN, a mariner, was admitted as a burgess of Kirkcaldy, Fife, on 20 March 1800. [KBR]

BROWN, JOHN, a mason, son of Robert Brown in Pittencrieff, Fife, was admitted as a burgess of Dunfermline on 19 December 1809 [DM]

BROWN, JOHN, born 1843, son of James Brown and his wife Janet Gardner, died in Namino, British Columbia, on 12 April 1886. [St Monance gravestone, Fife]

BROWN, JOHN, in East Wemyss, Fife, father of George Brown, born 1852, died in Runnel's Hotel, Texas, on 2 June 1885 [S.13090]

BROWN, JOSEPH, a Colonel in the Service of the East India Company, son and heir of Robert Brown a merchant in Kirkcaldy, Fife, in 1831. [NRS.S/H]

BROWN, ROBERT, a weaver, was admitted as a burgess of Crail, Fife, in 1791. [CBR]

BROWN, SIMON, born 1801, son of James Brown and his wife Margaret Arnot, a shipmaster who died in Port au Prince, Haiti, on 19 April 1829. [Ferry-port-on-Craig gravestone, Fife]

BROWN, THOMAS, a tailor, was admitted as a burgess of Cupar, Fife, on 4 October 1797. [CuBR]

BROWN, THOMAS, Quartermaster of the Royal Linlithgow Volunteers, was admitted as a burgess and guilds-brother of Dunfermline on 15 August 1804. [DM]

BROWN, THOMAS, born 1835, son of John Brown and his wife Mary Hodge, died in Australia, on 25 March 1862. [Kilrenny gravestone, Fife]

BROWN, THOMAS, born 1834, son of John and Jane Brown, died in Melbourne, Victoria, Australia, on 22 October 1879. [Kilconquhar gravestone, Fife]

BROWN, WILLIAM, a member of the Pittenweem Sea Box Society, Fife, in 1792. [NRS.B3.7.5]

BROWN, WILLIAM, a mariner in North Queensferry, Fife, testament, 1800, Comm. Edinburgh. [NRS]

BROWN, WILLIAM, born 1829, son of James Brown and his wife Janet Gardner, late in Leven, Fife, died in New York on 21 June 1866. [DA.1653][St Monance gravestone, Fife]

BROWNLEE, JAMES, a weaver, son of Robert Brownlee, was admitted as a burgess of Dunfermline on 4 July 1797. [DM]

BROWNLEE, ROBERT, a tinsmith, plumber and gasfittter in Kirkcaldy, Fife, later in Dunedin, New Zealand, a sasine, 1869. [NRS.R.S.Kirkcaldy.14/78]

BRUCE, ROBERT, born 1832, son of William Bruce and his wife Jean Anderson, died in Korrit, Victoria, Australia, on 16 October 1890. [Collessie gravestone, Fife]

BRUCE, WALTER, born 1845, second son of Walter Hamilton Tyndall Bruce of Falkland, Fife, died in Montreal, Quebec, on 17 March 1875. [EC.28227]

BRUCE, WILLIAM, and Company, operators of steamboats trading between Kirkcaldy, Grangemouth, Leven, Largo and Inverkeithing, papers, 1820-1821. [NRS.CS96.1419-1423]

BRUNTON, JAMES, a tailor, was admitted as a burgess of Cupar, Fife, on 3 October 1810. [CuBR]

BRYCE, ALEXANDER, born 1848, son of William Bryce, died at Charters Towers, Queensland, Australia, on 28 January 1884. [Aberdour gravestone, Fife]

BRYCE, ARCHIBALD, born 1843, son of Andrew Bryce and his wife Helen Munro, died in Cape Town, South Africa, on 5 February 1888. [Abbotshall gravestone, Kirkcaldy, Fife]

BRYCE, JAMES, a workman from Charlestown, Fife, son-in-law of George Aitken in South Lethens, Fife, was admitted as a burgess of Dunfermline on 25 February 1787. [DM]

BRYCE, WILLIAM, born 14 February 1830, son of William Bryce, a Lieutenant of the Madras Fusiliers, died in Calcutta, India, on 14 October 1852. [Aberdour gravestone, Fife]

BUCHAN, JOHN, a tailor, son of William Buchan, was admitted as a burgess of Dunfermline on 12 March 1795. [DM]

BUCHAN, JOHN, a tailor, son of John Buchan, was admitted as a burgess of Dunfermline on 21 August 1802. [DM]

BUCHAN, PETER, a tailor, son of John Buchan, was admitted as a burgess of Dunfermline on 28 July 1802. [DM]

BUCHAN, WALTER, a minister in Canongait, Edinburgh, was admitted as a burgess and guilds-brother of Dunfermline on 6 June 1792. [DM]

BUCHAN, WILLIAM, a merchant, was admitted as a burgess of Dunfermline on 20 August 1807. [DM]

BUCHANAN, ROBERT, a white-iron smith, was admitted as a burgess of Cupar, Fife, on 28 September 1801. [CuBR]

BUIK, ROBERT, born 1809, son of Robert Buik and his wife Jean Dick, died in San Luis, South America, on 28 October 1832. [Cupar gravestone, Fife]

BUIST, DAVID, born 1815, probably in Fife, emigrated via Liverpool to New York in March 1833, naturalised on 21 January 1841 in the Circuit Court of the District of Columbia.

BUIST, GEORGE, born 1769 or 1778, educated at Edinburgh University, settled in Charleston, South Carolina, a minister of the Old Scots Church there from 1793 to 1808, Principal of Charleston College in 1805, died on 31 August 1808. [Old Scots gravestone]

BUIST, HENRY, born 1804, son of Henry Buist and his wife Rachel Robertson, died in Canada on 19 December 1876. [Strathmiglo gravestone, Fife]

BUIST, ROBERT, born 1805 in Cupar, Fife, a horticulturalist who emigrated to Philadelphia, Pennsylvania, in 1828, died there on 13 July 1880. [AP]

BUIST, WILLIAM, born 1811, probably in Fife, emigrated via Liverpool to Philadelphia, Pennsylvania, in April 1832, naturalised on 20 January 1841 in the Circuit Court of the District of Columbia. [NARA]

BURNS, PATRICK, born in February 1807, Auditor General of the Leeward Islands, died on 2 July 1875. [St Andrews gravestone, Fife]

BURNS, THOMAS, Captain of the Aberdeenshire Fencibles, was admitted as a burgess and guilds-brother of Dunfermline on 8 June 1796. [DM]

BURNS, WILLIAM, a sieve-wright, was admitted as a burgess of Cupar, Fife, on 5 October 1808. [CuBR]

BURRELL, ALEXANDER, a mason, son-in-law pf William Wilson a slater, was admitted as a burgess of Dunfermline on 4 July 1797. [DM]

BURT, ANDREW, in Baltimore, Maryland, in 1812, eldest son of John Burt tacksman of the Pittencrieff Coalworks, Fife. [NRS.CS17.1.31/397]

BURT, GEORGE, a weaver, former apprentice to David Anderson a weaver burgess, was admitted as a burgess of Dunfermline on 22 July 1796. [DM]

BURT, JOHN, tacksman of the Baldridge Coalworks in Fife, was admitted as a burgess and guilds-brother of Dunfermline on 20 January 1795. [DM]

BUTTERS, JOHN H., born 2 April 1798 in Fife, emigrated to New York on 28 August 1829, naturalised there on 26 September 1840. [NARA]

CAIRNS, JAMES, a grocer, was admitted as a burgess of Kirkcaldy, Fife, on 9 July 1801. [KBR]

CAMERON, ALLEN, born in Auchtermuchty, Fife, husband of Mary Stewart, settled in Baker's Creek, Bladen County, North Carolina, died in 1800. [GBF]

CAMERON, JOHN, Captain of the 2nd Regiment of the Scots Brigade, was admitted as a burgess and guilds-brother of Dunfermline on 29 September 1794. [DM]

CAMPBELL, ALEXANDER, born 12 April 1778 in Creich, Fife, minister of St Andrew's, Jamaica, from 1803, died on 8 December 1858. [St Andrew's gravestone, Jamaica]

CAMPBELL, ALEXANDER, of Monzie, a Lieutenant General and a Member of Parliament, was admitted as a burgess of Dunfermline on 15 September 1807. [DM]

CAMPBELL, ALLAN, a merchant from Glasgow, was admitted as a burgess and guilds-brother of Dunfermline on 19 November 1792. [DM]

CAMPBELL, COLIN, Major of the 44th Regiment, was admitted as a burgess and guilds-brother of Dunfermline on 19 November 1792. [DM]

CAMPBELL, DAVID, formerly in the Service of the East India Company in Madras, India, died in St Andrews on 27 January 1828. [St Andrews gravestone, Fife]

CAMPBELL, Dr JAMES, from Calcutta, India, was admitted as a burgess and guilds-brother of Dunfermline on 19 November 1792. [DM]

CAMPBELL, JAMES DAVID LYON, died in Melbourne, Victoria, Australia, on 31 May 1844. [St Andrews gravestone, Fife]

CAMPBELL, JOHN, a weaver, son of James Campbell, was admitted as a burgess of Dunfermline on 17 August 1792. [DM]

CAMPBELL, JOHN, a Writer to the Signet from Edinburgh, was admitted as a burgess and guilds-brother of Dunfermline on 19 November 1792. [DM]

CAMPBELL, JOHN, minister of the Associate Congregation in Dunfermline, was admitted as a burgess and guilds-brother of Dunfermline on 1 August 1808. [DM]

CAMPBELL, MARGARET, born 1846, daughter of Alexander Campbell and his wife Agnes Reddoch, died in America on 23 March 1875. [Tulliallan gravestone, Fife]

CAMPBELL, PATRICK, of the Royal Navy, was admitted as a burgess and guilds-brother of Dunfermline on 19 November 1792. [DM]

CAMPBELL, THOMAS, from Methil, Fife, a sailor in the Royal Navy in 1799. [NRS.S/H]

CAMPBELL, WALTER, Captain of the Loyal Stirlingshire Volunteers, was admitted as a burgess and guilds-brother of Dunfermline in July 1804. [DM]

CAMPBELL, WILLIAM, a weaver, son of James Campbell, was admitted as a burgess and guilds-brother of Dunfermline on 30 July 1791. [DM]

CAMPBELL, WILLIAM, a surgeon, was admitted as a burgess and guilds-brother of Dunfermline on 4 June 1802. [DM]

CANT, DAVID, born 1807, son of Reverend George Cant, died in South Australia, on 13 May 1876. [Kingsbarns gravestone, Fife]

CANT, GEORGE, born 1765, schoolmaster at Dunino and a Licentiate of the Church of Scotland, died 31 May 1813, husband of Christian Robertson, born 1772, died in Kingsbarns on 23 May 1834. [Dunino gravestone, Fife]

CANT, JOHN, a weaver, son-in-law of Alexander Gib a wright burgess, was admitted as a burgess of Dunfermline on 8 August 1793. [DM]

CARNEGIE, ANDREW, born 25 November 1835 in Dunfermline, Fife, emigrated to America in 1848, a steel producer and philanthropist, a trust deed dated December 1913, died in Lenox, Massachusetts, on 11 August 1919. [NRS.RD15.1.4]

CARNOCHAN, SAMUEL, Ensign of the West Lowland Fencibles, was admitted as a burgess and guilds-brother of Dunfermline on 4 June 1798. [DM]

CARPHIN, JOHN, 2nd Lieutenant of the Royal Linlithgow Volunteers, was admitted as a burgess and guilds-brother of Dunfermline on 15 August 1804. [DM]

CARR, JOHN, agent in Dunfermline, Fife, for the Bank of Scotland in 1849. [POD]

CARSTAIRS, GEORGE, born 30 July 1776 in St Andrews, Fife, died in Leith on 1 December 1836, spouse of Helen Drysdale. [South Leith gravestone]

CARSTAIRS, JAMES, jr., a writer, was admitted as a burgess of Cupar, Fife, on 9 October 1808. [CuBR]

CASSEL, JOHN, born 1779 in Cupar, Fife, a student at the University of St Andrews, a teacher and minister in Nova Scotia, died in Bocca Bec, St Patricks, New Brunswick, on 18 July 1850. [StA.U.Library]

CATHCART, TAYLOR, son of James Cathcart of Pitcairly, Fife, was educated at Glasgow University in 1793, settled in Jamaica. [MAGU]

CATTON, JOHN EDWARD, born 1853, settled in the Punjab, India, died in Braemar, Aberdeenshire, on 17 August 1886. [Aberdour gravestone, Fife]

CHALMERS, ALEXANDER, a surgeon in Culross, was admitted as a burgess and guilds-brother of Dunfermline on 3 May 1791. [DM]

CHALMER, ALEXANDER, a weaver, son-in-law of David Sym a wight burgess, was admitted as a burgess and guilds-brother of Dunfermline on 11 September 1792. [DM]

CHALMERS, DAVID, from Auchtermuchty, Fife, a printer in New York by 1822. [NRS.NRAS.0462.10]

CHALMERS, GEORGE, born 1825, son of John Chalmers and his wife Elizabeth Geddes in Kirkcaldy, Fife, died in Havanna, Cuba, on 5 June 1862. [Benochy gravestone, Perthshire]

CHALMERS, Reverend PETER, in Dunfermline, Fife, married Marion Hay, youngest daughter of James Hay, in Portobello, Midlothian, on 10 October 1822. [SM.90.631]

CHALMER, ROBERT, a shoemaker, son-in-law of Andrew Henderson a weaver, was admitted as a burgess and guilds-brother of Dunfermline on 13 March 1793. [DM]

CHALMERS, THOMAS, a weaver, son-in-law of William Allaster a weaver burgess, was admitted as a burgess and guilds-brother of Dunfermline on 2 January 1788. [DM]

CHALMERS, THOMAS H., born 1793 in Fife, a grocer who was naturalised in New York on 7 May 1821. [N.Y. Court of Common Pleas]

CHALMERS, WILLIAM, born 1778, son of John Chalmers and his wife Elizabeth Hall, died aboard the Queen at Rio de Janeiro, Brazil, in 1800. [Anstruther Easter gravestone, Fife]

CHALMERS, WILLIAM, son of Andrew Chalmers a weaver burgess, was admitted as a burgess and guilds-brother of Dunfermline on 22 May 1801. [DM]

CHAPMAN, JAMES, son of Laurence Chapman a baker burgess, was admitted as a burgess and guilds-brother of Dunfermline on 13 March 1793. [DM]

CHAPMAN, WILLIAM, a weaver, son-in-law of Andrew Chalmers a weaver burgess, was admitted as a burgess and guilds-brother of Dunfermline on 13 May 1802. [DM]

CHARLES, A.H., and his wife Jeanne Steel, ere parents of Alexander H. Charles, born 1857, died on the Isle de Naos, Panama Bay, on 6 September 1885. [Burntisland gravestone, Fife]

CHEAP, JOHN, of Rossie, Fife, was admitted as a burgess and guilds-brother of Dunfermline onm20 September 1793. [DM]; was admitted as a burgess of Cupar, Fife, on 21 October 1795. [CuBR]

CHISHOLM, ALEXANDER, a skipper and manager of the Pittenweem Sea Box Society in 1787; husband of Mary Mortimer in 1793. [NRS.B3.7.5; B60.8.1]

CHISHOLM, ALEXANDER, son-in-law of Andrew Blair a burgess, was admitted as a burgess of Dunfermline on 21 March 1805. [DM]

CHISHOLM, WILLIAM, a merchant in Virginia, later in Pittenweem, Fife, by 1794. [NRS.CS17.1.13/450]

CHRISTIE, ALEXANDER, of Foodie, Fife, was admitted as a burgess of Cupar, Fife, on 4 September 1808. [CuBR]

CHRISTIE, ANDREW, born 1788, son of Andrew Christie and his wife Margaret Dempster, died in India on 26 November 1821. [Cupar gravestone, Fife]

CHRISTIE, BETSY, wife of Henry Christie and daughter of George Christie in the Mains of Lindores, Fife, died in Chelsea, Massachusetts, on 14 February 1859. [Fife Herald]

CHRYSTIE, GEORGE, son of Andrew Chrystie a weaver burgess, was admitted as a burgess of Dunfermline on 8 May 1790. [DM]

CHRISTIE, HENRY, was admitted as a burgess of Cupar, Fife, in October 1810. [CuBR]

CHRISTIE, JOHN, born 1833, son of George Christie and his wife Christine Strobie, died in Rio de Janeiro, Brazil, on 7 February 1853. [Ferryport on Craig, gravestone, Fife]

CHRISTIE, MARY, born 1824, daughter of C. M. Christie of Durie, wife of Francis Brown an advocate in Edinburgh, died 8 January 1848. [British Cemetery gravestone, Funchal, Madeira]

CHRISTIE, RALPH, a tailor, son of Robert Christie a tailor burgess, was admitted as a burgess of Dunfermline on 21 January 1789. [DM]

CHRISTIE, ROBERT, a farmer from Greenock, was admitted as a burgess of Dunfermline on 24 October 1809. [DM]

CHRISTIE, ROBERT, in Durie Fife, father of Charles Horace Christie, born 15 July 1852, died in Italy on 11 April 1877. [Protestant Cemetery gravestone in Rome]

CHRISTIE, ROBERT, of Durie, born 24 July 1818, a Captain of the 5th Bengal Cavalry in the Service of the East India Company, died 29 August 1896. [St Monance gravestone, Fife]

CHRISTIE, WILLIAM, son of Andrew Christie a weaver burgess, was admitted as a burgess of Dunfermline on 11 October 1792. [DM]

CHRISTIE, WILLIAM, born 16 December 1817, son of John Christie and his wife Janet Jamieson, died in Port of Spain, Trinidad, on 4 April 1838. [Tulliallan gravestone]

CHRISTIE, WILLIAM, eldest son of John Christie of the Royal Hotel in St Andrews, died in Minnesota Territory on 8 May 1852. [FJ.1018]

CHRYSTIE, WILLIAM, late in Kingston, Jamaica, youngest son of Alexander Chrystie of Balchrystie, died in Clifton on 5 June 1844. [AJ.5036] [EEC.21056] [W.5.481]

CHRISTIE, ..., of Durie, Fife, was admitted as a burgess and guilds-brother of Dunfermline on 25 June 1798. [DM]

CHRISTIE, Captain, of the Fife Militia, was admitted as a burgess and guilds-brother of Dunfermline on 25 June 1798. [DM]

CLARK, GEORGE, junior, a fisherman, was admitted as a burgess of Crail, Fife, in 1806. [CBR]

CLARK, THOMAS, a weaver, son in law of George Henderson in Lochend, was admitted as a burgess of Dunfermline on 16 August 1793. [DM]

CLARKSON, ADAM, son of John Clarkson sr., was admitted as a burgess of Kirkcaldy, Fife, on 5 September 1795. [KBR]

CLARKSON, JOHN, a dancing teacher, was admitted as a burgess of Kirkcaldy, Fife, on 5 September 1795. [KBR]

CLEGHORN, ALLAN MACKENZIE, son of Peter Cleghorn, of the 4th Madras Native Infantry, died in Hong Kong on 4 November 1844. [Dunino gravestone, Fife]

CLEGHORN, ISABELLA, born 1823, daughter of Peter Cleghorn, died in Rome, Italy, in 1888. [Dunino gravestone]

CLEGHORN, PETER, of Stravithie, a barrister in Madras, India, died 9 June 1863. [Dunino gravestone]

CLEPHANE, GEORGE, son of Andrew Clephane the Sheriff of Fife, died in Fergus, Canada, on 2 May 1851. [FJ.9621]

CLEPHANE, JAMES, born 20 October 1790, son of Thomas Clephane emigrated from Kirkcaldy to Norfolk, Virginia, in 1817, settled in Washington, DC, was naturalised on 10 December 1833 in the Circuit Court of the District of Columbia. [NARA]

COBBAN, JOHN, married Robina Hill, in Dunfermline, Fife, in 1830, a Process of Divorce in 1827. [NRS.CC8.6.167]

COCHRANE, Captain ALEXANDER F., of the Royal Navy, was admitted as a burgess and guilds-brother of Dunfermline on 21 March 1802. [DM]

COCHRANE, Captain ANDREW, of the Royal Navy, was admitted as a burgess and guilds-brother of Dunfermline on 8 April 1791. [DM]

COCHRANE, ARCHIBALD, Earl of Dundonald, was admitted as a burgess and guilds-brother of Dunfermline on 8 April 1791. [DM]

COCHRANE, JAMES CHURCH, of the Bengal Civil Service, died in Azamgarh, India, on 4 February 1874. [Cupar gravestone, Fife]

COCHRANE, JOHN, was admitted as a burgess and guilds-brother of Dunfermline on 8 June 1804. [DM]

COCKBURN, BARTHOLEMEW, a writer, was admitted as a burgess and guilds-brother of Cupar, Fife, on 24 September 1808. [CuBR]

COCKBURN, THOMAS, a merchant in Inverkeithing, Fife, was admitted as a burgess of Dunfermline on 19 November 1792. [DM]

COCKBURN, WILLIAM, son of William Cockburn and his wife Euphemia Hunter, a Lieutenant of the 24th Native Infantry, died in India in 1820. [Cupar gravestone, Fife]

COLDSTREAM, ALEXANDER, born 1766, son of Alexander Coldstream and his wife Janet Goodfellow, manager of Mitcham Estate on Dominica in 1799, [NRS.B65.5.8.104-106]; died on passage from Dominica on 6 August 1809. [St Andrews gravestone, Fife]

COLLIER, GEORGE, a weaver, was admitted as a burgess of Kirkcaldy, Fife, on 22 September 1792. [KBR]

COLLIER, ..., a Captain Lieutenant of the Fife Militia, was admitted as a burgess and guilds-brother of Dunfermline on 25 June 1798. [DM]

COLVILLE, ALEXANDER, son of Thomas Colville of Lambhill, was admitted as a burgess of Dunfermline on 4 August 1803. [DM]

COLVILLE, ANDREW, son of Thomas Colville of Lambhill, was admitted as a burgess of Dunfermline on 1 April 1803. [DM]

COMB, WILLIAM, a smith, was admitted as a burgess of Cupar, Fife, on 30 September 1800. [CuBR]

CONDIE, DAVID, jr., a tanner, was admitted as a burgess of Kirkcaldy, Fife, on 18 March 1790. [KBR]

CONNACHER, WILLIAM, born in 1844, son of William Connacher and his wife Helen Scott, died in Geelong, Victoria, Australia, on 12 September 1871. [Forgan gravestone, Fife]

CONNOLLY, M.F., agent in Anstruther, Fife, for the National Bank of Scotland in 1849. [POD]

CONSTABLE, ALEXANDER, a currier, was admitted as a burgess of Cupar, Fife, in 1811. [CuBR]

COOK, DANIEL, son of John Cook a weaver burgess, was admitted as a burgess of Dunfermline on 2 August 1792. [DM]

COOK, DAVID, son of John Cook a weaver burgess, was admitted as a burgess of Dunfermline on 5 July 1797. [DM]

COOK, JAMES, son of John Cook a weaver burgess, was admitted as a burgess of Dunfermline on 17 September 1790. [DM]

COOK, JOHN, born 8 August 1800, a master mariner, died 14 November 1831, buried in Holland. [Pittenweem gravestone, Fife]

COOK, JOSEPH, son of Professor Cook in St Andrews, Fife, died in Madeira on 6 February 1808. [ARM.70.317]

COOK, JOSEPH, born 1831, son of Joseph Cook and his wife Isabella Girdwood, died in Dunedin, Otago, New Zealand, on 20 January 1886. [St Andrews gravestone, Fife]

COOK, WALTER, born 1815, a Lieutenant of the 10th Madras Native Infantry Regiment, third son of Dr John Cook, Professor of Divinity in St Mary's College, University of St Andrews, died at the Cape of Good Hope, South Africa, on 7 November 1838. [AJ.4750] [St Andrews gravestone, Fife]

COOPER, GEORGE, a weaver, son of Charles Cooper a weaver burgess, was admitted as a burgess of Dunfermline on 26 September 1810. [DM]

COOPER, JAMES LUNDIN, of the Madras Fusiliers, died in Lucknow, United Provinces, India, on 25 October 1857. [Kirkcaldy gravestone, Fife]

CORBET, JAMES, a Lieutenant of the West Lowland Fencibles, was admitted as a burgess and guilds-brother of Dunfermline on 23 May 1798. [DM]

CORNFOOT, ANDREW JAMES, born 1807 in Largo, Fife, died in Surinam in 1830. [BM.28.574]

CORSTORPHINE, CHARLES, died in Georgetown, Demerara, on 12 August 1867. [St Andrews gravestone, Fife]

CORSTORPHINE, GEORGE, born 1806, son of Thomas Corstorphine and his wife Ann Johnston, died in Barbados on 20 September 1834. [St Andrews gravestone, Fife]

COUL, JOHN, born 1821, son of John Coul and his wife Ann Bissett, died in Windsor, California, on 3 December 1878. [Leuchars gravestone, Fife]

COUPAR, HENRY, a skipper in London, son and heir of Henry Coupar a sailor in Newburgh, Fife, in 1792. [NRS.S/H]

COUPAR, JAMES, son-in-law of George Anderson a weaver burgess, was admitted as a burgess of Dunfermline on 19 September 1797. [DM]

COUPAR, JOHN, son of George Coupar a weaver burgess, was admitted as a burgess of Dunfermline on 28 September 1792. [DM]

COUPAR, JOHN, son of David Coupar a tailor burgess, was admitted as a burgess and guilds-brother of Dunfermline on 4 July 1797. [DM]

COUPAR, THOMAS, a weaver, son of John Coupar a weaver burgess, was admitted as a burgess of Dunfermline on 4 September 1793. [DM]

COVENTRY, ROBERT, son of William Coventry a weaver burgess, was admitted as a burgess and guilds-brother of Dunfermline on 20 August 1802. [DM]

COWAN, THOMAS, Captain of the Royal Linlithgow Volunteers, was admitted as a burgess and guilds-brother of Dunfermline on 15 August 1804. [DM]

COWAN, WILLIAM, a baker, was admitted as a burgess of Crail, Fife, in 1790. [CBR]

COWBROUGH, Captain, master of the Sceptre of Burntisland from Leith to Quebec and Montreal in 1819. [NRS.E504.22.84]

COX, ELIZABETH, born 1819 in Elie, Fife, daughter of Henry Cox of the Royal Navy, wife of David Mason, died in Savanna la Mar,

Westmoreland, Jamaica, on 2 May 1850. [Petersville gravestone, Jamaica]

CRAIG, ALEXANDER, son of Adam Craig in Kilconquhar Mill, Fife, was apprenticed to Thomas Craig, a tailor in Edinburgh, for five years, on 29 November 1800. [ERA]

CRAIG, DAVID, at West 31st Street, New York, a sasine, 1854. [NRS.Auchtermuchty.Fife,5.8]

CRAIG, Captain, master of the Margaret of Kirkcaldy trading between Greenock and New York also Virginia in 1822. [NRS.E504.15.140]

CRAMBIE, SAMUEL, a skipper in Halketshall, Fife, testament, 21 August 1812, Comm. St Andrews. [NRS]

CRAWFORD, ANDREW, born 1827, son of Andrew Crawford and his wife Jean Davidson, died in Hong Kong, China, on 22 August 1861. [Kilrenny gravestone, Fife]

CRAWFORD, DAVID, son of James Crawford a burgess, was admitted as a burgess of Dunfermline on 25 March 1805. [DM]

CRAWFORD, JOHN, born 1828, son of Andrew Crawford and his wife Jean Davidson, died in Melbourne, Victoria, Australia, on 4 April 1864. [Kilrenny gravestone, Fife]

CRAWFORD, ROBERT, son of James Crawford a burgess, was admitted as a burgess of Dunfermline on 25 March 1805. [DM]

CRAWFORD, JAMES, son of James Crawford in Pitbaichly, Fife, was admitted as a burgess of Dunfermline on 15 February 1796. [DM]

CRAWFORD, JOHN, son of James Crawford, was admitted as a burgess and of Dunfermline on 15 February 1796. [DM]

CRAWFORD, WILLIAM, born 1794, son of William Crawford, a Lieutenant of the 16th Bengal Native Infantry, died in Calcutta, India, on 6 April 1818. [St Andrews gravestone, Fife]

CREE, MATTHEW, son-in-law of John Allaster a weaver burgess, was admitted as a burgess of Dunfermline on 13 August 1796. [DM]

CRERAR, JAMES, a bookseller, was admitted as a burgess of Kirkcaldy, Fife, on 14 June 1798. [KBR]

CRIGHTON, GEORGE, son of George Crighton a mason burgess, was admitted as a burgess of Dunfermline on 30 July 1791. [DM]

CROLL, ANDREW, born 1821, son of Charles Croll and his wife Janet Mitchell, died in Quebec on 18 June 1848. [St Andrews gravestone, Fife]

CUMING, ALEXANDER, 1at Lieutenant of the Royal Linlithgow Volunteers, was admitted as a burgess and guilds-brother of Dunfermline on 15 August 1804. [DM]

CUMMING, JAMES, a book-binder, was admitted as a burgess of Kirkcaldy, Fife, on 13 September 1794. [KBR]

CUMIN, JAMES, a mason, son-in-law of David Moir a weaver, was admitted as a burgess and guilds-brother of Dunfermline on 14 September 1807. [DM]

CUMMING, JAMES, born 1829, son of George and Janet Cumming, a skipper who died in Barbados on 27 May 1855. [Ferry-Port-on-Craig, Fife]

CUMMING, JOHN BALFOUR, born 1817, a Staff Sergeant of the Bengal Infantry, died on 12 January 1892. [Culross gravestone, Fife]

CUMMINGS, J., master of the *Fame of Kirkcaldy* trading between Greenock and Montreal, Quebec, in 1816. [NRS.E504.55.111]

CUNNINGHAM, DAVID H., youngest son of John Cunningham in Crail, Fife, died in Calcutta, India, on 4 June 1859. [EFR.4.8.1860]

CUNNINGHAM, JAMES, born 1722, a soldier of the Scots Brigade in Holland, died in Brompton in 1793. [Inverkeithing gravestone, Fife]

CURRIE, JAMES, a farmer in Rosyth, Fife, was admitted as a burgess and guilds-brother of Dunfermline on 13 April 1791. [DM]

CURRIE, JAMES, born 1774, a mariner, died on 29 October 1799. [Aberdour gravestone, Fife]

CURRIE, JOHN, a sailor in Aberdour, Fife, testament, 1820, Comm. Dunblane. [NRS]

CURROR, ANDREW B, born 1811, second son of Robert Curror of Wester Craigduckie, Fife, a surgeon of the Royal Navy, died at the River Gambia, West Africa, on 11 July 1844. [EEC.21095]

CURROR, ROBERT, of Craigduckie, Fife, was admitted as a burgess of Dunfermline on 27 March 1803. [DM]

CUSINE, JOHN, an Ensign of the 71st Regiment of Foot, son of John Cusine a merchant in Dunfermline, was admitted as a burgess and guilds-brother of Dunfermline on 1 August 1808. [DM]

CUTHBERT, JAMES, of Berthier, son of David Cuthbert, [1715-1781], HM Legislative Councillor in Canada. [Culross gravestone, Fife]

CUTHILL, ARCHIBALD, a Lieutenant of the Loyal Stirling Volunteers, was admitted as a burgess and guilds-brother of Dunfermline on 17 July 1794. [DM]

CUTLER, JAMES, a manufacturer in Pathhead, was admitted as a burgess of Kirkcaldy, Fife, on 17 July 1795. [KBR]

DAIRSIE, MARGARET, daughter of John Dairsie and his wife Agnes Robertson, husband of William Sturgeon, died in Westerly, Rhode Island, in May 1849. [Anstruther Easter gravestone, Fife]

DALGLEISH, Dr ROBERT, of Scotscraig, Fife, was admitted as a burgess and guilds-brother of Dunfermline on 27 October 1790. [DM]

DALGLEISH, WILLIAM, the younger of Scotscraig, Fife, was admitted as a burgess and guilds-brother of Dunfermline on 27 October 1790. [DM]

DALL, ALEXANDER, born 1815, son of James Dall, [died 1850], and his wife Agnes Black, [died 1869], a Customs officer who died in Falmouth, Jamaica, on 8 September 1840. [Leuchars gravestone, Fife] [Cupar gravestone, Fife] [FJ.12.11.1840]

DALL, THOMAS, son of David Dall a shoemaker burgess, was admitted as a burgess of Cupar, Fife, on 30 August 1796. [CuBR]

DALL, THOMAS, a shoemaker, was admitted as a burgess of Cupar, Fife, on 29 September 1800. [CuBR]

DALL, WILLIAM, born 1797, died in Racine, Wisconsin, on 24 May 1877. [Newburgh, Fife, gravestone]

DALLAS, JOHN, son-in-law of James Anderson a burgess, was admitted as a burgess of Dunfermline on 8 August 1801. [DM]

DALRYMPLE, JOHN HAMILTON, born 1777, the Customs Collector at Montego Bay, Jamaica, died there on 7 August 1804. [St Andrews gravestone, Fife] [Montego Bay gravestone]

DARLING, THOMAS, born 29 December 1834 in Dunfermline, son of John Darling and his wife Elizabeth Bonar, died in Rowayton, Connecticut, on 28 January 1909. [Dunfermline Abbey gravestone, Fife]

DAVIDSON, ALEXANDER, born 1788, son of John Davidson, a mariner who died in Bengal, India, on 23 October 1809. [Kilrenny gravestone, Fife]

DAVIDSON, Captain GEORGE, born 1774, son of John Davidson, died on Isle de France, [Mauritius], on 22 February 1810. [Kilrenny gravestone, Fife]

DAVIDSON, JAMES, a surgeon, was admitted as a burgess and guilds-brother of Dunfermline on 4 June 1792. [DM]

DAVIDSON, JAMES, a fisherman in Crail, Fife, in 1797. [SBC.19]

DAVIDSON, JAMES, a slater, was admitted as a burgess of Dunfermline on 18 May 1810. [DM]

DAVIDSON, JAMES, born 1823, son of John Davidson and Margaret Ramage in Dunfermline, Fife, emigrated to Canada in 1844. [SG.39.1.40]

DAVIDSON, JOHN, a member of the Pitteneem Sea Box Society, Fife, in 1792. [NRS.B3.7.5]

DAVIDSON, JOHN, born 1834, son of John Davidson and his wife Janet Sutherland, died in Adelaide, South Australia, on 22 July 1881. [Burntisland gravestone, Fife]

DAVIDSON, MARGARET, born 1805, wife of James Anderson, died in Calcutta, India, in 1843. [Kennoway gravestone, Fife]

DAVIDSON, SAMUEL, agent in Kirkcaldy, Fife, for the Commercial Bank of Scotland in 1849. [POD]

DAVIDSON, THOMAS, a waulker, son of William Davidson, was admitted as a burgess of Cupar, Fife, on 1 October 1800. [CuBR]

DAVIDSON, THOMAS, born 1760, a mariner in Pittenweem, Fife, husband of Elizabeth Henderson, died 27 May 1815, [Pittenweem gravestone]; testament, 13 November 1815, Comm. St Andrews. [NRS]

DAVIE, AMBROSE, born 1813 in Dunfermline, Fife, died in Boston, Massachusetts, on 13 July 1848. [Dunfermline Abbey gravestone]

DAVIE, THOMAS, a grocer, was admitted as a burgess of Kirkcaldy, Fife, on 18 September 1802. [KBR]

DAWSON, DAVID, born 1764, a ships mate and a member of the Pittenweem Sea Box Society in 1789, died on 25 August 1835. [NRS.B3.7.5][Anstruther Easter gravestone]

DAY, ALEXANDER, son-in-law of James Reid a shoemaker burgess, was admitted as a burgess of Dunfermline on 28 May 1795. [DM]

DEAS, DAVID, a wright, was admitted as a burgess of Cupar, Fife, on 9 December 1799. [CuBR]

DEAS, JAMES, a skipper in East Wemyss, Fife, testament, 1821, Comm. St Andrews. [NRS]

DEAS, Dr JAMES, youngest son of Frances Deas in Falkland, Fife, a surgeon of the Royal Navy, who died at the Cape of Good Hope, South Africa, on 29 September 1849. [SG.1879]

DEAS, ROBERT, a skipper in East Wemyss, Fife, testament, 1821, Comm. St Andrews. [NRS]

DEMPSTER, ALEXANDER, seventh son of James Dempster a surgeon in Cupar, Fife, died on Dunkley's Estate, Vere, Jamaica, on 24 October 1835. [FH]

DEMPSTER, Dr ANTHONY, fourth son of James Dempster a surgeon in Cupar, Fife, died in Manchester, Jamaica, in September 1847. [FH]

DEMPSTER, Dr DAVID THOMSON, fifth son of James Dempster a surgeon in Cupar, Fife, died in Spanish Town, Jamaica, on 3 December 1834. [FH]

DEMPSTER, JAMES, born 1760 in Cupar, Fife, died in Georgia on 18 October 1802. [Georgia gravestone]

DEMPSTER, Dr JAMES, fifth son of James Dempster a surgeon in Cupar, Fife, died in Spanish Town, Jamaica, on 3 December 1834. [FH]

DEMPSTER, SIMON, a merchant, was admitted as a burgess of Kirkcaldy, Fife, on 25 November 1793. [KBR]

DEWAR, Dr HENRY, of Lassodie, Fife, married Helen Spence, daughter of Andrew Spence in Philadelphia, Pennsylvania, in Dunfermline, Fife, on 24 May 1809. [SM.71.477]

DEWAR, JOHN, a skipper in Limekilns, Fife, testament, 1820, Comm. St Andrews. [NRS]

DEWAR, JOHN, born 1742, tenant of Cabbage Hall, died in December 1814, husband of Isobel Meiklejohn, born 1744, died in April 1810. [Dunino gravestone, Fife]

DEWAR, WILLIAM, a tailor, son-in-law of James Gilmour a labourer burgess, was admitted as a burgess of Dunfermline on 26 November 1807. [DM]

DICK, DAVID, a wright. was admitted as a burgess of Cupar, Fife, on 12 December 1799. [CuBR]

DICK, JOHN, a weaver, son-in-law of James Alison a weaver burgess, was admitted as a burgess and guilds-brother of Dunfermline on 19 September 1794. [DM]

DICK, JOHN, jr., a butcher, was admitted as a burgess of Cupar, Fife, in 1806. [CuBR]

DICKIE, WILLIAM, son of William Dickie a merchant in and baillie of Dunfermline, Fife, a writer in Dundee, was admitted as a notary public on 4 July 1799. [NRS.NP2.36.285]

DICKSON, Reverend DAVID, in Bothkennar, Fife, was admitted as a burgess and guilds-brother of Dunfermline on 6 June 179. [DM]

DICKSON, THOMAS, a skipper who died in Dieppe, France, on 16 June 1866. [Crail gravestone, Fife]

DINGWALL, WALTER, a saddler, was admitted as a burgess of Cupar, Fife, on 24 November 1802. [CuBR]

DINGWALL, WILLIAM, born 1777, son of Joh Dingwall and his wife Ann Sharp, a surgeon in the Royal Navy, died on 1 December 1815. [Kettle gravestone, Fife]

DINNIE, GEORGE, a land labourer, was admitted as a burgess of Kirkcaldy, Fife, on 17 July 1790. [KBR]

DIXON, Captain ROBERT, born 1783 in Fife, died in Yarmouth, Nova Scotia, on 27 September 1843. [HT.17.10.18.43]

DOBIE, ROBERT, born 1809 in Kirkcaldy, Fife, died in St John's, Newfoundland, in June 1837. [RGNA.27.6.1837]

DOIG, JOHN, born 1809, son of James Doig and his wife Anne Henderson, died in Hobart, Tasmania, Australia, on 12 December 1859. [Burntisland gravestone, Fife]

DOIG, ROBERT FLEMING, Captain of the 2nd Regiment of Infantry, died at Bolarum, Hyderabad Deccan, India, on 12 August 1871. [Torryburn gravestone, Fife]

DOIG, WILLIAM, born 1829, son of John Doig and his wife Elizabeth Watson, died in Williamstown, Victoria, Australia, on 17 October 1882. [Kilrenny gravestone, Fife]

DONALD, DAVID, son of David Donald a burgess, was admitted as a burgess of Dunfermline on 29 March 1805. [DM]

DONALD, DAVID, son of Thomas Donald, was admitted as a burgess and guilds-brother of Dunfermline on 8 June 1809. [DM]

DONALD, EBENEZER, born 1820, son of James Donald and his wife Helen Fotheringham, died at sea on 22 April 1848, was buried at Old Castle, the Dardanelles, Turkey. [Tulliallan gravestone, Fife]

DONALD, GEORGE, son of John Donald a weaver burgess, was admitted as a burgess of Dunfermline on 25 November 1801. [DM]

DONALD, JAMES, a weaver, former apprentice of David Allaster a weaver burgess, was admitted as a burgess of Dunfermline on 30 January 1797. [DM]

DONALD, JAMES, son of James Donald a weaver burgess, was admitted as a burgess of Dunfermline on 4 July 1797. [DM]

DONALD, JAMES, a shoemaker, son-in-law of James Hoggan a brewer burgess, was admitted as a burgess of Dunfermline on 14 October 1809. [DM]

DONALD, JOHN, son of John Donald a weaver burgess, was admitted as a burgess of Dunfermline on 25 November 1801. [DM]

DONALD, THOMAS, born 1823, son of James Donald and his wife Helen Fotheringham, died 27 February 1882, buried in Syria. [Tulliallan gravestone, Fife]

DONALDSON, JAMES, son of Henry Donaldson a weaver burgess, was admitted as a burgess and guilds-brother of Dunfermline on 5 June 1790. [DM]

DONALDSON, JOHN, son of Henry Donaldson a weaver burgess, was admitted as a burgess of Dunfermline on 5 September 1791. [DM]

DONALDSON, JOHN, son of John Donaldson a weaver burgess, was admitted as a burgess and guilds-brother of Dunfermline on 14 September 1803. [DM]

DONALDSON, JOHN, from Cupar, Fife, a theological student in 1808, emigrated to America. [UPC]

DONALDSON, THOMAS, from Cupar, Fife, emigrated via Belfast aboard the Perseverence bound for New York in 1811. [NWI.2.335]

DOTT, ANDREW, born 1756, a gunner in the Royal Navy, died on 10 August 1818. [Anstruther Easter gravestone, Fife]

DOUGLAS, ANDREW, Adjutant Lieutenant of the Scots Brigade, was admitted as a burgess and guilds-brother of Dunfermline on 4 June 1795. [DM]

DOUGLAS, ANDREW, Captain of the West Lowland Fencibles, was admitted as a burgess and guilds-brother of Dunfermline on 23 May 1798. [DM]

DOUGLAS, CHARLES HILL, born 1832, died in Melbourne, Victoria, Australia, on 30 March 1898. [Dunfermline gravestone, Fife]

DOUGLAS, DAVID, son of William Douglas a weaver burgess, was admitted as a burgess and guilds-brother of Dunfermline on 29 August 1791. [DM]

DOUGLAS, DAVID, a wright, son of Andrew Douglas, was admitted as a burgess of Cupar, Fife, on 3 October 1804. [CuBR]

DOUGLAS, GEORGE, a wright, son of Andrew Douglas, was admitted as a burgess of Cupar, Fife, on 24 September 1808. [CuBR]

DOUGLAS, JAMES, a writer, son of John Douglas the town clerk, was admitted as a burgess and guilds-brother of Dunfermline on 9 April 1790. [DM]

DOUGLAS, JAMES, son of James Douglas a burgess, was admitted as a burgess and guilds-brother of Dunfermline on 29 March 1805. [DM]

DOUGLAS, JOHN, bon 1784 in Dunfermline, Fife, a brewer, distiller and storekeeper, settled in Whitestown, Oneida County, New York, was naturalised there on 2 May 1821 and 11 October 1830. [NARA]

DOUGLAS, PATRICK, surgeon of the West Lowland Fencibles, was admitted as a burgess and guilds-brother of Dunfermline on 23 May 1798. [DM]

DOUGLAS, ROBERT, from Burntisland, Fife, died in Jamaica, testament, St Andrews, 20 August 1816. [NRS.SC.CC20.30.204]

DOUGLAS, ROBERT, agent in Dunfermline, Fife, for the British Linen Company in 1849. [POD]

DOUGLAS, WILLIAM, son-in-law of Robert Young a mason burgess, was admitted as a burgess and guilds-brother of Dunfermline on 14 September 1804. [DM]

DOUGLAS, WILLIAM, born in Dunfermline, Fife, emigrated to USA before 1834, a linen merchant in New York who was drowned on 8 January 1839. [ANY][DJ.22.6.1905]

DOVE, Mrs JEAN, widow of James Dove in Kingston, Jamaica, sister and heir of John Kirkcaldy, a landwaiter in Limekilns, Fife, in 1805. [NRS.S/H]

DOWIE, JAMES, a baker from Ballado, Kinross, former apprentice of George Meldrum a baker burgess, was admitted as a burgess of Dunfermline on 16 March 1794. [DM]

DOWIE, ..., a Lieutenant of the Loyal Tayside Fencibles, was admitted as a burgess and guilds-brother of Dunfermline on 4 June 1801. [DM]

DRUMMOND, JOHN, son of Robert Drummond, a weaver burgess, was admitted as a burgess of Dunfermline on 5 September 1791. [DM]

DRUMMOND, KATHERINE, daughter of James Drummond in Kelty, Fife, died in Kingston, Jamaica, in 1806. [SM.69.77]

DRUMMOND, ROBERT, son of Robert Drummond, a weaver burgess, was admitted as a burgess of Dunfermline on 5 September 1791. [DM]

DRUMMOND, WILLIAM, agent in Cupar, Fife, for the Western Bank of Scotland in 1849. [POD]

DRYSDALE, DAVID, son of burgess John Drysdale, was admitted as a burgess of Dunfermline on 5 July 1797. [DM]

DRYSDALE, GEORGE, son of Robert Drysdale a weaver burgess, was admitted as a burgess of Dunfermline on 22 July 1791. [DM]

DRYSDALE, JOHN, son-in-law of John Hepburn a weaver burgess, was admitted as a burgess of Dunfermline on 5 July 1797. [DM]

DRYSDALE, JOHN, tacksman of the Customs of Dunfermline, was admitted as a burgess of Dunfermline on 20 June 1792. [DM]

DRYSDALE, JOHN, son of burgess John Drysdale in Coaltown, was admitted as a burgess of Dunfermline on 5 July 1797. [DM]

DRYSDALE, JOHN, a meal-seller, was admitted as a burgess of Dunfermline on 18 April 1807. [DM]

DRYSDALE, ROBERT, son of Robert Drysdale a weaver burgess, was admitted as a burgess of Dunfermline on 10 September 1790. [DM]

DRYSDALE, ROBERT, a baker from Kirkcaldy, Fife, settled in USA, a sasine, 1863. [NRS.RS.Kirkcaldy.12.29]

DRYSDALE, THOMAS, a weaver, son-in-law of David Anderson a weaver, was admitted as a burgess of Dunfermline on 7 August 1793. [DM]

DRYSDALE, WILLIAM, a saddler, was admitted as a burgess of Dunfermline on 16 June 1802. [DM]

DRYSDALE, WILLIAM, son of Andrew Drysdale a travelling merchant, was admitted as a burgess of Dunfermline on 11 August 1802. [DM]

DUDDINGSTON, WILLIAM, in Earlsferry, Fife, a Rear Admiral of the Royal Navy, testament, 1822, Comm. St Andrews. [NRS]

DUN, DAVID, of Kilconquhar Mains, Fife, father of George Dun, born 1865, and his sister Mary Forsyth Dun, born 1869, who were both drowned in the New River Estuary, Invrcargill, New Zealand, on 20 March 1885. [S.13028]

DUNCAN, ALEXANDER, a mariner in Crail in 1798. [SBC.23]

DUNCAN, ARCHIBALD, a mariner in Kinghorn, Fife, testament, 10 August 1809, Comm. St Andrews. [NRS]

DUNCAN, ARCHIBALD, a seaman in Kinghorn, Fife, testament, 31 January 1811, Comm. St Andrews. [NRS]

DUNCAN, GEORGE, a land labourer, was admitted as a burgess of Crail, Fife, in 1800. [CBR]

DUNCAN, JAMES, born 1772, son of William Duncan and his wife Agnes Sime, died in Savannah, Georgia, in 1798. [Kilmany gravestone, Fife]

DUNCAN, JAMES, a Lieutenant of the Sutherland Fencibles, was admitted as a burgess and guilds-brother of Dunfermline on 5 December 1794. [DM]

DUNCAN, JAMES, born 1826, Paymaster of the 13th Regiment of Foot, died in South Africa on 5 November 1878. [St Andrews gravestone, Fife]

DUNCAN, JOHN, a merchant, was admitted as a burgess of Crail, Fife, in 1792. [CBR]

DUNCAN, ROBERT, a merchant in Cupar, Fife, a bankrupt in 1803. [NRS.CS96.3996]

DUNCAN, WILLIAM, a seaman in St Monance, Fife, testament, 1819, Comm. St Andrews. [NRS]

DUNCAN, WILLIAM, son of Henry Duncan, [died 1835], and his wife Catherine Bell, [died 1842], settled in Salem, Massachusetts. [St Andrews gravestone, Fife]

DUNDAS, R.B., Captain of the Perth Volunteers, was admitted as a burgess and guilds-brother of Dunfermline on 22 February 1804. [DM]

DURHAM, Admiral Sir PHILIP CHARLES HENDERSON CALDERWOOD, of Largo, Royal Navy, born 29 July 1763 in Largo, Fife, died in Naples, Italy, on 2 April 1845. [Largo gravestone]

DURIE, AGNES, youngest daughter of Captain Robert Durie of Craigluscar, Fife, married William Wilkinson Massiah of Strong Hope, Barbados, on 29 October 1839. [EEC.19972]

DURIE, ANDREW, born 1802, from Dunfermline, Fife, died in Jersey City, New Jersey, on 13 February 1888. [DJ]

DURIE, JAMES, schoolmaster in Leven, Fife, a testament, 1796, Comm. St Andrews. [NRS]

DUTCH, DAVID, born 1849, son of William Dutch and Hele Hay, died in Sydney, New South Wales, Australia, on 3 December 1873. [Ferry-Port-on-Craig gravestone, Fife]

DUTCH, JOHN, born 1837, son of William Dutch and Hele Hay, died at Cape Horn, Chile, on 18 May 1853. [Ferry-Port-on-Craig gravestone, Fife]

EADIE, WILLIAM, a skipper in Anstruther, Fife, a testament, 1821, Comm. St Andrews. [NRS]

EASON, JOHN, a shipbuilder, son of Thomas Eason and his wife Margaret Henderson, settled in Hobart, Van Diemen's Land, [Tasmania], Australia, before 1854. [Anstruther Easter gravestone, Fife]

ECKFORD, JOHN, son of John Eckford and his wife Janet Buntine, master of the East India Company ship Lady Jean Dundas, died 1809. [Dunfermline gravestone, Fife]

EDGAR, MARY-ANN KNIGHT, born 1814, widow of John Hay Horsburgh, from Cupar, Fife, died in Cape Town, South Africa, on 10 September 1884. [FH]

EDIE, ALEXANDER, born 1801, son of David Edie and his wife Mary Stark, a Lieutenant in the Service of the East India Company, died in India in 1825. [Kilmany gravestone, Fife]

ELDER, ALEXANDER, a merchant, was admitted as a burgess of Kirkcaldy, Fife, on 19 August 1795. [KBR]

ELDER, GEORGE, son-in-law of George Inglis a merchant burgess, was admitted as a burgess of Dunfermline on 6 October 1806. [DM]

ELDER, JAMES, a master mariner in the Royal Navy, son and heir of Peter Elder, a skipper in Inverkeithing, Fife, and his wife Janet Cowan, in 1798. [NRS.S/H]

ELDER, JOHN, a wright, was admitted as a burgess of Crail, Fife, in 1796. [CBR]

ELLIS, CHARLES, born 1824 in Netherton, Fife, emigrated to America in 1859, a foreman dyer on Long Island, New York, and on Staten Island, N.Y., died there on 19 October 1897. [DJ]

ELLIS, JAMES, born 28 January 1826 in Dunfermline, Fife, married Mary Cram in 1848, emigrated to America, a gardener on Long Island, New York, for 15 years, later a farmer in Minnesota, died in 1905. [DJ.28.10.1905]

ELLIS, WILLIAM, of Netherton, born 1780, emigrated from Dunfermline, Fife, to America in 1857, died on Staten Island, New York, on 10 June 1869. [PJ]

EMMERSON, JAMES, born 1809, son of Thomas Emmerson and his wife Elspeth Fleming, died in Melbourne, Victoria, Australia, on 17 September 1864. [Crail gravestone, Fife]

EMMERSON, THOMAS, born 1802, son of Thomas Emmerson and his wife Elspeth Fleming, died in Calcutta, India, on 3 August 1831. [Crail gravestone, Fife]

ERSKINE, CAMPBELL, son of Robert Erskine a weaver burgess, was admitted as a burgess of Dunfermline on 16 September 1796. [DM]

ERSKINE, Sir CHARLES, in Crail, Fife, testaments, 5 July 1791 and 22 December 1792, Comm. St Andrews. [NRS], Comm.St Andrews. [NRS]

ERSKINE, DAVID, in Cambo, Kingsbarns, Fife, testament, 16 November 1793, Comm, St Andrews. [NRS]

ERSKINE, JAMES, Ensign of the 26th Regiment of Foot, was admitted as a burgess and guilds-brother of Dunfermline on 13 April 1791. [DM]

ERSKINE, JOHN THOMAS, Major of the Clackmannan Volunteers, was admitted as a burgess and guilds-brother of Dunfermline on 22 February 1804. [DM]

ERSKINE, Sir WILLIAM, of Cambo, Fife, born 1759, son of Sir Charles Erskine of Cambo and his wife Margaret Chiene, died at Niagara on 2 October 1791. [SP.V.93]

ERSKINE, Colonel WILLIAM, of Torry, was admitted as a burgess and guilds-brother of Dunfermline on 20 January 1795. [DM]

ERSKINE, WILLIAM, of Kineddar, an Advocate, was admitted as a burgess and guilds-brother of Dunfermline on 8 August 1799. [DM]

ERSKINE, WILLIAM, a butcher, was admitted as a burgess of Dunfermline on 13 July 1808. [DM]

ERSKINE, WILLIAM, born 1843, from Netherton, Dunfermline, Fife, died in Bayside, New York, on 20 July 1875. [DJ]

EWAN, JOHN, a gardener in Carnbee, Fife, a testament, 2 October 1800, Comm. St Andrews. [NRS]

EWING, PATRICK, a Captain of the Scots Brigade, was admitted as a burgess and guilds-brother of Dunfermline on 4 June 1795. [DM]

EWING, WILLIAM, agent in Burntisland, Fife, for the National Bank of Scotland in 1849. [POD]

FAIR, JOHN, son of John Fair and his wife Helen, paymaster of the 63rd Regiment of Foot, died in Barbados on 4 July 1808. [Kilconquhar gravestone, Fife]

FAIR, THOMAS, son of John Fair and his wife Helen, a Lieutenant in the Service of the East India Company, died in Goa, India, on 24 December 1822. [Kilconquhar gravestone, Fife]

FAIRFULL, ALEXANDER S., from St Andrews, Fife, died in Kingston, Jamaica, on 21 July 1852. [FJ.1026]

FAIRLEY, THOMAS, born 1800, died in Marseilles, France, on 4 May 1855. [Culross gravestone, Fife]

FALCONER, THOMAS, a mason in Cupar, Fife, testament, 15 September 1796, Comm. St Andrews. [NRS]

FARNIE, JAMES, from St Andrews, Fife, in Canada by 1853. [NRS.B9.8.1.213/116]

FARQUHARSON, WILLIAM, was admitted as a burgess of Kirkcaldy, Fife, on 19 December 1795. [KBR]

FERGUS, DAVID, a weaver, son of David Fergus an innkeeper in Dunfermline, was admitted as a burgess of Dunfermline on 23 September 1807. [DM]

FERGUS, JESSIE, second daughter of Walter Fergus of Strathore in Fife, died in Rome, Italy, on 27 March 1863. [Rome Protestant gravestone]

FERGUSON, ANDREW, son of David Ferguson a burgess, was admitted as a burgess of Dunfermline on 16 September 1796. [DM]

FERGUSON, DRYSDALE, a weaver, was admitted as a burgess of Kirkcaldy, Fife, on 29 September 1796. [KBR]

FERGUSON, JAMES, son of George Ferguson a weaver burgess, was admitted as a burgess of Dunfermline on 9 September 1791. [DM]

FERGUSON, ROBERT, son of William Ferguson a weaver burgess, was admitted as a burgess of Dunfermline on 16 Ferguson 1796. [DM]

FERNIE, GEORGE, son of William Fernie of Tillywhandland, a Lieutenant of the 10th Bengal Native Infantry, died at Jallalabad, Afghanistan, on 29 July 1842. [St Andrews gravestone, Fife]

FERNIE, JAMES, son-in-law of William Beveridge a burgess, was admitted as a burgess of Dunfermline on 1 July 1808. [DM]

FERNIE, WILLIAM, tenant in Phincraig, Fife, was admitted as a burgess and guilds-brother of Dunfermline on 27 October 1790. [DM]

FERNIE, ROBERT, a merchant in Cupar, Fife, 1824. [NRS.SC20.50.1]

FERRIER, HAY, Colonel of the Scots Brigade, was admitted as a burgess and guilds-brother of Dunfermline on 29 June 1797. [DM]

FERRIER, JAMES, son of George Ferrier and his wife Elizabeth Bayne, settled in Montreal, Quebec, Canada, before 1841. [Auchtermuchty gravestone, Fife]

FINLAY, MAURICE, a mason, was admitted as a burgess of Cupar, Fife, in 1806. [CuBR]

FINLAYSON, JAMES, a shoemaker, son-in-law of William Bisset a burgess, was admitted as a burgess of Dunfermline on 24 February 1792. [DM]

FINLAYSON, JAMES, son-in-law of James Cooper former bailie of Dunfermline, was admitted as a burgess of Dunfermline on 29 July 1807. [DM]

FISHBICK, THOMAS, from Alloa, Clackmannanshire, was admitted as a burgess and guilds-brother of Dunfermline on 19 November 1792. [DM]

FISHER, JAMES, from Dunfermline, Fife, died in Jamaica in 1789, testament confirmed in Edinburgh on 4 October 1804. [NRS]

FAIRLEY, THOMAS, born 1800, died in Marseilles, France, on 4 May 1855. [Culross gravestone, Fife]

FALCONER, THOMAS, a mason in Cupar, Fife, testament, 15 September 1796, Comm. St Andrews. [NRS]

FARNIE, JAMES, from St Andrews, Fife, in Canada by 1853. [NRS.B9.8.1.213/116]

FARQUHARSON, WILLIAM, was admitted as a burgess of Kirkcaldy, Fife, on 19 December 1795. [KBR]

FERGUS, DAVID, a weaver, son of David Fergus an innkeeper in Dunfermline, was admitted as a burgess of Dunfermline on 23 September 1807. [DM]

FERGUS, JESSIE, second daughter of Walter Fergus of Strathore in Fife, died in Rome, Italy, on 27 March 1863. [Rome Protestant gravestone]

FERGUSON, ANDREW, son of David Ferguson a burgess, was admitted as a burgess of Dunfermline on 16 September 1796. [DM]

FERGUSON, DRYSDALE, a weaver, was admitted as a burgess of Kirkcaldy, Fife, on 29 September 1796. [KBR]

FERGUSON, JAMES, son of George Ferguson a weaver burgess, was admitted as a burgess of Dunfermline on 9 September 1791. [DM]

FERGUSON, ROBERT, son of William Ferguson a weaver burgess, was admitted as a burgess of Dunfermline on 16 Ferguson 1796. [DM]

FERNIE, GEORGE, son of William Fernie of Tillywhandland, a Lieutenant of the 10th Bengal Native Infantry, died at Jallalabad, Afghanistan, on 29 July 1842. [St Andrews gravestone, Fife]

FERNIE, JAMES, son-in-law of William Beveridge a burgess, was admitted as a burgess of Dunfermline on 1 July 1808. [DM]

FERNIE, WILLIAM, tenant in Phincraig, Fife, was admitted as a burgess and guilds-brother of Dunfermline on 27 October 1790. [DM]

FERNIE, ROBERT, a merchant in Cupar, Fife, 1824. [NRS.SC20.50.1]

FERRIER, HAY, Colonel of the Scots Brigade, was admitted as a burgess and guilds-brother of Dunfermline on 29 June 1797. [DM]

FERRIER, JAMES, son of George Ferrier and his wife Elizabeth Bayne, settled in Montreal, Quebec, Canada, before 1841. [Auchtermuchty gravestone, Fife]

FINLAY, MAURICE, a mason, was admitted as a burgess of Cupar, Fife, in 1806. [CuBR]

FINLAYSON, JAMES, a shoemaker, son-in-law of William Bisset burgess, was admitted as a burgess of Dunfermline on 24 February 1792. [DM]

FINLAYSON, JAMES, son-in-law of James Cooper former bailie of Dunfermline, was admitted as a burgess of Dunfermline on 29 July 1807. [DM]

FISHBICK, THOMAS, from Alloa, Clackmannanshire, was admitted as a burgess and guilds-brother of Dunfermline on 19 November 1792. [DM]

FISHER, JAMES, from Dunfermline, Fife, died in Jamaica in 1789, testament confirmed in Edinburgh on 4 October 1804. [NRS]

FISHER, JOHN, a weaver, son of Thomas Fisher a burgess, was admitted as a burgess and guilds-brother of Dunfermline on 17 August 1792. [DM]

FISHER, JOHN, son of John Fisher a weaver burgess, was admitted as a burgess of Dunfermline on 8 August 1794. [DM]

FISHER, JOHN, born 1805, from Newburgh, Fife, a master mariner in Liverpool, England, died in Ann Arbor, Michigan, on 20 February 1851. [FJ.9521]

FITCHIE, WILLIAM, a weaver, was admitted as a burgess of Cupar, Fife, on 26 September 1795. [CuBR]

FLEMING, ANDREW, a wright in Kirkcaldy, Fife, emigrated to America after 1824. [SG.33.2.184]

FLEMING, DAVID, a cabinet maker in Toronto, Canada, a sasine, 1849. [NRS.RS.Kirkcaldy.9.164]

FLEMING, JAMES, a wright, was admitted as a burgess of Crail, Fife, in 1790. [CBR]

FLEMING, ROBERT, a manufacturer, was admitted as a burgess and guilds-brother of Dunfermline on 13 April 1797. [DM]

FLEMING, WILLIAM, a currier, was admitted as a burgess of Kirkcaldy, Fife, on 29 May 1792. [KBR]

FLEMING, WILLIAM, a shipowner in Dysart, Fife, died there on 15 September 1822. [SM.90.632]

FLEMINGSTONE, JAMES, a land labourer, was admitted as a burgess of Crail, Fife, in 1805. [CBR]

FLOCKHART, DAVID, of Craigduckie Easter, Fife, was admitted as a burgess and guilds-brother of Dunfermline on 29 May 1805. [DM]

FLOCKHART, WILLIAM, of Arnafreuch, son-in-law of Robert Moodie of Balmile, was admitted as a burgess of Dunfermline on 28 June 1805. [DM]

FOGGO, JOHN, a teacher, was admitted as a burgess and guilds-brother of Dunfermline on 26 April 1798. [DM]

FORBES, ALEXANDER, born 1830, son of John Forbes and his wife Jean Dick, died in Berbice, British Guiana, on 23 October 1876. [Anstruther Easter gravestone, Fife]

FORBES, ANDREW, a wright, son of David Forbes, was admitted as a burgess of Kirkcaldy, Fife, on 18 February 1803. [KBR]

FORBES, WILLIAM, and his wife Margaret Hopkins, parents of Robert Forbes, born 1855, died in Leadville, Colorado, on 10 December 1891. [St Andrews gravestone, Fife]

FORD, ARCHIBALD, son of James Ford, was admitted as a burgess of Dunfermline on 15 September 1810. [DM]

FORD, DAVID, a weaver, son of James Ford a weaver burgess, was admitted as a burgess of Dunfermline on 5 July 1797. [DM]

FORD, LAURENCE, son of James Ford, was admitted as a burgess of Dunfermline on 5 July 1797. [DM]

FORDYCE, or BALFOUR, EUPHEMIA KATHERINE, died in Pau Basse in the Pyrenees, France, on 9 January 1852. [Markinch gravestone, Fife]

FORREST, JAMES NAIRNE, born 1842, son of Thomas Forrest and his wife Janet Alexander, a surgeon who died in Nagasaki, Japan, on 29 July 1873. [Elie gravestone, Fife]

FORRESTER, ARCHIBALD, master of the David of Kincardine, Fife, trading between Leith and Miramachi, New Brunswick, in 1816. [NRS.E504.22.73]

FORRESTER, ROBERT, a skipper in Kinghorn, died on 6 February 1817, husband of Catherine Menzies, died on 24 June 1824. [Kinghorn gravestone, Fife]

FORTESQUE, JAMES, second son of ..... Fortesque in Cameron, Fife, died at Orange Park, St David, Jamaica, on 7 October 1837. [DPCA.1845]

FORTUNE, JOHANNA WILHELMINA, in Grenada, daughter of John Fortune a surgeon there, late of Wester Craigfoodie, Fife, wife of David Basden Otway a merchant in Grenada, in 1868. [NRS.SC20.34.38.86-91]

FORTUNE, JOHN, son of John Fortune and his wife Margaret Gray, died in Kingston, Jamaica, on 1 October 1853. [St Andrews gravestone, Fife]

FORTUNE, LOUISA ELLEN, born 1835, fifth daughter of Dr John Fortune in Grenada, died at Wester Craigfoodie, Fife, on 29 August 1853. [FH]

FOSTER, ANDREW, born 25 June 1772, son of John Foster and his wife Barbara Fairnie in Kinghorn, Fife, a merchant in New York by 1798, died there on 25 December 1849. [ANY]

FOTHERINGHAM, JOHN, a merchant grocer, was admitted as a burgess and guilds-brother of Dunfermline on 29 January 1796. [DM]

FOULIS, PETER, born 1836, son of Robert Foulis, an engineer in the Royal Navy who died in Bermuda on 31 October 1875. [Aberdour gravestone, Fife]

FOWLER, ALEXANDER, born 1830, son of Robert Fowler and his wife Elizabeth Rodger, died aboard the Northern Bride on the River Hooghly, West Bengal, India, on 5 September 1856. [Kilrenny gravestone, Fife]

FOWLER, ANDREW, junior, a sloop-master, was admitted as a burgess of Crail, Fife, in 1805. [CBR]

FOWLER, GEORGE SWAN, born 9 March 1835, son of James Fowler and Rhea Anderson, died in Mitcham, South Australia, on 1 October 1896. [Kilrenny gravestone, Fife]

FOWLER, JANET, born 1827, third daughter of James Fowler in Nethergate, Crail, Fife, wife of David Webster a sugar planter in Victoria County, died in Durban, Natal, South Africa, on 27 February 1901. [EFR]

FOWLER, JOHN, a baker, was admitted as a burgess of Crail, Fife, in 1791. [CBR]

FOWLER, ROBERT, a land labourer, was admitted as a burgess of Crail, Fife, in 1792. [CBR]

FRANKE, ALEXANDER, a distiller, was admitted as a burgess and guilds-brother of Dunfermline on 16 June 1796. [DM]

FRASER, ALEXANDER, a baker in New York, brother and heir of James Fraser a corn-dealer in Markinch, Fife, who died 4 September 1851. [NRS.S/H]

FRAZER, DAVID, son of Peter Frazer, was admitted as a burgess of Cupar, Fife, on 4 October 1814. [CuBR]

FRASER, FINLAY, bon 1826, a gardener from Fife, landed in Hobart, Tasmania, Australia, aboard the John Bell on 4 December 1855. [SRA.TD292]

FRAZER, PETER, a butcher, was admitted as a burgess of Cupar, Fife, on 4 September 1795. [CuBR]

FRAZER, PETER, a butcher, was admitted as a burgess of Cupar, Fife, on 14 September 1804. [CuBR]

FRASER, RODERICK, a Lieutenant of the West Lowland Fencibles, was admitted as a burgess and guilds-brother of Dunfermline on 23 May 1798. [DM]

FRASER, WILLIAM, agent in Inverkeithing, Fife, for the Eastern Bank in 1849. [POD]

GAIRNS, ROBERT, an engineer in Chicago, Illinois, son and heir of Janet Johnston, wife of Andrew Gairns in Cupar, Fife, 1857. [NRS.S/H]

GALL, JOHN, son of Robert Gall a mason burgess, was admitted as a burgess and guilds-brother of Dunfermline on 4 July 1797. [DM]

GALLATLY, JOHN, a baker in Geelong, Australia, a sasine, 1863. [NRS.RS.Kirkcaldy, Fife,.12/141]

GALLOWAY, DAVID, a smith, was admitted as a burgess of Cupar, Fife, on 4 October 1814. [CuBR]

GALLOWAY, DEWAR, son-in-law of James Cousin a burgess, was admitted as a burgess and guilds-brother of Dunfermline on 25 March 1805. [DM]

GALLOWAY, JAMES, born 1829, son of James Galloway in Springfield, Fife, died in Melbourne, Victoria, Australia, on 7 July 1860. [Collessie gravestone, Fife]

GALLOWAY, THOMAS, was admitted as a burgess of Cupar, Fife, in 1802. [CuBR]

GALLOWAY, WILLIAM, a labourer, was admitted as a burgess of Crail, Fife, in 1791. [CBR]

GALLOWAY, WILLIAM, a wright, was admitted as a burgess of Cupar, Fife, in 1802. [CuBR]

GALLOWAY, William, jr., was admitted as a burgess of Cupar, Fife, on 6 October 1810. [CuBR]

GARDNER, DAVID, son of Alexander Gardner a weaver burgess, was admitted as a burgess and guilds-brother of Dunfermline on 31 July 1790. [DM]

GARDNER, JOHN, a wright, son in law of James Kelty a burgess, was admitted as a burgess and guilds-brother of Dunfermline on 19 December 1809. [DM]

GARDNER, WILLIAM, was admitted as a burgess of Cupar, Fife, on 4 October 1808. [CuBR]

GAVIN, JOHN, a witer, was admitted as a burgess of Cupar, Fife, in 1806. [CuBR]

GAY, ALEXANDER, in Fredericton, New Brunswick, nephew and heir, of William Gay in Anstruther Easter, Fife, who died 25 April 1853. [NRS.S/H]

GAY, or RUMGAY, WILLIAM, in Barbados, later in London, heir to his great grandfather John Rumgay in Arncroach, Fife,1844. [NRS.S/H]

GEDDES, JOHN, born 1829, son of Alexander Geddes, [died 1841], and his wife Jean Ramsay, [died 1848], died in Westmoreland, Jamaica, on 27 August 1857. [Cupar gravestone, Fife]

GEDDIE, DAVID, a mariner in Pittenweem, Fife, husband of Alison Knowles, in 1790. [NRS.GD62.406]

GIB, CHARLES, son of Lawrence Gib a merchant burgess, was admitted as a burgess of Dunfermline on 4 August 1794. [DM]

GIBB, DAVID, a painter in Philadelphia, Pennsylvania, son and heir of Alexander Gibb a weaver in Dunikier, Fife, 1842. [NRS.S/H]

GIBB, HENRY, son of Lawrence Gibb a merchant burgess, was admitted as a burgess of Dunfermline on 14 September 1804. [DM]

GIBB, HENRY WILLIAM, born 1813, son of Henry Gibb, died in Port Adelaide, South Australia, on 8 January 1842. [Dunfermline gravestone, Fife]

GIBB, JOHN, jr., a manufacturer from Leslie, was admitted as a burgess of Kirkcaldy, Fife, on 29 September 1792. [KBR]

GIBB, JOHN, the third, a manufacturer from Leslie, was admitted as a burgess of Kirkcaldy, Fife, on 29 September 1792. [KBR]

GIBB, LAWRENCE, a merchant, was admitted as a burgess of Dunfermline on 25 September 1786. [DM]; testament, 28 October 1799, Comm. St Andrews. [NRS]

GIBB, WALTER, born 1838, son of Thomas Gibb, died in India on 15 October 1870. [Kennoway gravestone, Fife]

GIBB, WILLIAM, son of Lawrence Gibb a merchant burgess, was admitted as a burgess of Dunfermline on 10 April 1789. [DM]

GIBB, WILLIAM, a weaver in Dunfermline, was admitted as a burgess of Dunfermline on 9 August 1808. [DM]

GIBSON, ANDREW, a weaver, son-in-law of John Houston a weaver burgess, was admitted as a burgess of Dunfermline on 27 September 1790. [DM]

GIBSON, ANDREW, a weaver, son of John Gibson a weaver burgess, was admitted as a burgess of Dunfermline on 29 August 1791. [DM]

GIBSON, JAMES, a Writer to the Signet, was admitted as a burgess and guilds-brother of Dunfermline on 3 May 1791. [DM]

GIBSON, JAMES, son of James Gibson a weaver burgess, was admitted as a burgess of Dunfermline on 31 July 1801. [DM]

GIBSON, Reverend JAMES, sometime in Dunfermline, Fife, later in New York, died on 7 April 1860. [Inventory, 1860, Edinburgh, NRS]

GIBSON, JOHN, a writer, son of John Gibson a carrier burgess, was admitted as a burgess of Dunfermline on 5 July 1797. [DM]

GIBSON, JOHN, a grocer, was admitted as a burgess of Cupar, Fife, on 24 November 1802. [CuBR]

GIBSON, JOHN, an ironmaster in Halbeath, Fife, sederunt books, 1820-1824. [NRS.CS96.14.1-4]

GIBSON, THOMAS, a feuar in Torryburn, Fife, testament, 22 November 1800, Comm. St Andrews. [NRS]

GIBSON, WILLIAM, son of James Gibson a carrier burgess, was admitted as a burgess of Dunfermline on 17 August 1802. [DM]

GIBSON, WILLIAM, jr., a merchant in Edinburgh, son of William Gibson a weaver burgess, was admitted as a burgess of Dunfermline on 10 September 1810. [DM]

GILCHRIST, WILLIAM, from Tecomseh, Michigan, married Catherine Swan, youngest daughter of William Swan, in Dunfermline, Fife, on 3 February 1846. [EEC.21304]

GILLESPIE, ANDREW, a mariner from Crail, Fife, who was lost when bound for the West Indies, testament, 1811, Comm. St Andrews. [NRS]

GILLESPIE, JAMES, a clerk in Inverkeithing, Fife, son-in-law of John Cusine a merchant in Dunfermline, was admitted as a burgess of Dunfermline on 13 January 1795. [DM]

GILLESPIE, JOHN, a cooper, was admitted as a burgess of Crail, Fife, in 1794. [CBR]

GILLESPIE, WILLIAM, Major of the Scots Brigade, was admitted as a burgess and guilds-brother of Dunfermline on 22 May 1795. [DM]

GILMORE, THOMAS, son of James Gilmore a burgess, was admitted as a burgess of Dunfermline on 9 August 1796. [DM]

GILMOUR, ALLAN, in Lundin Links, Fife, father of John Gilmour who married Henrietta Gilmour, second daughter of David Gilmour in Quebec, there on 18 September 1873. [EC.27766]

GILMOUR, WILLIAM, a butcher, was admitted as a burgess of Kirkcaldy, Fife, on 18 November 1790. [KBR]

GLASS, CUDBERT THORNHILL, born 1793, eldest son of Lieutenant Colonel Glass in St Andrews, Fife, died in India on 14 December 1830. [South Park gravestone, Calcutta, India]

GLASS, WALTER STIRLING, Captain of the Loyal Stirling Volunteers, was admitted as a burgess and guilds-brother of Dunfermline on 17 July 1804. [DM]

GOLDIE, JOHN, a skipper in Pittenweem, Fife, master and manager of the Pittenweem Sea Box Society on 11 January 1796. [NRS.B3.7.5]

GOODFELLOW, JOHN, born 1800, son of Thomas Goodfellow and his wife Catherine Farquharson, died in New Granada in 1860. [Ceres gravestone, Fife]

GOODSON, Dr DAVID, a physician in Leven, Fife, testament, 23 October 1793, Comm. St Andrews. [NRS]

GOODSON, JAMES, a brewer in Leven, Fife, testament, 7 January 1796, Comm. St Andrews. [NRS]

GORDON, DAVID, a fisher in Pittenweem, testament, 1816, Comm. St Andrews. [NRS]

GORDON, JAMES, from Edinburgh, was admitted as a burgess and guilds-brother of Dunfermline on 19 November 1791. [DM]

GORDON, JOHN, in Providence Mission, Chicago, Illinois, son and heir of Margaret Bell, wife of Andrew Gordon a weaver in Cupar, 1870. [NRS.S/H]

GORDON, JOHN SUTHERLAND, born 1821, a planter in Demerara, died on 19 August 1880. [Burntisland gravestone]

GORDON, ROBERT, a Lieutenant of the Northern Fencible Highlanders, was admitted as a burgess and guilds-brother of Dunfermline on 27 February 1799. [DM]

GORDON, THOMAS, a Captain of the West Lowland Fencibles, was admitted as a burgess and guilds-brother of Dunfermline on 23 May 1798. [DM]

GORDON, WALTER, Captain of the Northern Fencible Highlanders, was admitted as a burgess of Dunfermline on 27 February 1799. [DM]

GORRIE, WILLIAM, born 1842, son of David Gorrie and his wife Barbara Bett, died in Rio de Janeiro, Brazil, on 26 September 1872. [Ferry-Port-on-Craig gravestone, Fife]

GOURLAY, DAVID, an engineer from Kirkcaldy, Fife, son of George Gourlay, died in Singapore in 1870. [FH.26.1.1871]

GOURLAY, JOHN, from Lebanon, Cupar, Fife, later in Jamaica by 1835. [NRS.SC20.34.18.175-180]

GOURLAY, WILLIAM, of Kincraig, Fife, testament, 24 August 1792, Comm. St Andrews. [NRS]

GOVAN, JOHN GEORGE, died in Darjeeling, Bengal, India, on 5 March 1850. [Cupar gravestone, Fife]

GOW, GEORGE, in Johnsonville, New Hampshire, nephew and heir of John Gow a builder in Kirkcaldy, Fife, who died 2 October 1871. [NRS.S/H]

GOWAN, ALEXANDER, agent in Markinch, Fife, for the Commercial Bank of Scotland in 1849. [POD]

GOWIE, WILLIAM, a tailor, was admitted as a burgess of Dunfermline on 14 October 1809. [DM]

GRACE, CHARLES, jr., was admitted as a burgess and guilds-brother of Cupar, Fife, on 10 October 1810. [CuBR]

GRACE, HUGH DOUGLAS, third son of Dr Charles Grace in Cupar, Fife, married Henrietta Geddes, daughter of Lieutenant Colonel William Geddes of the 83rd Regiment, at St George's Chapel in Edinburgh on 14 September 1822. [SM.90.519]

GRACE, PETER, son of Dr Grace in Cupar, Fife, died in Jamaica on 26 April 1824. [FH][EA]

GRAHAME, ANDREW, master of the sloop Margaret of Dysart testament, 1816, Comm. St Andrews. [NRS]

GRAHAM, GEORGE, a merchant, was admitted as a burgess of Kirkcaldy, Fife, on 13 September 1794. [KBR]

GRAHAM, JAMES, a weaver, son of Hugh Graham a weaver burgess, was admitted as a burgess of Dunfermline on 4 July 1797. [DM]

GRAHAM, JOHN, a weaver, son of Hugh Graham a weaver burgess, was admitted as a burgess of Dunfermline on 4 July 1797. [DM]

GRANT, ALEXANDER, MD, born 7 November 1827, died in Bombay, India, on 18 November 1853. [Kennoway gravestone, Fife]

GRANT, CHARLES, Ensign of the Sutherland Fencibles, was admitted as a burgess and guilds-brother of Dunfermline on 5 December 1794. [DM]

GRANT, FRANCIS ROBERT, born 1849, a shipbroker, eldest son of John Grant a banker in Inverkeithing, Fife, sailed from Inverkeithing aboard the Swiftsure bound for New York on 3 September 1870, lost at sea. [S.8605]

GRANT, HUMPHREY, a Lieutenant of the Northern Fencible Highlanders, was admitted as a burgess and guilds-brother of Dunfermline on 27 February 1799. [DM]

GRANT, WILLIAM, a wright, son of John Grant, was admitted as a burgess of Kirkcaldy, Fife, on 28 February 1798. [KBR]

GRAY, CHARLES, born 1818, son of George Gray, a Major of the Royal Marines, and his wife Ann Roger, died in Narreb Narreb, Victoria, Australia, on 27 January 1905. [Anstruther Wester gravestone, Fife]

GRAY, CLEMENTINA, born 1812, daughter of Reverend Thomas Gray in Kirkcaldy, Fife, died in Edinburgh on 19 October 1838. [NBRG.16.1.1839]

GRAY, MARY ANN, daughter of George Gray, a Major of the Royal Marines, and his wife Ann Roger, died in Melbourne, Victoria, Australia, on 21 February 1903. [Anstruther Wester gravestone, Fife]

GRAY, ROBERT, a skipper in Anstruther Easter, testament, 1795, Comm. St Andrews. [NRS]

GRAY, ROBERT, a skipper in Anstruther, Fife, in 1799. [NRS.S/H]; testament, 5 March 1795, Comm.St Andrews. [NRS]

GRAY, ROBERT, son-in-law of David Mackie a burgess, was admitted as a burgess of Dunfermline on 10 July 1804. [DM]

GRAY, THOMAS, born 1746, son of David Gray and his wife Agnes Mitchell, a skipper who died on 25 November 1816. [Tulliallan gravestone, Fife]

GRAY, THOMAS CARSTAIRS, born 17 January 1817 in Anstruther, Fife, a Lieutenant of the 29th Bengal Native Infantry, died at Meerut, United Provinces, India, on 11 October 1829. [Kingsbarns gravestone, Fife]

GREENHILL, DAVID, son of David Greenhill and his wife Agnes Hill in Russell Mill, died in Hamilton, Canada West, on 23 November 1873. [Cupar gravestone, Fife]

GREENHILL, JOHN, son of David Greenhill and his wife Agnes Hill in Russell Mill, died in Binbrook, Canada West, on 15 February 1868. [Cupar gravestone, Fife]

GREIG, or MITCHELL, ANNIE DAVIDSON, in Nashville, Tennessee, heir to her grandfather George Greig a reed-maker in Cupar, Fife, who died in January 1848. [NRS.S/H]

GREIG, DAVID, a candlemaker, was admitted as a burgess of Kirkcaldy, Fife, on 21 November 1795. [KBR]

GREIG, DAVID, a baker, son of John Greig a skipper burgess of Inverkeithing, Fife, was admitted as a burgess of Dunfermline on 19 September 1810. [DM]

GREIG, DAVID, born 1801 from Kilrenny, died in Greenland on 10 August 1832. [Boarhills gravestone, Fife]

GREIG, GEORGE, a porter in New York, heir to his grandfather George Greig a reed-maker in Cupar, Fife, who died in January 1848. [NRS.S/H]

GREIG, JAMES FORTUNE, a bookseller in Almonte, Ontario, heir to Christian Burnett, widow of James Fortune a baker in Kirkcaldy, Fife, who died on 7 May 1833. [NRS.S/H]; a sasine in 1871. [NRS.RS.Kirkcaldy.14.256]

GREIG, JAMES, an engineer in Paterson, New Jersey, son of Simon Greig in East Wemyss, Fife, in 1853. [NRS.SC20.34.29.275/278]

GREIG, JOHN, a merchant, son of John Greig a skipper in Inverkeithing, Fife, was admitted as a burgess of Dunfermline on 8 February 1810. [DM]

GREIG, ROBERT, born 1811, son of David Greig, [1786-1859], and his wife Anna ....., [1786-1848], a machinist who settled in Mobile, Alabama, by 1840. [Kinghorn gravestone, Fife]

GREIG, SIMON, in East Wemyss, Fife, father of James Greig an engineer in Paterson, New Jersey, 1853. [NRS.SC20.34.275/278]

GREIG, WALTER, master of the Clyde of Kirkcaldy trading between Greenock and Newfoundland in 1816. [NRS.E504.15.111]

GREIG, Captain, in Burntisland, Fife, father of George Greig, born 1853, died in the Punjab, India on 29 August 1880. [PJ]

GRUBB, HENRY, a shoemaker, was admitted as a burgess of Crail, Fife, in 1808. [CBR]

GRUBB, JAMES, a grazier from Colinsburgh, Fife, was admitted as a burgess of Kirkcaldy, Fife, on 2 April 1793. [KBR]

GRUBB, JAMES, born 1815, a shipmaster, died in Philadelphia, Pennsylvania, on 21 May 1849. [Ferry-port-on-Tay gravestone, Fife]

GRUBB, Mrs JANET, born 1788 in Fife, wife of George Grubb, their son John Thornton Melville Dow born 1813, emigrated via Leith to America, they were naturalised in New York on 20 May 1828. [NY Court of Common Pleas]

GULD, JAMES, a sailor in Kirkcaldy, Fife, in 1794. [NRS.S/H]

GULLAND, JAMES, was admitted as a burgess and guilds-brother of Dunfermline on 25 September 1792. [DM]

GUTHRIE, ROBERT, a merchant, was admitted as a burgess of Cupar, Fife, on 19 April 1796. [CuBR]; a bankrupt in 1818. [NRS.CS9.6.359]

HAIN, MARGARET, born 1827, daughter of George Hain a merchant in Auchtermuchty, Fife, wife of Alexander Lawrie, manager of the Kowno Steam Mills in Russia, died on 1 July 1855. [FH]

HAIN, THOMAS, in Balmullo, Leuchars, Fife, a testament, 3 October 1797, Comm, St Andrews. [NRS]

HALIBURTON, JOHN, a skipper in Newburgh, Fife, testament, 14 May 1798, Comm. St Andrews. [NRS]

HALKERSTON, DAVID, died in Falkland, Fife, on 14 September 1822. [SM.90.632]

HALKERSTON, ROBERT, son of David Halkerston, a tobacconist in Leven, Fife, was apprenticed to Innes and Wallace, gunsmiths in Edinburgh, for six years on 22 February 1798. [ERA]

HALKETT, FREDERICK, Lieutenant Colonel of the Scots Brigade, was admitted as a burgess and guilds-brother of Dunfermline on 4 June 1794. [DM]

HALKETT, HENRY in the Service of the East India Company, was admitted as a burgess and guilds-brother of Dunfermline on 6 June 1798. [DM]

HALKETT, JOHN, of Pitfirran, Fife, born 1769, Governor of the Bahamas, died in 1852. [Dunfermline gravestone, Fife]

HALL, JAMES, a weaver, son-in-law of Andrew Stevenson a weaver burgess, was admitted as a burgess of Dunfermline on 18 August 1792. [DM]

HALYBURTON, ALEXANDER, was admitted as a burgess of Dunfermline on 25 September 1792. [DM]

HALLIBURTON, JOHN, a skipper in Newburgh, Fife, in 1792. [NRS.S/H]

HALLIDAY, ..., , was admitted as a burgess of Kirkcaldy, Fife, on 10 September 1792. [KBR]

HAMILTON, DAVID, born 1769, a seaman, husband of Elspet Oswald, died on 28 November 1835. [Kingsbarns gravestone, Fife]

HARDY, JAMES, a weaver, son-in-law of William Henderson, a land labourer in Newton, was admitted as a burgess of Dunfermline on 23 August 1791. [DM]

HARDIE, JOHN, a skipper in Pittenweem, Fife, manager of the Pittenweem Sea Box Society, on 11 July 1791. [NRS.B3.7.5]

HARDIE, RICHARD, a tailor, was admitted as a burgess of Dunfermline on 5 December 1808. [DM]

HARDY, THOMAS, son-in-law of George Hunter a weaver burgess, was admitted as a burgess of Dunfermline on 17 September 1790. [DM]

HARDIE, THOMAS, from Ceres, Fife, a theological student in 1815, emigrated to America as a teacher. [UPC]

HARDIE, WILLIAM, a skipper in Pittenweem, Fife, manager of the Pittenweem Sea Box Society, on 14 January 1793. [NRS.B3.7.5]

HARLEY, ARCHIBALD, son of John Harley, was admitted as a burgess of Dunfermline on 24 November 1796. [DM]

HARMER, JOHN, a member of the Pittenweem Sea Box Society, in 1792. [NRS.B3.7.5]

HARROWER, JOHN, son-in-law of John Henderson a tapster in Kirkgate, Dunfermline, was admitted as a burgess of Dunfermline on 19 March 1795. [DM]

HARROWER, JOHN, a weaver, son-in-law of John Anderson a burgess, was admitted as a burgess of Dunfermline on 20 August 1802. [DM]

HART, JAMES, son-in-law of John Donaldson a burgess, was admitted as a burgess of Dunfermline on 30 April 1801. [DM]

HASTIE, JAMES, died in Boarhills, Fife, on 30 November 1850. [Dunino gravestone, Fife]

HASTIE, JOHN, born 1827, son of James Hastie and his wife Agnes Cairns, died in New Zealand, on 12 February 1868. [Kettle gravestone, Fife]

HAXTON, JOHN, a sailor, was admitted as a burgess of Kirkcaldy, Fife, on 17 July 1790. [KBR]

HAY, ALEXANDER, Captain of the Royal Regiment of Foot, in Cupar, Fife, a testament, 1792. Comm, St Andrews. [NRS]

HAY, ALEXANDER, an innkeeper, was admitted as a burgess of Cupar, Fife, on 24 November 1802. [CuBR]

HAY, HENRY, born 1838, son of David Hay and his wife Helen Morris, died in New Zealand on 20 August 1893. [Leuchars gravestone, Fife]

HAY, JAMES, born 1809, son of Alexander Hay and his wife Jeannie Scott, died in New Orleans, Louisiana, on 10 December 1835. [Kilconquhar gravestone, Fife]

HAY, ROBERT, son of Robert Hay, was admitted as a burgess of Dunfermline on 13 August 1796. [DM]

HEAD, JAMES, master of the East India Company ship Canning, died in the Calcutta River, India, in 1824. [Balcarres gravestone, Fife]

HEDDERWICK, JOHN, tenant in Kemback, Fife, testament, 18 January 1798, Comm. St Andrews. [NRS]

HEDDERWICK, JOHN, of Denhead, tenant in Blebo, Fife, testament, 17 June 1799, Comm. St Andrews. [NRS]

HEGGIE, ISOBEL, in Lady's Mill of Pittencrieff, Dunfermline, testament, 23 April 1791, Comm. St Andrews. [NRS]

HEGGIE, JAMES, of Pitlessie, Kirkcaldy, testament, 22 April 1791, Comm. St Andrews. [NRS]

HEGGIE, ROBERT, factor to James Townsend Oswald of Dunnikier, Kirkcaldy, testament, 12 June 1799, Comm. St Andrews. [NRS]

HEMPSEED, JAMES, son of James Hempseed a baker burgess, was admitted as a burgess of Dunfermline on 28 June 1792. [DM]

HEMPSEED, JAMES, a baker in Dunfermline, testament, 31 December 1799, Comm. St Andrews. [NRS]

HEMPSEED, JOHN, son of James Hempseed a baker burgess, was admitted as a burgess of Dunfermline on 20 January 1796. [DM]

HENDERSON, ANDREW, son of John Henderson, was admitted as a burgess of Dunfermline on 4 July 1797. [DM]

HENDERSON, ANDREW, a cooper, was admitted as a burgess of Kirkcaldy, Fife, on 9 February 1801. [KBR]

HENDERSON, DAVID, a weaver, was admitted as a burgess of Kirkcaldy, Fife, on 13 August 1791. [KBR]

HENDERSON, GEORGE, servant of George Purves of Lochend, son of John Henderson a burgess, was admitted as a burgess of Dunfermline on 14 August 1793. [DM]

HENDERSON, GEORGE, son of John Henderson a watchmaker burgess, was admitted as a burgess of Dunfermline on 14 December 1809. [DM]

HENDERSON, JAMES, was admitted as a burgess of Kirkcaldy, Fife, on 16 May 1793. [KBR]

HENDERSON, JAMES, a weaver, son-in-law of William Knox a merchant guilds-brother, was admitted as a burgess of Dunfermline on 31 March 1792. [DM]

HENDERSON, JAMES, son of John Henderson, was admitted as a burgess of Dunfermline on 4 July 1797. [DM]

HENDERSON, JAMES, born 1839, son of John Henderson and his wife Elizabeth Orchard, died in India on 1 June 1878. [Cupar gravestone, Fife]

HENDERSON, Sir JOHN, of Fordell, Fife, was admitted as a burgess and guilds-brother of Dunfermline on 8 April 1791. [DM]

HENDERSON, JOHN, son-in-law of George Coupar, was admitted as a burgess of Dunfermline on 28 September 1792. [DM]

HENDERSON, JOHN, son of John Henderson a burgess, was admitted as a burgess of Dunfermline on 15 September 1802. [DM]

HENDERSON, JOHN, born 1768, son of John Henderson and his wife Elizabeth Hay, a Captain of the 42nd [Black Watch] Regiment, who died in Paullace, France, on 7 July 1814. [Logie gravestone, Fife]

HENDERSON, JOHN, a wool merchant, was admitted as a burgess of Kirkcaldy, Fife, on 23 November 1793. [KBR]

HENDERSON, ROBERT, a shoemaker from Milnathort, Kinross, was admitted as a burgess of Dunfermline on 5 December 1794. [DM]

HENDERSON, ROBERT BRUCE, of Earlshall, Fife, was admitted as a burgess and guilds-brother of Dunfermline on 16 June 1796. [DM]

HENDERSON, ROBERT, son of John Henderson a burgess, was admitted as a burgess of Dunfermline on 15 September 1802. [DM]

HENDERSON, THOMAS, son of John Henderson a burgess, was admitted as a burgess of Dunfermline on 15 September 1802. [DM]

HENDERSON, THOMAS, born 1802, son of George Henderson and his wife Janet Tod, died in Leghorn/Livorno, Italy, on 11 October 1854. [Pittenweem gravestone, Fife]

HENDERSON, THOMAS, born 1831, son of David Henderson and his wife Margaret Miller, died in Windermere, Victoria, Australia, on 19 July 1866. [Balmerino gravestone, Fife]

HENDERSON, WALTER, a block-maker in Kincardine, Fife, versus his wife Janet Hamilton, a Process of Divorce in 1817. [NRS.CC8.6.113]

HENDERSON, WILLIAM, son of Andrew Henderson a weaver burgess, was admitted as a burgess of Dunfermline on 30 July 1790. [DM]

HENDERSON, WILLIAM, son-in-law of David Kennedy a weaver and guilds-brother, was admitted as a burgess of Dunfermline on 17 April 1793. [DM]

HENDERSON, WILLIAM, son of John Henderson a weaver burgess, was admitted as a burgess of Dunfermline on 5 July 1797. [DM]

HENDERSON, WILLIAM, a farmer at Hatton of Largo, Fife, testament, 28 December 1800 and 2 February 1801, Comm. St Andrews. [NRS]

HENDERSON, WILLIAM, a farmer at Banks, was admitted as a burgess of Dunfermline on 24 October 1809. [DM]

HENDRY, WILLIAM, a merchant from St Andrews, Fife, died in Shortwood, Jamaica, in 1805. [AJ.2981]

HENRY, GEORGE, tenant in St Nicolas, St Andrews, testament, 25 September 1792, Comm. St Andrews. [NRS]

HENRY, JAMES, a vintner in St Andrews, testament, 23 December 1795, Comm. St Andrews. [NRS]

HERIOT, Mrs JEAN, in Ramornie, Kettle, Fife, a testament, 6 July 1792, Comm. St Andrews. [NRS]

HERIOT, ROBERT, of Ramornie, Fife, a testament, 26 May 1790, Comm. St Andrews. [NRS]

HERON, GEORGE, jr., was admitted as a burgess of Kirkcaldy, Fife, on 14 January 1797. [KBR]

HERON, GILBERT, a stocking maker, was admitted as a burgess of Kirkcaldy, Fife, on 14 January 1797. [KBR]

HERRON, JAMES, died in Melbourne, Victoria, Australia, on 24 February 1853. [Cairneyhill gravestone, Fife]

HERON, ROBERT, a baker, was admitted as a burgess of Kirkcaldy, Fife, on 13 September 1794. [KBR]

HILL, JAMES, a farmer in Scotscraig, Fife, testaments, 23 April 1795, and 6 December 1797, Comm. St Andrews. [NRS]

HILL, JAMES, son of James Hill. was admitted as a burgess and guilds-brother of Cupar, Fife, on 4 August 1798. [CuBR]

HILL, Colonel JOHN, of the Madras Army, died in Winberg, Cape of Good Hope, South Africa, on 14 May 1866. [St Andrews gravestone, Fife]

HODGE, HENRY, son of Andrew Hodge in Anstruther, Fife, was apprenticed to Henry Band, a baker in Edinburgh, for five years on 20 February 1793. [ERA]

HODGE, JOHN, a shoemaker, was admitted as a burgess of Cupar, Fife, on 2 October 1799. [CuBR]

HODGE, ROBERT, son of Robert Hodge a tailor burgess, was admitted as a burgess of Dunfermline on 15 August 1794. [DM]

HOG, DAVID, son of Alexander Hog a tailor burgess, was admitted as a burgess of Dunfermline on 29 March 1805. [DM]

HOG, JAMES, son of Peter Hog a weaver burgess, was admitted as a burgess of Dunfermline on 25 July 1796. [DM]

HOG, M., an Ensign of the Kinross Volunteer Infantry, was admitted as a burgess and guilds-brother of Dunfermline on 27 October 1804. [DM]

HOGARTH, GEORGE, agent in Cupar, Fife, for the Commercial Bank of Scotland in 1849. [POD]

HOGGAN, ANDREW, son of Thomas Hoggan a weaver burgess, was admitted as a burgess of Dunfermline on 1 March 1795. [DM]

HOGGAN, JAMES, a brewer in Dunfermline, was admitted as a burgess of Dunfermline on 12 January 1808. [DM]

HOGGAN, JOHN, a weaver, son-in[law of John Main a mason burgess, was admitted as a burgess of Dunfermline on 6 May 1796. [DM]

HOGGAN, THOMAS, son of Andrew Hoggan a weaver burgess, was admitted as a burgess of Dunfermline on 4 July 1797. [DM]

HOGGAN, THOMAS, son of Thomas Hoggan a weaver burgess, was admitted as a burgess of Dunfermline on 13 August 1797. [DM]

HOGGAN, WILLIAM, a mason, son-in-law of William Beveridge a wright burgess, was admitted as a burgess of Dunfermline on 4 July 1797. [DM]

HOGGAN, WILLIAM, son of Thomas Hoggan a weaver burgess, was admitted as a burgess of Dunfermline on 25 November 1801. [DM]

HOME, WILLIAM, a slater, was admitted as a burgess of Kirkcaldy, Fife, on 22 February 1792. [KBR]

HONEYMAN, CHRISTINE, born 1796, died 27 July 1835, wife of David Mare. [Dunbog gravestone, Fife]

HONEYMAN, DAVID, born 1827, son of Charles Honeyman and his wife Angela Philp, died in America in August 1849. [Monimail gravestone, Fife]

HONYMAN, JOHN, a mason, was admitted as a burgess of Cupar, Fife, on 4 October 1808. [CuBR]

HONYMAN, ROBERT, a grocer, was admitted as a burgess of Cupar, Fife, on 3 October 1804. [CuBR]

HOOD, JENNIE, in Los Guillicos Ranch, Santa Rosa, California, heir to her grand-father James Hood a wright in Drybriggs, Cupar, Fife, who died on 7 October 1853. [NRS.S/H]

HOOPER, ..., a surgeon, was admitted as a burgess and guilds-brother of Dunfermline on 4 June 1798. [DM]

HOPE, GEORGE, of Craigiehall, Fife, a Captain in the Royal Navy in 1795. [NRS.S/H]

HOPE, HARRY, born 28 December 1800 in Falkland, Fife, died in Howrah, Bengal, India, on 2 November 1840. [Howrah gravestone]

HOPE, WILLIAM, born 1803 in Falkland, Fife, died in Howrah, Bengal, India, on 18 June 1841. [Howrah gravestone]

HORNE, DAVID, of Thomanean, residing in Kirkcaldy, testament, 20 February 1795, Comm. St Andrews. [NRS]

HORN, JAMES, a Writer to the Signet, was admitted as a burgess of Dunfermline on 26 August 1796. [DM]

HORN, JOHN, son of William Horn a weaver burgess, was admitted as a burgess of Dunfermline on 25 August 1790. [DM]

HORN, JOHN, a weaver, son-in-law of David Morison a weaver burgess, was admitted as a burgess of Dunfermline, on 5 July 1797. [DM]

HORSBURGH, DAVID, a shoemaker, was admitted as a burgess of Crail, Fife, in 1791. [CBR]

HORSBURGH, JAMES, born 23 September 1762 in Elie, Hydrographer of the East India Company in Bombay, India, died on 14 May 1836. [Elie gravestone, Fife]

HORSBURGH, JOHN, a shoemaker, was admitted as a burgess of Crail, Fife, in 1790. [CBR]

HORSBURGH, THOMAS PATE, born 1819, son of Andrew Horsburgh of Firth and his wife Christian Pollock, died on Chatham Island, New Zealand, in November 1855. [Pittenweem gravestone, Fife]

HOSTLER, DAVID, born in East Fife, a lessee of the Kellie Colliery, died at his son's residence in Leeds, Canada, on 6 March 1873. [FH]

HOUSTON, Lieutenant HUGH, was admitted as a burgess and guilds-brother of Dunfermline on 4 March 1793. [DM]

HOUSTON, P., from Crail, Fife, died in Shanghai, China, on 15 October 1865. [FH]

HOWARD, Mrs KATHERINE, daughter of James Drummond in Kelty, Fife, died in Kingston, Jamaica, on 3 October 1806. [SM.69.77]

HOWDEN, JOHN, born 1783, son of Archibald Howden and his wife Joan Manderston, a merchant who died in Savannah, Georgia, on 26 October 1806. [St Monance gravestone, Fife] [Savannah Death Register]

HOWIE, JOHN, a mariner, was buried in Crail on 28 March 1798. [SBC.24]

HOWIESON, WILLIAM, son-in-law of John Couston a burgess, was admitted as a burgess of Dunfermline on 21 July 1809. [DM]

HUGH, BETSY, a merchant in Cupar, Fife, 1823. [NRS.SC20.58.1]

HUGH, THOMAS, from Wemyss, Fife, father of a daughter born at Little Sawmill Run, Pennsylvania, on 31 March 1870. [FA]

HUME, WILLIAM, from Auchtermuchty, Fife, a theological student in 1796, a missionary in America around 1800, later a minister in Nashville. [UPC]

HUNT, CHARLES, son of Thomas Hunt a burgess, was admitted as a burgess of Dunfermline on 21 March 1805. [DM]

HUNT, JAMES, son of William Hunt, was admitted as a burgess of Dunfermline on 10 April 1799. [DM]

HUNT, JOHN, son of Alexander Hunt, was admitted as a burgess of Dunfermline on 5 October 1793. [DM]

HUNT, JOHN, from Dunfermline, Fife, arrived in Charleston, S.C., in November 1803, applied to become a citizen of South Carolina on 7 January 1808. [S.C.Court of Common Pleas, 23/15]

HUNT, WILLIAM, son of Alexander Hunt a merchant, was admitted as a burgess and guilds-brother of Dunfermline on 5 October 1793. [DM]

HUNTER, FRANCIS JEFFREY, born 1802, son of James Hunter and his wife Jane Wilson, a Lieutenant in the Service of the East India

Company in Bengal, died in Calcutta, India, on 10 March 1833. [St Andrews gravestone, Fife]

HUNTER, GEORGE, a weaver, son of George Hunter a weaver burgess, was admitted as a burgess of Dunfermline on 3 February 1792. [DM]

HUNTER, JAMES, born 1849, died in Mobile, Alabama, on 31 January 1886. [St Andrews gravestone, Fife]

HUNTER, JOHN, eldest son of Professor John Hunter of the University of St Andrews, Fife, died in Jamaica on 29 October 1794. [EA.3225.343]

HUNTER, JOHN, a slater, son of Robert Hunter a causeylayer burgess, was admitted as a burgess of Dunfermline on 20 December 1805. [DM]

HUNTER, MICHAEL, a baker, former apprentice to Alexander Kilgour a baker burgess, was admitted as a burgess of Dunfermline on 28 July 1802. [DM]

HUNTER, ROBERT, a slater, son of Robert Hunter a causeylayer burgess, was admitted as a burgess of Dunfermline on 20 December 1805. [DM]

HUNTER, THOMAS, son of Thomas Hunter and his wife Christina Morrison in Elie, Fife, settled in New Zealand, before 1847. [Newburn gravestone, Fife]

HUNTER, WILLIAM, a watch-maker, former apprentice to Mathew Parker a watch-maker burgess, was admitted as a burgess of Dunfermline on 27 May 1803. [DM]

HUTCHISON, ALEXANDER, a butcher, son of John Hutchison, was admitted as a burgess of Kirkcaldy, Fife, on 18 November 1790. [KBR]

HUTCHISON, ALEXANDER, a shipbuilder, was admitted as a burgess of Kirkcaldy, Fife, on 13 February 1797. [KBR]

HUTCHESON, ANDREW, born 1786, son of Andrew Hutcheson and his wife Mary Malcolm, a surgeon aboard HMS Sapphire died at Chagres, Columbia, on 17 September 1819. [Burntisland gravestone, Fife]

HUTCHISON, JAMES, a butcher, was admitted as a burgess of Kirkcaldy, Fife, on 18 November 1790. [KBR]

HUTCHISON, JOHN, MD, born 1797, from Kirkcaldy, Fife, died in Montreal, Quebec, on 1 August 1847. [AJ.520] [EEC.21554]

HUTCHISON, ROBERT, a shoemaker, son of John Hutchison, was admitted as a burgess of Dunfermline on 2 July 1795. [DM]

HUTTON, ALEXANDER, son of James Hutton a weaver burgess, was admitted as a burgess of Dunfermline on 29 August 1791. [DM]

HUTTON, ALEXANDER, son of David Hutton, was admitted as a burgess of Dunfermline on 12 September 1799. [DM]

HUTTON, ALEXANDER, born 25 January 1821, youngest son of James Hutton in Greenside Place, St Andrews, Fife, a merchant in New York, died at 59 Morton Street, N.Y., on 5 June 1863. [S.2503][ANY]

HUTTON, ANDREW, a writer in Stirling, son of William Hutton a burgess, was admitted as a burgess of Dunfermline on 24 October 1809. [DM]

HUTTON, DAVID, son of David Hutton, was admitted as a burgess of Dunfermline on 12 September 1799. [DM]

HUTTON, ANDREW, a writer in Stirling, son of William Hutton a burgess, was admitted as a burgess of Dunfermline on 24 October 1809. [DM]

HUTTON, DAVID, son of David Hutton, was admitted as a burgess of Dunfermline on 12 September 1799. [DM]

HUTTON, DAVID, son of Alexander Hutton in Kinghorn, Fife, a merchant in Trinidad, died at Savanna Grance on 25 February 1862. [FJ.15.4.1852]

HUTTON, GEORGE, a weaver in Netherton, Fife, son-in-law of James Thomson a weaver burgess, was admitted as a burgess of Dunfermline on 16 September 1808. [DM]

HUTTON, JAMES, born 1747, a factor from Fife, was naturalised in South Carolina on 20 April 1796. [NARA.M1183.1]

HUTTON, JAMES, a wright, son of Robert Hutton a mason, was admitted as a burgess of Dunfermline on 11 December 1809. [DM]

HUTTON, JAMES, and his wife Margaret Rogers, parents of John Hutton, born 1852, died at sea when bound from New York to Leith in November 1868. [Crombie gravestone, Fife]

HUTTON, JOHN, a farmer at the Mill of Torry, Fife, was admitted as a burgess of Dunfermline on 24 October 1809. [DM]

HUTTON, JOHN, born 1808 in St Andrews, Fife, settled in New York by 1827, a merchant in N.Y., died at West 34th Street, N.Y., on 13 July 1874. [ANY]

HUTTON, MARY, born 1816, daughter of Mary Hutton, died in California on 25 January 1854. [Cupar gravestone, Fife]

HUTTON, ROBERT, an Ensign of the West Lowland Fencibles, was known as a burgess and guilds-brother of Dunfermline on 4 June 1798. [DM]

HUTTON, ROBERT, son of David Hutton a burgess, was admitted as a burgess of Dunfermline on 12 September 1799. [DM]

HUTTON, ROBERT, a wright from Blair Drummond, Stirlingshire, son of William Hutton a burgess, was admitted as a burgess of Dunfermline on 24 October 1809. [DM]

HUTTON, WILLIAM, son of David Hutton, was admitted as a burgess of Dunfermline on 12 September 1799. [DM]

HYND, DAVID, a skipper in Newburgh, Fife in 1796. [NRS.S/H]

IMRIE, ANDREW, a land labourer, was admitted as a burgess of Kirkcaldy, Fife, on 29 August 1791. [KBR]

IMRIE, JAMES, a baker in Inverkeithing, Fife, son of John Imrie a butcher burgess, was admitted as a burgess of Dunfermline on 22 September 1807. [DM]

INCH, DAVID, tenant in Gallowridgehill, was admitted as a burgess of Dunfermline on 26 September 1791. [DM]

INCH, JAMES, son-in-law of Andrew Chalmers a weaver burgess, was admitted as a burgess of Dunfermline on 24 August 1791. [DM]

INCH, WILLIAM, a weaver, son-in-law of Robert Drummond a weaver burgess, was admitted as a burgess of Dunfermline on 28 May 1795. [DM]

INGLES, ANDREW, the Customs Controller in Kirkcaldy, testament, 1 April 1793, Comm. St Andrews. [NRS]

INGLES, DAVID, from Glasgow, was admitted as a burgess and guilds-brother of Dunfermline on 22 March 1796. [DM]

INGLIS, DAVID, born 1780, a power loom manufacturer from Dunfermline, Fife, died in Paterson, New Jersey, on 14 May 1868, his wife died there on 1 August 1868, and their youngest son James died there on 9 August 1860. [DP][S.7751]

INGLES, HENRY, son of George Ingles a weaver burgess, was admitted as a burgess of Dunfermline on 4 July 1797. [DM]

INGLIS, HENRY, a merchant in Cupar, Fife, a bankrupt in 1805. [NRS.CS96.20.7.9]

INGLES, JAMES, son of George Ingles a weaver burgess, was admitted as a burgess of Dunfermline on 4 July 1797. [DM]

INGLIS, JAMES, a merchant, was admitted as a burgess and guilds-brother of Cupar, Fife, on 14 November 1798. [CuBR]

INGLES, JAMES, a mason, son of deacon John Ingles a mason burgess, was admitted as a burgess of Dunfermline on 5 July 1809. [DM]

INGLIS, JAMES, son of John Inglis and his wife Annie Robertson, died in Australia on 9 November 1884. [Burntisland gravestone, Fife]

INGLES, JOHN, son of John Ingles a weaver burgess, was admitted as a burgess of Dunfermline on 1 September 1796. [DM]

INGLES, JOHN, son-in-law of James Scott a baker burgess, was admitted as a burgess of Dunfermline on 10 July 1804. [DM]

INGLIS, JOHN WILLIAM, son of John Bethune Inglis in Crail, Fife, died in Howrah near Calcutta, India, on 26 April 1856.

INGLIS, ROBERT, a shoemaker, was admitted as a burgess of Kirkcaldy, Fife, on 11 June 1790. [KBR]

INGLIS, ROBERT, a land labourer, was admitted as a burgess of Kirkcaldy, Fife, on 20 July 1793. [KBR]

INGLES, ROBERT, son of John Ingles a weaver burgess, was admitted as a burgess of Dunfermline on 4 July 1797. [DM]

INGLES, ROBERT, son of Robert Ingles a burgess, was admitted as a burgess of Dunfermline on 29 March 1805. [DM]

INGLIS, ROBERT, of Kirkmay, born 1813, died in Allahabad, United Provinces, India, in 1841. [Crail gravestone, Fife]

INGLIS, THOMAS, a merchant, was admitted as a burgess of Kirkcaldy, Fife, on 22 September 1792. [KBR]

INGLES, THOMAS, a police officer, son of William Ingles a weaver burgess, was admitted as a burgess of Dunfermline on 7 August 1795. [DM]

INGLES, WILLIAM, son of William Ingles a weaver in Nethertown, Dunfermline, was admitted as a burgess of Dunfermline on 7 July 1791. [DM]

INGLES, WILLIAM, a sailor at Crombie Point, Fife, son-in-law of John Mackie a burgess and guilds-brother, was admitted as a burgess of Dunfermline on 21 December 1795. [DM]

INGLIS, WILLIAM, a horse hirer in North Queensferry, Fife, 1806. [NRS.CS97.104.3]

INNES, ANDREW, a skipper in St Monance, Fife, testament, 13 October 1800, Comm. St Andrews. [NRS]

INNES, CAMPBELL, a merchant from Queensferry, Fife, was admitted as a burgess and guilds-brother of Dunfermline on 15 August 1804. [DM]

INNES, DAVID, a weaver, son of Andrew Innes, was admitted as a burgess of Cupar, Fife, on 29 September 1795. [CuBR]

INNES, DAVID, born 1812, died aboard the Home on the Banks of Newfoundland on 30 November 1835. [Anstruther Easter gravestone, Fife]

INNES, JAMES, a mason, was admitted as a burgess of Cupar, Fife, on 3 October 1810. [CuBR]

INNES, JOHN, a skipper in St Monance, Fife, testament, 13 October 1800, Comm. St Andrews. [NRS]

IRELAND, GEORGE, born 1804, son of John Ireland and his wife Mary Jackson, died in St Petersburg, Russia, on 7 October 1819. [Ferry-Port-on-Craig gravestone, Fife]

IRELAND, ISABELLA, born 1818, from Fife, landed in Hobart, Tasmania, Australia, aboard the Ocean Chief on 25 March 1855. [SRS.TD292]

IRELAND, JAMES, born 1827, son of William Ireland and his wife Euphemia Roger, died in East Oakland, California, on 16 March 1884. [Ferry-Port-on-Craig gravestone, Fife]

IRELAND, JOHN, son of Robert Ireland a baillie, was admitted as a burgess of Dunfermline on 28 October 1791. [DM]

IRELAND, PETER, born 1817, a ploughman from Fife, landed in Hobart, Tasmania, Australia, aboard the Ocean Chief on 25 March 1855. [SRS.TD292]

IRELAND, ROBERT, a merchant in Dunfermline, testament, 22 December 1791, Comm. St Andrews. [NRS]

IRELAND, WALTER FOGGO, son of Walter Foggo Ireland, a Captain of the Bengal Police, died in Narsinghpur, Central Provinces, India, on 6 July 1865. [St Andrews gravestone, Fife]

IRELAND, W. F., agent in St Andrews, Fife, for the Edinburgh and Glasgow Bank in 1849. [POD]

IZATT, ANDREW, born 1820, a labourer from Fife, landed in Hobart, Tasmania, Australia, aboard the Ocean Chief on 25 March 1855. [SRS.TD292]

JACK, DAVID WILLIAM, born 25 February 1785, son of William Jack in Cupar, Fife, settled in St Andrews, New Brunswick. [American Armory and Blue Book, London, 1903]

JACKSON, DAVID, born 1800 in Kirkcaldy, Fife, emigrated to America in 1822, settled in Richmond, Virginia, naturalised on 7 July 1825 in the Eastern District of Virginia. [Va. District Court RB5.492]

JACKSON, GEORGE, born 1803, son of James Jackson and his wife Margaret Bread, died Baltimore, Maryland, on 15 July 1830. [Burntisland gravestone, Fife]

JAMIESON, FRANCIS, a weaver in Pittencrieff, Fife, a former apprentice to Andrew Stevenson a weaver burgess, was admitted as a burgess of Dunfermline on 25 March 1790. [DM]

JAMESON, JOHN, youngest son of John Jameson the town clerk of Dysart, Fife, died in Bellmont, Jamaica, on 4 November 1819. [BM.6.726] [EEC.16950] [S.4.159]

JAMIESON, ROBERT, a grocer, was admitted as a burgess of Cupar, Fife, on 10 May 1804. [CuBR]

JAMIESON, WILLIAM, born 1837, son of James Jamieson and his wife Catherine Hutcheson, died in Kobe, Japan, on 2 May 1882. [Kirkcaldy gravestone, Fife]

JAMIESON, ..., a Lieutenant of the Fife Militia, was admitted as a burgess and guilds-brother of Dunfermline on 25 June 1798. [DM]

JOBSON, JOHN, agent in St Andrews, Fife, for the Eastern Bank in 1849. [POD]

JOHNSTON, DANIEL, born 1764, lately from White Bluff, Savanna, Georgia, died in Leslie, Fife, on4 December 1809. [PC.43]

JOHNSTON, FRANCES WEMYSS, daughter of Dr Johnston, married John Forbes Inverarity, from Mantanzas Isle, Cuba, in Kirkcaldy, Fife, on 25 September 1837. [DPCA.1835]

JOHNSTONE, HELEN WALKER, born 14 November 1839, daughter of Reverend Robert John Walker in Auchtermuchty, Fife, married Daniel Gibb from San Francisco, California, in Logie, Stirlingshire, on 14 November 1855. [F.4.357] [EEC.788818]

JOHNSTON, HENRY, Captain of the Scots Brigade, was admitted as a burgess and guilds-brother of Dunfermline on 4 June 1795. [DM]

JOHNSTON, JAMES, Quartermaster of the Scots Brigade, was admitted as a burgess and guilds-brother of Dunfermline on 29 September 1794. [DM]

JOHNSTONE, JOHN, in Knoxville County, Illinois, husband of Ann Mitchell, daughter of Captain Andrew Mitchell late of the Fife Militia [he died on 26 March 1837], a deed 2 July 1842, and a power of attorney, 15 November 1837. [NRS.B13.8.2/163; SC20.34.20/61]

JULIAN, ELEANOR, born 1792, wife of David Maitland Makgill of Rankeillor, Fife, died in Madeira on 9 January 1823. [ARM]

KAY, ALEXANDER, a mercantile clerk, was admitted as a burgess of Kirkcaldy, Fife, on 13 September 1794. [KBR]

KAY, JAMES, born 1780, a skipper in Torry, died on 21 January 1819. [Torryburn gravestone, Fife]

KAY, WILLIAM, a skipper in South Ferry, Fife, testament, 23 April 1804, Comm. St Andrews. [NRS]

KEAY, JOHN, farmer at Hilton of Carslogie, [1782-1859], husband of Margaret Melville, a farmer at Terre Haute, Indiana. [Moonzie gravestone, Fife]

KEAY, WILLIAM, born 1732, a skipper, husband of Euphan Pryde, died on 17 February 1804. [Ferry-port-on-Craig gravestone, Fife]

KEELER, ALEXANDER, a Lieutenant in the Royal Navy, was admitted as a burgess and guilds-brother of Dunfermline on14 June 1803. [DM]

KEIR, JOHN, a Captain of the Royal Linlithgow Volunteers, was admitted as a burgess and guilds-brother of Dunfermline on 15 August 1804. [DM]

KEIR, JOHN, master of the *Resolution of Kirkcaldy* from Greenock to Quebec in 1813. [NRS.E504.15.100]

KEITH, JAMES, born 1763, schoolmaster in Dunbog for 48 years, died 6 December 1838. [Dunbog gravestone, Fife]

KELLOCK, GEORGE, son of George Kellock a shoemaker burgess, was admitted as a burgess of Dunfermline on 17 August 1792. [DM]

KELLOCK, JOHN, son of George Kellock a shoemaker burgess, was admitted as a burgess and guilds-brother of Dunfermline on 15 April 1796. [DM]

KELLOCK, JOHN, son of David Kellock a weaver burgess, was admitted as a burgess of Dunfermline on 3 July 1797. [DM]

KELLOCK, JOHN, a merchant in Inverkeithing, Fife, testament, 26 February 1798, Comm. St Andrews. [NRS]

KELLY, ALEXANDER, son of Alexander Kelly and his wife Ann Tod, died in Ballarat, Australia, on 5 April 1882. [Aberdour gravestone, Fife]

KELTIE, JOHN, a weaver, son of James Keltie a burgess, was admitted as a burgess and guilds-brother of Dunfermline on 4 July 1797. [DM]

KENNEDY, DAVID, born 1773, son of Thomas Kennedy and his wife Ann Gibb in Falkland, a merchant in Philadelphia, Pennsylvania, died in Germantown, Pa., in 1798. [Falkland gravestone, Fife]

KENNEDY, RICHARD MOWBRAY, born 1840, third son of Peter Kennedy, a butcher in Aberdour, Fife, died 1861, and his wife Margaret Chisholm, died 1860, died in Kimberley, Cape of Good Hope, South Africa, on 7 December 1879. [S.11383][FJ]

KENNEDY, ROBERT, a Lieutenant of the Scots Brigade was admitted as a burgess and guilds-brother of Dunfermline on 29 September 1794. [DM]

KENNELL, JAMES, a weaver, son-in-law of James Anderson a weaver burgess, was admitted as a burgess of Dunfermline on 16 September 1803. [DM]

KER, ALEXANDER, a piper from Doune, Stirlingshire, was admitted as a burgess and town officer of Dunfermline on 30 July 1791. [DM]

KER, ALEXANDER, son of John Ker a manufacturer burgess, was admitted as a burgess of Dunfermline on 4 July 1797. [DM]

KER, JAMES, son of John Ker a manufacturer burgess, was admitted as a burgess of Dunfermline on 4 July 1797. [DM]

KERR, JOHN, in Coaltown, Markinch, Fife, father of David Kerr, born 1858, died in McCook, Nebraska, on 8 July 1885. [DCA.3540]

KERR, PETER, a merchant, was admitted as a burgess of Cupar, Fife, on 10 October 1797. [CuBR]

KER, ROBERT, son of John Ker a manufacturer burgess, was admitted as a burgess of Dunfermline on 4 July 1797. [DM]

KETTLE, THOMAS YOUNG, born 27 November 1778, son of Reverend Thomas Kettle and his wife Sarah Young in Leuchars, Fife, settled in Savanna, Georgia, died there on 6 August 1832. [F.5.222] [EEC.18861]

KEY, DAVID, a tailor in Falkland, Fife, testament, 26 January 1800, Comm. St Andrews. [NRS]

KEY, JAMES, a brewer, was admitted as a burgess of Crail, Fife, in 1800. [CBR]

KEY, WILLIAM INGLIS, born 1816, son of John Key a merchant in New Orleans, Louisiana, grandson and heir of James Key in Crail, 1856. [NRS.S/H]; died in New Orleans on 5 April 1868. [Crail gravestone, Fife]

KYD, JAMES, in Elie, Fife, formerly master of the Customs cutter Osnaburgh, testament, 1793, Comm. St Andrews. [NRS]

KID, JAMES, son of James Kid a tailor burgess, was admitted as a burgess of Dunfermline on 4 August 1795. [DM]

KYD, JAMES, son of David Kyd, was admitted as a burgess of Cupar, Fife, on 6 October 1807. [CuBR]

KIDD, JANET, born 1800, daughter of Thomas Kidd and his wife Margaret Anderson, died in Horsham, Victoria, Australia. On 17 November 1855. [Newburn gravestone, Fife]

KIDD, JOHN, born 1808, son of Thomas Kidd and his wife Margaret Anderson, died in Melbourne, Victoria, Australia, on 18 March 1853. [Newburn gravestone, Fife]

KIDD, ROBERT, born 1832, son of Robert Kidd and his wife Elizabeth Smith, died in Epucha, Victoria, Australia, on 23 September 1882. [Forgan gravestone, Fife]

KYD, WILLIAM, son of David Kyd, was admitted as a burgess of Cupar, Fife, on 10 October 1797. [CuBR]

KILGOUR, ALEXANDER, a weaver, son of David Kilgour a smith burgess, was admitted as a burgess of Dunfermline on 31 July 1790. [DM]

KILGOUR, CHRISTIAN, relict of Andrew Chalmers, sr., a weaver in Dunfermline, testament, 20 December 1791, Comm. St Andrews. [NRS]

KILGOUR, DAVID, son of Robert Kilgour, was admitted as a burgess of Kirkcaldy, Fife, on 28 February 1798. [KBR]

KILGOUR, JAMES, a tailor and staymaker in Dunfermline, testament, 14 April 1797, Comm. St Andrews. [NRS]

KILGOUR, RICHARD, a weaver, son of David Kilgour a smith burgess, was admitted as a burgess of Dunfermline on 27 September 1790. [DM]

KILGOUR, JOHN, a wright in Cupar, Fife, testament, 10 November 1795, Comm. St Andrews. [NRS]

KILGOUR, ROBERT, a wright, son of George Kilgour, was admitted as a burgess of Kirkcaldy, Fife, on 3 September 1798. [KBR]

KILPATRICK, DAVID, son of David Kilpatrick a weaver burgess was admitted as a burgess of Dunfermline on 28 November 1792. [DM]

KING, JAMES, born 1797, son of James King and his wife Helen Skinner, a vine grower in New South Wales, Australia, died in London, England, on 29 November 1857. [Kilconquhar gravestone, Fife]

KING, MARY, wife of William Carstairs, died at the Cape of Good Hope, South Africa, on 7 March 1834. [Cupar gravestone, Fife]

KING, MITCHELL, born 1783 in Crail, Fife, emigrated to America in 1805, a teacher and judge in Charleston, S.C., was naturalised in South Carolina on 6 February 1810, died in Charleston, S.C., on 12 November 1862. [NARA.M1183-1][Old Scots gravestone, Charleston]

KINLOCH, DAVID, son of David Kinloch a burgess, was admitted as a burgess of Dunfermline on 23 September 1801. [DM]

KINLOCH, JOHN, son of David Kinloch a burgess, was admitted as a burgess of Dunfermline on 3 August 1802. [DM]

KINNEAR, CHRISTOPHER, born 1794 in Dysart, Fife, formerly in Halifax, Nova Scotia, died in Baltimore, Maryland, on 26 September 1821. [FP.13.11.1821]

KINNEAR, THOMAS, born 1803, son of Thomas Kinnear of Kinloch, Fife, was admitted to the Society of Writers to the Signet on 25 May 1826, died at Richmond Hill, Yonge Street, Toronto, Ontario, on 27 July 1843. [WS] [EEC.20653]

KINNINMONT, JOHN, born 1769, husband of Catherine Carstairs, died in France in 1815. [Kilconquhar gravestone, Fife]

KIRK, ALEXANDER, son of John Kirk a wright in Dunfermline, Fife, was apprenticed to David Finlay, a barber in Edinburgh, for six years on 21 November 1799. [ERA]

KIRKE, CATHERINE, born 1821, daughter of David Kirk and his wife Janet Walls, died in America in 1856. [Burntisland gravestone, Fife]

KIRK, CHARLES, son of Charles Kirk a smith burgess was admitted as a burgess of Dunfermline on 7 August 1795. [DM]

KIRK, DAVID, son of John Kirk a burgess, was admitted as a burgess of Dunfermline on 18 March 1805. [DM]

KIRK, DOUGAL, son of Charles Kirk a smith burgess, was admitted as a burgess of Dunfermline on 24 September 1793. [DM]

KIRK, GEORGE, born 1836, son of Alexander Kirk and his wife Elizabeth Clark, died at Hawke's Bay, New Zealand, on 2 September 1894. [St Andrew's gravestone, Fife]

KIRK, JAMES, son of former Provost John Kirk, was admitted as a burgess of Dunfermline on 2 August 1797. [DM]

KIRK, JAMES, son of James Kirk, [1749-1829], and his wife Elspeth Russell, [1751-1832], a merchant who settled in St John's, New Brunswick, before 1832. [Pittenweem gravestone] [St Andrews gravestone, Fife]

KIRK, JAMES, born 1825, son of Alexander Kirk and his wife Elizabeth Clark, died in Braidwood, New South Wales, Australia, on 27 January 1859. [Pittenweem gravestone, Fife]

KIRK, ROBERT, son of John Kirk a burgess, was admitted as a burgess of Dunfermline on 29 March 1805. [DM]

KIRK, ROBERT, born 1841, son of Alexander Kirk and his wife Elizabeth Clark, died at sea off Cape Colony, South Africa, on 9 March 1880. [Pittenweem gravestone, Fife]

KIRKE, ROBERT, born 1816, son of Robert Kirke and his wife Helen Balfour, later of Greenmount, Burntisland, and of Waterloo, Nickery, Surinam, died 3 January 1894. [Cairneyhill gravestone, Fife]

KIRK, WILLIAM, born 1746 in Dunfermline, Fife, served in the first American War, then settled in Pictou, Nova Scotia, died in St Mary's, Antigonish, N.S., on 9 August 1843. [SG.XI.1228]

KIRK, WILLIAM, a smith, son of Charles Kirk a feuar burgess, was admitted as a burgess of Dunfermline on 3 January 1810. [DM]

KIRKCALDY, or DOVE, widow of James Dove, in Kingston, Jamaica, sister and heir of John Kirkcaldy a landwaiter in Limekilns, Fife, 1805. [NRS.S/H]

KIRKCALDY, THOMAS, son of Thomas Kirkcaldy a guilds-brother, was admitted as a burgess of Dunfermline on 9 July 1799. [DM]

KIRKCALDIE, THOMAS, in Burntisland, Fife, father of William Kirkcaldie, born 1862, died in Johannesburg, South Africa, on 15 December 1898. [S.17335]

KIRKLAND, JOHN, a baker, was admitted as a burgess of Dunfermline on 29 June 1798. [DM]

KNOX, HENRY, a weaver, was admitted as a burgess of Kirkcaldy, Fife, on 18 September 1801. [KBR]

KNOX, JOHN, a weaver, was admitted as a burgess of Kirkcaldy, Fife, on 18 September 1801. [KBR]

LAING, ANDREW, in Black Diamond, Pennsylvania, heir to Andrew Laing, a collier in New Gilston, Fife, who died on 25 January 1854. [NRS.S/H]

LAING, GEORGE, a writer in Edinburgh, was admitted as a burgess and guilds-brother of Dunfermline on 16 June 1796. [DM]

LAING, PETER, a draper in Newburgh, Fife, later at the Cape of Good Hope, South Africa, husband of Annie Anderson, born 1786, died 1813. [Abdie gravestone, Fife]

LAING, WILLIAM, in Springfield, Fife, father of Annie Laing, born 1862, wife of John Watt of the Bank of Africa, died in Alewal, Cape Colony, South Africa, on 27 May 1888. [FH.30.5.1888]

LAING, ..., agent in Newburgh, Fife, for the Commercial Bank of Scotland in 1849. [POD]

LAIRD, MATTHEW, born 1825, son of Matthew Laird and his wife Margaret Tavendale, died on a voyage from Manilla in the Phillipines to Sydney, New South Wales, Australia, on 3 September 1846. [Burntisland gravestone, Fife]

LAMB, ELOISE, in Fredericton, New Brunswick, heir of Robert Lamb of Templehall, Fife, her grandfather, in 1829. [NRS.S/H]

LANDALE, CHRISTIAN, spouse of James Landale tacksman of the coal of Kingsmuir, Dunino, Fife, testament, 12 February 1772, Comm. St Andrews. [NRS]

LANDALE, JAMES, tacksman of the coat at Kingsmuir, Dunino, testament, 7 December 1790, testament, 7 December 1790, Comm. St Andrews. [NRS]

LANSMAN, JOHN, a mariner in Anstruther, Fife, testament, 13 December 1792, Comm. St Andrews. [NRS]

LATOU, ROBERT, born 10 July 1799 in Cupar, Fife, son of Peter Latou and his wife Janet Henderson, a shipbuilder who emigrated to Montreal in 1816, settled in New York before 1851, died 12 January 1869. [Leuchars gravestone, Fife] [ANY]

LATTO, ALEXANDER, in Winthank, Cameron, Fife, testament, 29 June 1790, Comm. St Andrews. [NRS]

LATTO, DAVID, born 1838, from Pittenweem, Fife, master of the <u>Persian</u> died in Kranken Anstalt, Bremen, Germany, on 16 August 1880. [EFR]

LATTO, JOHN, a brewer in Kettle, Fyfe, testament, 13 January 1797, Comm. St Andrews. [NRS]

LAURENCE, HENRY, a merchant, was admitted as a burgess of Cupar, Fife, on 3 October 1804. [CuBR]

LAURIE, JOHN, a miller from Strathmiglo, Fife, settled in America by 1809. [NRS.CS17.1.29/442]

LAVEROCK, JOHN, a skipper in Dysart, Fife, testament, 13 August 1812, Comm. St Andrews. [NRS]

LAW, GEORGE, a tailor from Achtererderran, Fife, was admitted as a burgess of Dunfermline on 12 March 1791. [DM]

LAW, JAMES, son-in-law of Robert Drummond a weaver burgess, was admitted as a burgess of Dunfermline on 24 September 1806. [DM]

LAW, WILLIAM, a weaver, son of David Law a weaver burgess, was admitted as a burgess of Dunfermline on 2 Octosber 1807. [DM]

LAW, WILLIAM, a weaver, son of David Law a weaver burgess, was admitted as a burgess of Dunfermline on 2 October 1807. [DM]

LAW, WILLIAM, a skipper in Burntisland, Fife, testament, 15 February 1808, Comm. St Andrews. [NRS]

LAW, WILLIAM, born 1829, son of Reverend John Law and his wife Jane Murray, died in Trinidad on 21 August 1855. [Dunfermline gravestone, Fife]

LAW, WILLIAM, born 1830, son of John and Mary Law, died in Rio de Janeiro, Brazil, in 1852. [Crail gravestone, Fife]

LAWRENCE, DAVID, a baillie of Culross, Fife, was admitted as a burgess and guilds-brother of Dunfermline on 3 July 1790. [DM]

LAWRIE, DAVID, son of David Lawrie a soapboiler burgess, was admitted as a burgess of Dunfermline on 24 September 1802. [DM]

LAWRIE, JAMES, son of Robert Lawrie, was admitted as a burgess of Dunfermline on 2 May 1797. [DM]

LAWRIE, JAMES, minister at Ballingry, Fife, testaments, 6 February 1789 and 23 December 1805, Comm. St Andrews. [NRS]

LAWRIE, WILLIAM, a weaver, son of David Lawrie a weaver burgess, was admitted as a burgess of Dunfermline on 2 October 1807. [DM]

LAWSON, DAVID, born 1778 in Fife, a blacksmith who settled in Kingston, King's County, New Brunswick, was drowned on 10 June 1804. [SJG.18.6.1804]

LAWSON, DAVID, a wright, son of James Lawson, was admitted as a burgess of Kirkcaldy, Fife, on 31 July 1800. [KBR]

LAWSON, DAVID, a baker in Leslie, Fife, son-in-law of Alexander Aitken a burgess, was admitted as a burgess of Dunfermline on 14 September 1808. [DM]

LAWSON, THOMAS, son of Thomas Lawson of Pitlethie, Fife, a writer in Edinburgh, later a judge and magistrate in Grahamstown, Cape of Good Hope, South Africa, died on 19 June 1828. [FH.25.9.1828]; testament, 1829, Comm. Edinburgh. [NRS]

LAWSON, WALTER, in Buckhaven, Fife, settled in Nova Scotia by 1809. [NRS.B41.7.9]

LAWSON, WILLIAM, sr., late of Pitlethia, later in Cupar, Fife, testament, 16 March 1795, Comm. St Andrews. [NRS]

LAWSON, WALTER, in Buckhaven, Fife, settled in Nova Scotia by 1809. [NRS.B41.7.9]

LAWSON, WILLIAM, sr., late of Pitlethia, later in Cupar, Fife, testament, 16 March 1795, Comm. St Andrews. [NRS]

LEAR, WILLIAM, a watchmaker, was admitted as a burgess of Dunfermline on 2 July 1801. [DM]

LEARMONTH, ALEXANDER, a weaver, son-in-law of William Anderson a weaver burgess, was admitted as a burgess of Dunfermline on 18 August 1792. [DM]

LEE, JAMES, born in St Andrews, Fife, settled in New York, husband of Mary Crookshank, died 9 October 1795. [ANY]

LEES, HENRY, born 1839, son of James Lees, died in Chicago, Illinois, in 1867. [Kilconquhar gravestone, Fife]

LEIL, THOMAS, a sailor in Burntisland, Fife, son of Thomas Leil, was admitted as a burgess of Kirkcaldy, Fife, on 14 May 1794. [KBR]

LEITCH, JANET, wife of Malcolm McGibbon in Manchester, North America, daughter and heir of Andrew Leitch an engineer in Lochgelly, Fife, who died on 11 January 1863. [NRS.S/H]

LEITCH, Reverend WILLIAM, born 1815, was Principal of Queen's College, Kingston, Ontario, for eighteen years, died in Monimail on 9 May 1864. [Monimail gravestone, Fife]

LEITH, ROBERT, former baillie of Pittenweem, Fife, settled in Philadelphia, Pennsylvania, before 1851. [NRS.SC16.1.85]

LESLIE, ALEXANDER, born 1767, a farmer from Fife, settled in Richmond City, Virginia, naturalised in the Eastern District of Virginia in 1799. [Va. District Court 1799.34]

LESLIE, ALEXANDER, born 1765, son of Andrew Leslie and his wife Jean Orrock, died in America in 1818. [Burntisland gravestone, Fife]

LESLIE, DAVID, a merchant, was admitted as a burgess of Kirkcaldy, Fife, on 25 November 1793. [KBR]

LESLY, DAVID, son of David Lesly and Jane Kinnear, a shipmaster who settled in New York before 1826. [Monimail gravestone, Fife]

LESLIE, JOHN, a police officer, was admitted as a burgess of Dunfermline on 17 August 1793. [DM]

LESLIE, JOHN, born 1772, son of Andrew Leslie and his wife Jean Orrock, died in America in 1818. [Burntisland gravestone, Fife]

LESLIE, ROBERT, a grocer from Burntisland, Fife, later in America by 1810. [NRS.CS17.1.30/7]

LESSELS, ALEXANDER, a sailor in Burntisland, in 1791. [NRS.S/H]

LESSELS, ANDREW, born 1829, son of George Lessels and his wife Martha Henderson, died in Panama on 27 August 1868. [Newburgh gravestone, Fife]

LESSELS, GEORGE, born 1825, son of George Lessels and his wife Martha Henderson, died in America in 1847. [Newburgh gravestone, Fife]

LESSELLS, JAMES, a sloop-master, was admitted as a burgess of Crail, Fife, in 1801. [CBR]

LESSELS, JAMES, born 1839, son of George Lessels and his wife Martha Henderson, died in India on 3 November 1845. [Newburgh gravestone, Fife]

LESSELLS, JAMES, a sloopmaster burgess of Crail in 1801. [CBR]

LETHAM, JOHN, a baker, son of William Letham a burgess, was admitted as a burgess of Dunfermline on 9 August 1804. [DM]

LETHIAN, JAMES, son of John Lethian a weaver burgess, was admitted as a burgess of Dunfermline on 4 July 1797. [DM]

LETHIAN, JAMES, son of William Lethian a weaver burgess, was admitted as a burgess of Dunfermline on 4 July 1797. [DM]

LETHIAN, JOHN, son of John Lethian, was admitted as a burgess of Dunfermline on 4 July 1797. [DM]

LEWIS, PHILIP, born 1832, son of William Lewis and his wife Helen Rust, died in Queensland, Australia, in August 1863. [Abbotshall gravestone, Fife]

LIDDEL, DAVID, a tenant in Urquhart, son-in-law of William Davison a butcher burgess, was admitted as a burgess of Dunfermline on 4 February 1799. [DM]

LIDDELL, DAVID, born 1806, son of James Liddell and his wife Agnes Leighton, a Captain of the 10th Bombay Native Infantry, died at sea on 21 April 1829. [Aberdour gravestone, Fife]

LIDDELL, HENRY, born 1801, son of James Liddell and his wife Agnes Leighton, a Major of the 11th Native Infantry, died in Bombay, India, on 27 December 1841. [Aberdour gravestone, Fife]

LIDDELL, HENRY, born 1807, of the Bombay Civil Service, died in Culross on 29 September 1873. [Auchtertool gravestone, Fife]

LIDDELL, JAMES, born 1798, son of James Liddell and his wife Agnes Leighton, a Major of the 1st Bombay Cavalry, died at Kotra, Bombay, India, on 3 June 1841. [Aberdour gravestone, Fife]

LIDDELL, JOHN, born 1805, son of James Liddell and his wife Agnes Leighton, a Lieutenant of the 10th Bombay Artillery, died at the Cape of Good Hope, South Africa, on 14 October 1824. [Aberdour gravestone, Fife]

LIDDELL, JOHN, born 1811, a Major General of the Bombay Army, died on 12 April 1879. [Auchtertool gravestone, Fife]

LIDDELL, JOHN, born 1847, son of David Liddell and his wife Elizabeth Davidson, died in Sydney, New South Wales, Australia, on 15 January 1873. [Auchtertool gravestone, Fife]

LINDSAY, ADAM, of Nativity, born 1754, a Lieutenant Colonel of the 7th Bengal Native Infantry in the Service of the East India Company, died 12 March 1812. [Dunfermline gravestone, Fife]

LINDSAY, Captain DAVID, of Kirkforthar, Markinch, Fife, testaments, 11 July 1799 and 23 March 1804, Comm. St Andrews. [NRS]

LINDESAY, HENRY, youngest son of Patrick Lindesay of Wormiston, Crail, a Major of the 3rd Bengal Light Cavalry, died in Mussoorie, Bengal, India, on 22 June 1856. [FH]

LINDSAY, JAMES, born 1794, son of John Lindsay and his wife Margaret Jackson, a joiner who died in New Orleans, Louisiana, on 28 August 1822. [Falkland gravestone, Fife]

LINDSAY, JAMES HEAD, born 2 November 1828, son of Robert Lindsay and his wife Frances Henderson, died in Barrackpore, Bengal, India, on 14 August 1856. [St Andrews gravestone, Fife]

LINDSAY, JOHN, born 1801, son of John Lindsay and his wife Margaret Jackson, a joiner who died in New York on 22 May 1855. [Falkland gravestone, Fife]

LINDSAY, JOHN, born 1803, son of William Lindsay of Balmunzie and his wife Mary Adamson, a Lieutenant of the 34th Madras Native Infantry, died in Rangoon, Burma, on 12 October 1824. [St Andrews gravestone, Fife]

LINDSAY, ROBERT, in Kirkcaldy, Fife, testament, 25 July 1791, Comm. St Andrews. [NRS]

LINDSAY, ROBERT, born 19 May 1827, son of Robert Lindsay and Frances Henderson, died in Trichinopoly, Madras, India, on 18 January 1849. [St Andrews gravestone, Fife]

LINDSAY, ROBERT, son of Lieutenant General James Lindsay, died in Genoa, Italy, on 18 December 1856. [Balcarres gravestone, Fife]

LISTER, JAMES, a mariner in St Andrews, Fife, testament, 1825, Comm. St Andrews. [NRS]

LISTON, Reverend ROBERT, in Aberdour, Fife, was admitted as a burgess and guilds-brother of Dunfermline on 4 June 1792. [DM]

LOCHHEAD, JANET, relict of John Hunter a feuar in Torry, Fife, testament, 28 November 1800, Comm. St Andrews. [NRS]

LOCHTY, JAMES, born 1823, son of John Lochty and his wife Isobel Moyes, died in Sydney, New South Wales, Australia, on 23 October 1856. [Aberdour gravestone, Fife]

LOCK, ANN, daughter of John Lock, sister of David Lock of Carnbee, Fife, residing in Kirkcaldy, testament, 7 March 1800, Comm. St Andrews. [NRS]

LOCK, MARGARET, daughter of John Lock, sister of David Lock of Carnie, Fife, residing in Kirkcaldy, testament, 7 March 1800, Comm. St Andrews. [NRS]

LOGIE, JAMES, a fisherman in Buckhaven, Fife, in 1799. [NRS.S/H]

LORIMER, DAVID, a tailor, son of David Lorimer, was admitted as a burgess of Cupar, Fife, on 28 August 1807. [CuBR]

LORIMER, Professor JAMES, and his wife Hannah Stoddart, were parents of James Lorimer born 1852, died in Grahamstown, Cape of Good Hope, South Africa, in 1898. [Newburn gravestone, Fife]

LORIMER, WILLIAM, was admitted as a burgess of Cupar, Fife, on 3 October 1809. [CuBR]

LOUDEN, ALEXANDER, a weaver, son of Alexander Louden, was admitted as a burgess of Cupar, Fife, on 2 October 1799. [CuBR]

LOURIE, DAVID, a sailor, was admitted as a burgess of Kirkcaldy, Fife, on 3 March 1790. [KBR]

LOURIE, WILLIAM, a sailor, was admitted as a burgess of Kirkcaldy, Fife, on 3 March 1790. [KBR]

LOUSON, JOHN, son of James Louson a weaver burgess, was admitted as a burgess of Dunfermline on 4 July 1797. [DM]

LOUSON, THOMAS, son of James Louson a weaver burgess, was admitted as a burgess of Dunfermline on 4 July 1797. [DM]

LOUSON, WILLIAM, son of James Louson a weaver burgess, was admitted as a burgess of Dunfermline on 7 August 1795. [DM]

LOVE, ADAM, a weaver, son of John Love a butcher burgess, was admitted as a burgess of Dunfermline on 5 July 1797. [DM]

LOVE, GAVIN, a butcher, son of William Love the deacon of the butchers, was admitted as a burgess of Dunfermline on 24 September 1794. [DM]

LOVE, ROBERT, a butcher, son of William Love a butcher burgess, was admitted as a burgess of Dunfermline on 9 September 1807. [DM]

LOW, IRVINE, a Major of the Bengal Cavalry, died in Simla, Punjab, India, on 26 June 1881. [Kemback gravestone, Fife]

LOW, JAMES, a wright, son of David Low, was admitted as a burgess of Kirkcaldy, Fife, on 1 January 1798. [KBR]

LOW, JOHN, died 15 April 1839, husband of Mary Geddie, born 1735, died 1 December 1813. [Dairsie gravestone, Fife]

LOWSON, ROBERT, a butcher, son of Robert Lowson an innkeeper in Dunfermline, was admitted as a burgess of Dunfermline on 15 June 1810. [DM]

LUKE, JOHN, and his wife Elisabeth Simson in St Monance, were parents of David Luke born 13 May 1858, died in Melbourne, Victoria, Australia, on 17 September 1909. [Abercrombie gravestone, Fife]

LUKE, JOHN, and his wife Elisabeth Simson in St Monance, were parents of Robert Luke born 26 October 1859, died in Coolgardie, Western Australia, on 13 October 1894. [Abercrombie gravestone, Fife]

LUMSDEN, F. R., schoolmaster of Wood's school in Newburn, Fife, and his wife Janet W. Hill, parents of Janet Hill Lumsden, born 1861, died in Treves, Rhenish Prussia, Germany, on 30 April 1879. [S.11167][FH]

LUMSDEN, JAMES, in Newton of Falkland, testament, 24 February 1798, Comm. St Andrews. [NRS]

LUMSDEN, JAMES, a wright in Kirkcaldy, Fife, emigrated to America after 1827. [SG.33.2.184]

LUMSDAIN, JOHN, son-in-law of David Kesson, was admitted as a burgess of Dunfermline on 28 April 1797. [DM]

LUNDIN, BETTY, daughter of Captain James Lundin of Auchtermairnie, Kennoway, Fife, testament, 22 June 1792, Comm.St Andrews. [NRS]

LYAL, ANDREW, a flax-dresser, son of Thomas Lyal a tailor burgess, was admitted as a burgess of Dunfermline on 18 July 1791. [DM]

LYON, JASPER, born 17 February 1777, son of Reverend George Lyon and his wife Sophia Marshall in Strathmiglo, Fife, a merchant in the West Indies. [F.5.175]

LYON, THOMAS, a surgeon aboard the Pigot, son and heir of Reverend George Lyon in Strathmiglo, Fife, in 1793. [NRS.S/H]

MCALPIN, WILLIAM, a skipper in Pittenweem, Fife, manager and master of the Pittenweem Sea Box Society, on 14 January 1799. [NRS.B3.7.5]

MCANDREW, DAVID, from Culross, Fife, later in America by 1824, a sasine. [NRS.RS.Culross i.40]

MCARRA, JAMES, son of James McArra a flaxdresser in Edinburgh, was admitted as a burgess of Dunfermline on 9 October 1809. [DM]

MCARRA, JOHN, son of James McArra a merchant, was admitted as a burgess of Dunfermline on 28 October 1791. [DM]

MCARRA, ROBERT, a watchmaker, son of James McArra a merchant burgess, was admitted as a burgess of Dunfermline on May 1798. [DM]

MCARTHUR, Reverend ALEXANDER, born 1780, minister in Dairsie, died 4 February 1841, husband of Isabella Alison, born 1793, died 28 August 1870. [Dairsie gravestone, Fife][F.5.149]

MCBEAN, JAMES, son-in-law of James Beveridge a writer, was admitted as a burgess of Dunfermline on 11 September 1802. [DM]

MCBEATH, ARCHIBALD, son-in-law of Charles Kirk sr. a smith burgess, was admitted as a burgess of Dunfermline on 22 February 1808. [DM]

MCBRIAR, ALEXANDER, born 1847, from Kirkcaldy, Fife, died in Montreal, Quebec, on 1 April 1878. [EC.29191]

MCCONNEL, MARGARET, servant to Sir John Halket of Pitfirran, Dunfermline, testament, 16 January 1790, Comm. St Andrews. [NRS]

MCCREDIE, WILLIAM, born 1806, a staff assistant surgeon, died in Bermuda on 13 October 1840. [Kirkcaldy gravestone, Fife]

MCCULLOCH, Reverend ROBERT, born 1740, minister at Dairsie for 52 years, died 2 September 1824, husband of Janet ..., born 1741, died 28 November 1811. [Dairsie gravestone, Fife]

MCDONALD, ALEXANDER, a wright, was admitted as a burgess of Dunfermline on 15 May 1810. [DM]

MACDONALD, CHARLES, son of Professor MacDonald in St Andrews, Fife, died at Lake View, Hamilton, Canada West, on 7 April 1851. [FJ.959]

MCDONALD, DONALD ALEXANDER, born 1820, son of Angus McDonald and his wife Robina MacFarlane, died in Furreedport in the East Indies on 20 September 1845. [Dysart gravestone, Fife]

MCDONALD, GORDON, late of Plantation Moy, Corome, Surinam, died in Burntisland on 28 June 1859. [Burntisland gravestone, Fife]

MCDONALD, JOHN, a wright, , was admitted as a burgess of Dunfermline on 16 March 1810. [DM]

MCEWIN, JOHN, a weaver, son-in-law of George Ferguson a weaver burgess, was admitted as a burgess of Dunfermline in July 1797. [DM]

MCFADYEN, JOHN, a surgeon, was admitted as a burgess and guilds-brother of Dunfermline on 4 June 1792. [DM]

MCFARLANE, JOHN, a shoemaker, son-in-law of Andrew Williamson a shoemaker burgess, was admitted as a burgess of Dunfermline on 5 December 1794. [DM]

MACFARLANE, JOHN, born 1814 in Fife, died in India on 29 May 1834. [Scotch Burial Ground gravestone, Calcutta, India]

MAKGILL, Sir JOHN, born 6 February 1836, son of George Makgill of Kemback, died in Brackmont, Waiuka, New Zealand, on 14 November 1906. [Kemback gravestone, Fife]

MCGLASHAN, CHARLES, was admitted as a burgess and guilds-brother of Cupar, Fife, on 10 October 1808. [CuBR]

MCGREGOR, DAVID, son of Mungo McGregor a weaver burgess, was admitted as a burgess of Dunfermline on 8 August 1795. [DM]

MCGREGOR, WILLIAM, son of William McGregor a weaver burgess, was admitted as a burgess of Dunfermline on 16 August 1793. [DM]

MCGUGAN, DAVID, a mason, was admitted as a burgess of Dunfermline on 23 December 1807. [DM]

MCINTOSH, ALEXANDER, born 1760, a skipper, died 4 February 1805. [Tulliallan gravestone, Fife]

MCINTOSH, ROBERT, a shoemaker, was admitted as a burgess of Dunfermline on 21 October 1809. [DM]

MCINTYRE, PETER, a skipper at Crombie Point, Fife, testament, 1819, Comm. St Andrews. [NRS]

MCKECHNIE, STUART, eldest son of A. McKechnie, in St Austine, Fife, died on Canada West, on 5 May 1853. [GM.ns40.98]

MCKEIRLY, PETER, son of John McKeirly a weaver burgess, was admitted as a burgess of Dunfermline on 3 August 1797. [DM]

MCKENZIE, COLIN, born 1811, son of Colin McKenzie and his wife Marjory Lumsden, a carpenter on the **Firth of Alloa**, died in the China Seas in 1836. [Dysart gravestone, Fife]

MCKENZIE, ROBERT, born 1803, '21 years in America', died in Leslie on 24 April 1854. [Leslie gravestone, Fife]

MACKERSIE, ANDREW, from Auchtermuchty, Fife, an employee of the Bank of the Republic in New York, died in Whitestone, Long Island, New York, on 1 September 1863. [S.2577]

MACKEY, CHARLES, born 1772, a skipper in Rosyth, Fife, died in 1812, died in 1812, husband of Elizabeth Thomson. [Rosyth gravestone]

MCKIBBIN, ROBERT, born 1840, son of William and Janet McKibbin, died in Calcutta, India, on 7 May 1867. [St Andrews gravestone, Fife]

MACKIE, DAVID, a manufacturer in Dunfermline, testament, 3 December 1798, Comm. St Andrews. [NRS]

MACKIE, ELIZABETH, relict of Dr Henry Miller in Jamaica, died in Kirkcaldy, Fife, on 28 October 1853. [FH]

MACKIE, JAMES, son-in-law of Adam Beveridge a weaver burgess, was admitted as a burgess of Dunfermline on 4 July 1797. [DM]

MCKIE, JOHN, son of Andrew McKie a farmer in St Monance, Fife, was apprenticed to Henry Watson, a hardware merchant in Edinburgh, for five years on 31 October 1799. [ERA]

MACKIE, MARGARET, born 1793 in Fife, residing in Charleston, S.C., was naturalised in South Carolina on 29 September 1837. [NARA.M1183.1]

MACKIE, WILLIAM, a stoneware merchant, was admitted as a burgess of Kirkcaldy, Fife, on 9 July 1801. [KBR]

MCKILY, ..., son of ...... McKily a weaver burgess, was admitted as a burgess of Dunfermline on 7 October 1799. [DM]

MCKINLAY, DANIEL, master of the Concord of Dysart trading between Greenock and Quebec in 1811. [NRS.E504.15.92]

MCKINLAY, JAMES, a mason in Kirkcaldy, Fife, emigrated to America in 1827. [SG.33.2.183]

MCLACHLAN, JOHN, a weaver, son-in-law of John Paton a burgess, was admitted as a burgess of Dunfermline on 30 July 1791. [DM]

MCLACHLAN, JOHN, son of John McLachlan a burgess, was admitted as a burgess of Dunfermline on 1 May 1795. [DM]

MCLAREN, JAMES, a vintner, was admitted as a burgess of Cupar, Fife, on 10 October 1801. [CuBR]

MCLAREN, JAMES, a coal grieve at Townhill of Dunfermline, was admitted as a burgess of Dunfermline on 31 August 1810. [DM]

MCLAREN, JOHN, a mariner in Torryburn, Fife, testament, 18 August 1814, Comm. St Andrews. [NRS]

MCLAREN, WALTER, born 1848, son of Walter McLaren and his wife Agnes Meiklejohn, died in the Indian Ocean in March 1876. [Tulliallan gravestone, Fife]

MCLAUCHLAN, THOMAS, a wright, was admitted as a burgess of Kirkcaldy, Fife, on 4 October 1802. [KBR]

MCLEISH, JOHN, a tailor, was admitted as a burgess of Kirkcaldy, Fife, on 13 January 1798. [KBR]

MCNAIR, GEORGE, son of James McNair a labourer burgess, was admitted as a burgess of Dunfermline on 4 July 1797. [DM]

MCNAUGHTON, PETER, a weaver, son of Daniel McNaughton a burgess, was admitted as a burgess of Dunfermline on 17 August 1792. [DM]

MCNEIL, NEIL, son-in-law of Robert Bonnar a wright burgess, was admitted as a burgess of Dunfermline on 20 August 1802. [DM]

MCNEISH, JOHN, born 1785 in Largo, Fife, a merchant in Falkirk, with his wife Janet, and five children, emigrated to USA, and was naturalised in New York on 5 February 1828. [NARA]

MCPHERSON, JAMES, an innkeeper, was admitted as a burgess of Cupar, Fife, on 7 December 1795. [CuBR]

MCPHERSON, JOHN, son-in-law of David Turnbull a burgess and a guilds-brother, was admitted as a burgess of Dunfermline on 10 April 1799. [DM]

MCRITCHIE, ANDREW, a mariner in North Queensferry, Fife, testament, 1823, Comm. St Andrews. [NRS]

MCRITCHIE, JAMES, a sailor in North Queensferry, Fife, in 1797. [NRS.S/H]

MCRUVIE, WILLIAM, son of Duncan McRuvie, [1805-1821], and his wife Agnes Scott, [1800-1888], died in Ballston Spa, USA, on 2 April 1888. [Kilconquhar gravestone, Fife]

MCTAGGART, ROBERT, the town officer and drummer, was admitted as a burgess of Dunfermline on 17 August 1793. [DM]

MCVEY, ARCHIBALD, a skipper in Limekilne, Dunfermline, Fife, testament, 19 February 1811, Comm. St Andrews. [NRS]

MAILLER, JAMES, son of William Mailler a carrier, was admitted as a burgess of Dunfermline on 12 August 1791. [DM]

MAILLER, JOHN, son of William Mailler a carrier, was admitted as a burgess of Dunfermline on 12 August 1791. [DM]

MAILLER, ROBERT, son of William Mailler a carrier, was admitted as a burgess of Dunfermline on 5 July 1797. [DM]

MAIN, ANDREW, son of Robert Main, was admitted as a burgess of Dunfermline on 22 July 1796. [DM]

MAIN, ANDREW, son of Andrew Main, was admitted as a burgess of Dunfermline on 5 July 1797. [DM]

MAIN, DAVID, son of Robert Main the deacon of the shoemakers, was admitted as a burgess of Dunfermline on 23 March 1795. [DM]

MAIN, JAMES, a weaver, son-in-law of William Mailler, was admitted as a burgess of Dunfermline on 12 August 1791. [DM]

MAIN, JOHN, son of John Main a wright burgess, was admitted as a burgess of Dunfermline on 21 July 1790. [DM]

MAIN, JOHN, son of Andrew Main a dyer burgess, was admitted as a burgess of Dunfermline on 25 January 1796. [DM]

MAIN, JOHN, son of Robert Main a shoemaker burgess, was admitted as a burgess of Dunfermline on 22 July 1796. [DM]

MAIN, ROBERT, son of Robert Main a shoemaker burgess, was admitted as a burgess of Dunfermline on 4 July 1797. [DM]

MAIN, ROBERT, son of John Main a wright burgess, was admitted as a burgess of Dunfermline on 3 September 1802. [DM]

MAIR, JOHN, from Dunfermline, Fife, a theological student in 1794, settled in America as a teacher. [UPC]

MAIR, WILLIAM, son of John Mair from London, was admitted as a burgess and a guilds-brother of Dunfermline on 15 September 1794. [DM]

MALCOLM, GEORGE, a skipper, was admitted as a burgess of Kirkcaldy, Fife, on 5 December 1795. [KBR]

MALCOLM, JAMES, a manufacturer, was admitted as a burgess of Kirkcaldy, Fife, on 27 September 1791 [KBR]

MALCOLM, JAMES, a weaver, son-in-law of John Ingles a mason burgess, was admitted as a burgess of Dunfermline on 17 August 1793. [DM]

MALCOLM, JAMES, born 1809, son of Alexander Malcolm and his wife Janet Allison, died in Adelaide, South Australia, on 28 October 1865. [Kirkcaldy gravestone, Fife]

MALCOLM, JOHN, jr., was admitted as a burgess of Kirkcaldy, Fife, in 1795. [KBR]

MALLOCH, JAMES, a shoemaker, son-in-law of Andrew Williamson a shoemaker, was admitted as a burgess of Dunfermline on 14 March 1793. [DM]

MANSON, PETER, a mariner in Crail in 1799. [SBC.27]

MARR, THOMAS, born 1850, youngest son of Thomas Marr in Crossgates, Peat Inn, Fife, was drowned at Scott's Barr, Siskyow County, California, on 29 April 1875. [PJ]

MARSHALL, ALEXANDER, born 1752, a wright in Newburgh, Fife, died 2 February 1826, husband of Ann Scott, born 1758, died 13 September 1824. [Dunbog gravestone, Fife]

MARSHALL, JOHN, was admitted as a burgess and guilds-brother of Cupar, Fife, on 10 October 1810. [CuBR]

MARSHALL, ROBERT, born 1848, son of Alexander Marshall in Ladybank, Fife, a draper who drowned at St John, Newfoundland, on 5 August 1871. [PJ]

MARSHALL, Reverend WILLIAM, born 1740 in Fife, emigrated to America in 1762, a minister in Pennsylvania, died in Philadelphia, Pennsylvania, on 17 November 1802. [AP]

MARTIN, ALEXANDER, born 15 October 1761, son of Thomas Martin and his wife Elizabeth Bridges, a surgeon in the Royal Navy, died in July 1797. [Pittenweem gravestone, Fife]

MARTIN, ALEXANDER, a land surveyor from Cupar, Fife, died in Brooklyn, New York, on 26 December 1842. [FH]

MARTIN, DAVID, a grocer, son-in-law of David Syme a wright burgess, was admitted as a burgess of Dunfermline on 22 December 1809. [DM]

MARTIN, DAVID, in Brooklyn, New York, son of Alexander Martin a land surveyor in Cupar, Fife, died in Torquay, Devon, on 30 October 1847. [EEC.21574]

MARTIN, PETER, born 1831, eldest son of John Martin in Kelty, died in Algana, Iowa, on 8 February 1874. [FJ]

MARTIN, WILLIAM, born 1810 in Dunfermline, died in Patterson, New Jersey, on 28 March 1872. [PJ]

MASON, WILLIAM, born 1764, a merchant in Jamaica, died on 1 December 1841. [St Andrews gravestone, Fife]

MASTERTON, ALEXANDER, a bailie of Culross, Fife, was admitted as a burgess and guilds-brother of Dunfermline on 24 February 1804. [DM]

MASTERTON, DAVID, son-in-la of James Cooper a baillie of Dunfermline, was admitted as a burgess of Dunfermline on 1 August 1806. [DM]

MATHER, ARCHIBALD, son of James Mather and his wife Christine Melville, died in Hamburg, Germany, on 10 March 1850. [Ferry-Port-on-Craig gravestone, Fife]

MATHER, THOMAS, son of James Mather and his wife Christine Melville, a shipmaster who died in the River Gaillegos, South America, on 23 October 1850. [Ferry-Port-on-Craig gravestone, Fife]

MATTHEW, JOHN, born 11 June 1815 in Cupar, Fife, a carpenter who emigrated to USA in 1860, died in Indiana in December 1895. [FH.8.1.1896]

MATTHEWSON, AGNES, born 1817, widow of William Gowan Dobie, of Comely Park Place, Dunfermline, Fife, died at the residence of Mrs H. T. Woods, 1405 Agnes Avenue, Kansas City, Missouri, on 27 December 1898. [S.17333][Dunfermline gravestone]

MATTHEWSON, JOHN, son of George Matthewson and his wife Elizabeth Melville, settled in New York before 1854. [Dunnikier gravestone, Fife]

MATHIE, JOHN, a baker, former apprentice of John Stenhouse a burgess, was admitted as a burgess of Dunfermline on 6 June 1806. [DM]

MAXWELL, Captain ANDREW, was admitted as a burgess and guilds-brother of Dunfermline on 30 July 1793. [DM]

MAXWELL, ANDREW, a tanner, was admitted as a burgess of Cupar, Fife, in 1796. [CuBR]

MAXWELL, JOHN, a merchant from Dunkeld, Perthshire, was admitted as a burgess and guilds-brother of Dunfermline on 30 July 1793. [DM],

MAXWELL, JOHN, born 1812, son of Alexander Maxwell and his wife Elizabeth Dutch, died in the Davis Strait, Canada, on 8 May 1837. [Ferry-Port-on-Craig gravestone, Fife]

MAYES, ALEXANDER, born 1740, son of Philip Mayes and Margaret Key his wife, settled in Newark, Carriacou, near Grenada, died in Elie, Fife, on 21 April 1791. [St Monance gravestone, Fife]

MEIKLEJOHN, JOHN, from Eyemouth, Berwickshire, was admitted as a burgess and guilds-brother of Dunfermline on 16 June 1796. [DM]

MEIKLEJOHN, ROBERT, born 1818, son of George Meiklejohn and his wife Mary Anderson, died on the Aghuay Coast of Guinea, on 11 April 1842. [Tulliallan gravestone, Fife]

MELDRUM, DAVID, of Easter Craigfoodie, born 1770, died 30 November 1848, husband of Wilhelmina Menzies, born 1772, died 9 February 1814, parents of David Meldrum of Easter Craigfootie, born 5 April 1805, died 23 November 1876. [Dairsie gravestone, Fife]

MELDRUM, GEORGE, son of George Meldrum a baker burgess, was admitted as a burgess of Dunfermline on 11 August 1802. [DM]

MELDRUM, JEAN STENHOUSE SCOTLAND, born 1811, daughter of George Meldrum and his wife Janet Stenhouse, died at Kulladehee in the East Indies, in April 1833. [Dunfermline gravestone, Fife]

MELDRUM, JOHN BALFOUR, born 1810, son of James Meldrum, died in Paterson, New Jersey, in March 1883. [Leuchars gravestone, Fife]

MELDRUM, MARTIN, a weaver, son of William Meldrum a weaver burgess, was admitted as a burgess of Dunfermline on 29 August 1791. [DM]

MELDRUM, WILLIAM, son of Henry Meldrum a weaver burgess, was admitted as a burgess of Dunfermline on 27 September 1810. [DM]

MELVILLE, ALEXANDER, a baker, son of Alexander Melville, was admitted as a burgess of Cupar, Fife, on 25 November 1795. [CuBR]

MELVILLE, ALEXANDER, a manufacturer, was admitted as a burgess of Cupar, Fife, on 18 September 1809. [CuBR]

MELVILLE, DAVID, a sailor in Cellardyke, Fife, son and heir of David Melville there, in 1797. [NRS.S/H]

MELVILL, DAVID, a fisherman in St Andrews, Fife, testament, 1811, Comm. St Andrews. [NRS]

MELVILLE, JAMES, a mariner in St Andrews, Fife, testament, 1821, Comm. St Andrews. [NRS]

MELVILLE, JAMES, a livery stable keeper in Cape Town, South Africa, eldest son of James Melville and his wife Rachel Latto in the Kirkton of Balmerino, Fife, 1862. [NRS.SC20.34.34.160/161]

MELVILLE, JANET, born 19 May 1809 in St Andrews, Fife, daughter of John Melville, a smith, and his wife Janet Miller, settled in Ohio in 1819, died in La Porte County, Indiana, in 1889. [SG]

MELVILLE, JOHN, born 1794, a shipmaster who died in St Vincent, West Indies, on 18 June 1834, husband of Willemina Durie. [Pittenweem gravestone, Fife]

MELVILLE, ROBERT, a carpenter, youngest son of George Melville in Pitscottie, Fife, died in Nassau in the Bahamas on 24 August 1862. [FH.4.6.1863]

MELVILLE, WILLIAM, born 1761, a skipper, master and manager of the Pittenweem Sea Box Society on 12 January 1795, died on 1 March 1803. [NRS.B3.7.5][Pittenweem gravestone]

MELVILLE, WILLIAM, son of Alexander Melville of Hallfields, Fife, [1784-1842], and his wife Grace Babington, [1779-1823], died in Austin, Texas, aged 25. [St Michael's, Dumfries, gravestone]

MELVILLE, WILLIAM, a shoemaker, was admitted as a burgess of Cupar, Fife, on 2 October 1799. [CuBR]

MELVILLE, WILLIAM, a mason, son of Thomas Melville, was admitted as a burgess of Cupar, Fife, on 11 May 1805. [CuBR]

MERCER, JAMES, a shoemaker from Kincardine-on-Forth, son-in-law of William Kellock a tailor burgess, was admitted as a burgess of Dunfermline on 20 January 1790. [DM]

MERCER, WILLIAM, a shipmaster who died in Port au Prince, San Domingo, in January 1833. [Tulliallan gravestone, Fife]

METHVEN, ALEXANDER, son of Thomas Methven, [1742-1790], and his wife Euphemia Meldrum, [1749-1826], a surgeon who died in South Carolina in 1807. [St Andrews gravestone, Fife]

METHVEN, ALEXANDER MELDRUM, born 1806, son of Thomas Methven and his wife Helen Larbert, a Lieutenant of the 56th Bengal Native Infantry, died in Mhow, India, on 24 August 1833. [St Andrews gravestone, Fife]

METHVEN, Captain CATHCART, son of Thomas Methven and his wife Mary Symers, died in Calcutta, India, in 1832. [St Andrews gravestone, Fife]

METHVEN, ..., a writer, , was admitted as a burgess of Cupar, Fife, in 1810. [CuBR]

MILES, THOMAS, born 1832, son of Thomas Miles and Margaret Thomson, died at North Fork on the America River, California, on 24 May 1852. [St Andrews gravestone, Fife]

MILL, THOMAS, of Blair, son-in-law of Reverend George Adie in Carnock, Fife, was admitted as a burgess of Dunfermline on 10 May 1798. [DM]

MILLER, ADAM, a weaver, son of Ralph Miller a weaver burgess, was admitted as a burgess of Dunfermline on 20 September 1792. [DM]

MILLER, ANDREW, son-in-law of James Stewart a flaxdresser burgess, was admitted as a burgess of Dunfermline on 7 December 1801. [DM]

MILLER, DAVID, master of the Trusty of Inverkeithing bound from Leith to New York in 1819. [NRS.E504.22.86]

MILLER, GEORGE, a merchant, was admitted as a burgess of Kirkcaldy, Fife, on 21 February 1797. [KBR]

MILLER, GEORGE, son of George Miller and his wife Janet Morrison, died in Savannah, Georgia, on 28 September 1839. [Tulliallan gravestone, Fife,]

MILLER, GEORGE S., an engineer in Melbourne, Victoria, Australia, a sasine, 1867. [NRS.RS.Kirkcaldy. Fife, 13/143]

MILLER, HARRIET, born 1839, wife of John Davidson, died in Adelaide, South Australia, on 21 December 1883. [Burntisland gravestone, Fife]

MILLER, JAMES, born 1735, a skipper, died 13 June 1808. [Tulliallan gravestone]

MILLER, JAMES, son of James Miller a mason burgess, was admitted as a burgess of Dunfermline on 7 September 1790. [DM]

MILLER, JAMES, a gardener, son of James Miller a gardener burgess, was admitted as a burgess of Dunfermline on 24 March 1797. [DM]

MILLER, JAMES, a merchant, was admitted as a burgess of Cupar, Fife, on 3 October 1797. [CuBR]

MILLER, JAMES, a grocer, was admitted as a burgess of Cupar, Fife, in 1802. [CuBR]

MILLER, JANET, youngest daughter of Henry Miller, died in Kirkcaldy, Fife, on 15 October 1819. [AM.85]

MILLER, JEAN, in America by 1809, widow of John Lawrie a miller in Strathmiglo, Fife. [NRS.CS17.1.28/442]

MILLER, JOHN, a merchant, was admitted as a burgess of Kirkcaldy, Fife, on 1 October 1791. [KBR]

MILLER, JOHN, a shoemaker, was admitted as a burgess of Cupar, Fife, in December 1799. [CuBR]

MILLAR, JOHN, a skipper in Kirkcaldy, Fife, testament, 1802, Comm. St Andrews. [NRS]

MILLER, JOHN, a stationer, was admitted as a burgess of Dunfermline on 19 September 1808. [DM]

MILLAR, JOHN, a skipper in Kirkcaldy, Fife, was admitted as a burgess of Kirkcaldy in 1773, KBR]; testament, 15 November 1809, Comm. St Andrews. [NRS]

MILLER, JOHN, master of the Sisters of Kirkcaldy from Dundee to Philadelphia, Pennsylvania, in 1818. [NRS.CE70.1.15]

MILLER, JOHN, son of Alexander Miller, died at Cape Ras Haffoon, north east Africa, on 18 August 1858. [Tulliallan gravestone, Fife]

MILLER, LAWRENCE, son of James Miller a mason burgess, was admitted as a burgess of Dunfermline on 23 September 1796. [DM]

MILLER, RALPH, son of Ralph Miller a weaver burgess, was admitted as a burgess of Dunfermline on 21 September 1790. [DM]

MILLER, ROBERT, a merchant, was admitted as a burgess of Kirkcaldy, Fife, on 1 October 1791. [KBR]

MILLER, STOCKS, son of Walter Miller and his wife Sarah Stocks, died in Moorcroft, Wyoming, in August 1890. [Logie gravestone, Fife]

MILLER, WILLIAM, a shipbuilder, was admitted as a burgess of Kirkcaldy, Fife, on 213 February 1797. [KBR]

MILLER, WILLIAM, son of George Miller and his wife Janet Morrison, died in Melbourne, Victoria, Australia, on 5 April 1871. [Tulliallan gravestone, Fife]

MILLIE, HENRY, messenger at arms, Cupar, Fife, 1849. [POD]

MILLIE, WILLIAM JAMES, born 1842 died in Chittagong, India, on 10 April 1874. [Dunnikier gravestone, Fife]

MILLIGAN, GEORGE, son of Reverend George Milligan and his wife Agnes Colville, a Captain of the Bengal Horse Artillery, died at Buyukdere, India, on 24 June 1865. [Elie gravestone, Fife]

MILNE, JAMES, a skipper in Newburgh, Fife, testament, 5 May 1803, Comm. St Andrews. [NRS]

MILNE, THOMAS, of Blair, was admitted as a burgess of Dunfermline on 113 April 1797. [DM]

MILNE, THOMAS, of Blair, jr., was admitted as a burgess of Dunfermline on 113 April 1797. [DM]

MITCHELL, ALEXANDER, a sailor in Dysart, Fife, son and heir of John Mitchell there, in 1790. [NRS.S/H]

MITCHELL, ALEXANDER, born 1799, son of George Mitchell and Elizabeth Chiene, a Lieutenant of the Madras Native Infantry, died at sea on 31 March 1827. [St Andrews gravestone, Fife]

MITCHELL, ANDREW, a day labourer, son-in-law of Robert Grieve a weaver burgess, was admitted as a burgess of Dunfermline on 26 March 1790. [DM]

MITCHELL, ANNE, daughter of Captain Andrew Mitchell in Cupar, wife of John Johnston in Illinois, 1837. [NRS.SC20.34.20.61-63]

MITCHELL, BRUCE, in the Service of the East India Company, was admitted as a burgess and guilds-brother of Dunfermline on 5 June 1797. [DM]; in Hull House, Dunfermline, Fife, former Commander of the East Indiaman Marquis Wellesley, testament, 3 July 1815, Comm. St Andrews. [NRS]

MITCHELL, DAVID, son of Andrew Mitchell a day labourer burgess, was admitted as a burgess of Dunfermline on 3 March 1792. [DM]

MITCHELL, DAVID, a banker, was admitted as a burgess of Cupar, Fife, in 1811. [CuBR]

MITCHELL, JOHN, and his wife Janet Nicolson, parents of Archibald Mitchell, born 1856, a marine engineer, died in Singapore, Malaya, in 1904. [Ceres gravestone, Fife]

MITCHELL, ROBERT, born 24 August 1817, late in Auckland, New Zealand, died 3 March 1898. [St Monance gravestone, Fife]

MITCHELL, THOMAS, born 1800, son of George Mitchell and Elizabeth Chiene, Commander of the <u>Sultan of Calcutta</u> died off Saugar Island on 22 May 1833. [St Andrews gravestone, Fife]

MITCHELL, THOMAS, son of Robert Mitchell and his wife Margaret Carmichael, died in Montreal, Quebec, on 10 August 1848. [St Andrews gravestone, Fife]

MITCHELL, WILLIAM, a cabinetmaker, was admitted as a burgess of Kirkcaldy, Fife, on 9 February 1801. [KBR]

MOFFAT, WILLIAM, a grocer, was admitted as a burgess of Kirkcaldy, Fife, on 18 November 1793. [KBR]

MOIR, ALEXANDER, a farmer in Thornhill, was admitted as a burgess of Dunfermline on 24 October 1809. [DM]

MOIR, JAMES, son of David Moir a weaver burgess, was admitted as a burgess of Dunfermline on 11 September 1802. [DM]

MOIR, JOHN, son of David Moir a weaver burgess, was admitted as a burgess of Dunfermline on 13 September 1802. [DM]

MOIR, ROBERT, a baker, was admitted as a burgess of Cupar, Fife, on 29 September 1795. [CuBR]

MONRO, or JONES, CATHERINE, born 1798 in Fife, residing in Charleston, S.C., was naturalised in South Carolina on 21 March 1828. [NARA.M1183.1]

MONRO, JOHN, born 1830, son of Arthur Monro and his wife Helen Reid, died in Hamburg, Germany, on 5 December 1859. [Rosyth gravestone, Fife]

MONTEATH, ANDREW, son-in-law of Robert Westwood a weaver burgess, was admitted as a burgess of Dunfermline in January 1797. [DM]

MONTEATH, HARRY, a merchant from Glasgow, was admitted as a burgess and guilds-brother of Dunfermline on 24 January 1793. [DM]

MOODIE, JAMES, in Aberdour, Fife, in 1792. [NRS.S/H]

MOODIE, JAMES, son of John Moodie of Cocklaw a burgess, was admitted as a burgess of Dunfermline on 8 February 1810. [DM]

MOODIE, ROBERT, son of George Moodie a labourer burgess, was admitted as a burgess of Dunfermline on 5 July 1797. [DM]

MOODIE, WILLIAM, son of George Moodie a labourer burgess, was admitted as a burgess of Dunfermline on 5 July 1797. [DM]

MORE, ROBERT, and his wife Jessie Berwick, were parents of John Berwick More, born 1860, died in Adelaide, South Australia, in 1884. [St Andrews gravestone, Fife]

MORE, THOMAS, a wright in Dunfermline, was admitted as a burgess of Dunfermline on 27 May 1810. [DM]

MORGAN, A. G., agent in Kirkcaldy, Fife, for the Bank of Scotland in 1849. [POD]

MORGAN, DAVID, agent in Kirkcaldy, Fife, for the Bank of Scotland in 1849. [POD]

MORGAN, WILLIAM, a weaver, former apprentice to Robert K …., a weaver burgess, was admitted as a burgess of Dunfermline on 8 October 1790. [DM]

MORRIS, ALEXANDER, born 1795, a farmer in Stravithie Cotton, died 17 August 1842, husband of Mary Briggs, born 1794, died 15 September 1874. [Dunino gravestone, Fife]

MORRES, DAVID, son of Andrew Morres a wright burgess, was admitted as a burgess of Dunfermline on 22 March 1793. [DM]

MORRES, DAVID, son of Adam Morres a weaver burgess, was admitted as a burgess of Dunfermline on 7 September 1804. [DM]

MORRIS, DAVID, born 1793, son of William Morris and his wife Elizabeth Simpson, died in Dominica on 18 May 1818. [Kemback gravestone, Fife]

MORRIS, DAVID, born 1824, youngest son of Robert Morris in Pittenweem, Fife, an engineer who died in Jamaica on 5 November 1849. [PR.29.12.1849]

MORRES, JOHN, son of James Morres, was admitted as a burgess of Dunfermline on 30 July 1791. [DM]

MORRES, JOHN, a brewer, son-in-law of Michael Anderson a weaver burgess, was admitted as a burgess of Dunfermline on 7 August 1795. [DM]

MORRIS, ROBERT, a weaver, son-in-law of John Somerville a weaver burgess, was admitted as a burgess of Dunfermline on 31 May 1797. [DM]

MORRIS, ROBERT, son of James Morris a burgess, was admitted as a burgess of Dunfermline on 10 August 1797. [DM]

MORRIS, THOMAS, son of Thomas Morris a shoemaker, was admitted as a burgess of Dunfermline on 5 January 1797. [DM]

MORRIS, THOMAS, a land labourer, was admitted as a burgess of Crail, Fife, in 1801. [CBR]

MORRES, WILLIAM, son of William Morres of Brierly Hill, was admitted as a burgess of Dunfermline on 29 January 1796. [DM]

MORRISON, ADAM, a weaver, son of Adam Morrison a weaver burgess, was admitted as a burgess of Dunfermline on 4 July 1797. [DM]

MORRISON, GEORGE, son of David Morrison a burgess and guilds-brother, was admitted as a burgess of Dunfermline on 28 August 1792. [DM]

MORRISON, HENRY, a smith in Inverkeithing, Fife. Son-in-law of Thomas Gibson a wright in Dunfermline, was admitted as a burgess of Dunfermline on 5 September 1796. [DM]

MORRISON, JOHN, son of Thomas Morrison a shoemaker burgess, was admitted as a burgess of Dunfermline on 7 October 1791. [DM]

MORISON, JOHN, born 1781 in Fife, a merchant who was naturalised in South Carolina on 18 March 1807. [NARA.M1183.1]

MORRISON, JOHN, born 1854 in Kinghorn, Fife, a plumber who died in Kimberley, South Africa, on 2 June 1884. [S.12787]

MORRISON, MARGARET, versus her husband Charles Black a carpenter in Inverkeithing, Fife, married in February 1807, a Process of Divorce in November 1808. [NRS.CC8.6.103]

MORISON, SIMON, born 1796 in Fife, a cabinetmaker in Charleston, S.C., who was naturalised in South Carolina on 13 April 1830. [NARA.M1183.1]

MORISON, THOMAS, born 1803, son of Thomas Morrison a cabinetmaker in Anstruther, Fife, a cabinetmaker in Charleston, S.C., who was naturalised in South Carolina on 15 January 1841. [NARA.M1183.1] [NRS.SC20.34.23.36-39]

MORRISON, WILLIAM, a pensioner of the Pittenweem Sea Box Society in 1793. [NRS.B3.7.5]

MORRISON, WILLIAM, a grocer, was admitted as a burgess of Cupar, Fife, on 9 December 1799. [CuBR]

MORTON, ALEXANDER, a mason, son-in-law of Thomas Bonnar a wright in Dunfermline, was admitted as a burgess of Dunfermline on 9 March 1807. [DM]

MORTON, ALEXANDER, eldest son of Henry Morton a grocer in Kirkcaldy, Fife, in Raubsville, USA, 1866. [NRS.SC20.34.36.265-266]

MORTON, J. A. THOMSON, son of Robert Morton and his wife Elizabeth Anderson, died in Bermuda on 7 May 1861. [Strathmiglo gravestone, Fife]

MOUBRAY, DAVID, son of Henry Moubray a weaver burgess, was admitted as a burgess of Dunfermline on 20 September 1806. [DM]

MOUBRAY, JOHN, of Cockenzie, was admitted as a burgess and guilds-brother of Dunfermline on 5 June 1797. [DM]

MOYES, GEORGE, son of James Moyes a weaver burgess, was admitted as a burgess of Dunfermline on 5 July 1797. [DM]

MOYES, JAMES, a weaver, son-in-law of Andrew Strachan a weaver burgess, was admitted as a burgess of Dunfermline on 3 March 1792. [DM]

MOYES, JOHN, a wright, eldest son of Patrick Moyes, was admitted as a burgess of Kirkcaldy, Fife, on 25 November 1793. [KBR]

MOYES, WILLIAM, sr., a skipper in Kinghorn, Fife, testament, 7 May 1815, Comm. St Andrews. [NRS]

MUDIE, JAMES, son of George Mudie a merchant in Dunfermline, was admitted as a burgess of Dunfermline on 15 September 1807. [DM]

MUDIE, JOHN, of Cocklaw, jr., son-in-law of John Aitken of Thornton, Fife, was admitted as a burgess of Dunfermline on 14 November 1791. [DM]

MUIR, JOHN, jr., a writer from Edinburgh, was admitted as a burgess and guilds-brother of Dunfermline on 5 May 1791. [DM]

MULTERY, GEORGE, a mason, was admitted as a burgess of Dunfermline on 15 May 1810. [DM]

MUNRO, CATHERINE, born 1778, daughter of Robert and Margaret Munro, settled in Charleston, South Carolina, before 1807, naturalised there in 1828. [NARA.M1183.1][Crail gravestone, Fife]

MUNROE, JAMES, a mariner from Fife, was admitted as a citizen of South Carolina on 7 February 1797. [NARA.M1183.1]

MUNRO, JOHN, a merchant, was admitted as a burgess of Cupar, Fife, on 19 April 1796. [CuBR]

MURCHIE, ALLAN BARBOUR, born 1797 in Dunfermline, Fife, son of William Murchie, a blacksmith in Glasgow in 1820, sentenced to transportation to Australia for his part in the Uprising of 1820, a blacksmith in government service in New South Wales, later a dealer at 88 Kent Street, Sydney. [TSR]

MURIE, JAMES, a wright, son-in-law of James Norie a weaver burgess, was admitted as a burgess of Dunfermline on 3 August 1791. [DM]

MURRAY, ALEXANDER, born in May 1797, son of Reverend Andrew Murray and his wife Janet Mackie, died in Jamaica on 21 October 1821. [Auchterderran gravestone, Fife] [F.5.77] [AJ.3861]

MURRAY, ANDREW, born 1806, son of Andrew Murray and his wife Janet Mackie, died in Bombay, India, in 1833. [Auchterderran gravestone, Fife]

MURRAY, CHARLES, born 1812, son of Andrew Murray and his wife Janet Mackie in Auchterderran, Fife, settled in New Orleans, Louisiana, died at Pass Christian, La., in 1853. [Auchterderran gravestone, Fife] [S.24.9.1853]

MURRAY, Captain DAVID, from Kirkcaldy, Fife, died in Sierra Leone on 31 May 1859. [CM.21779]

MURRAY, Captain GEORGE, born 1844, son of James Murray, died in Shanghai, China, on 9 March 1882. [Cupar gravestone, Fife]

MURRAY, WILLIAM, a merchant, was admitted as a burgess of Cupar, Fife, on 3 October 1804. [CuBR]

MURRAY, ..., agent in St Andrews, Fife, for the Edinburgh and Glasgow Bank in 1849. [POD]

MUTTRIE, DAVID, a skipper in Limekilns, Fife, a witness in 1804. [NRS.CC8.8.135]

MYLES, ELIZA CRAIG, born 1848, daughter of Robert Myles and his wife Helen Cellars, wife of John Honyman, died in Emerson, Mills County, Iowa, on 15 May 1874. [Cupar gravestone, Fife]

NAIRNE, WILLIAM F., son of J. T. Nairne an artist in Kirkcaldy, Fife, died at the Cape of Good Hope, South Africa, on 29 December 1843. [W.5.444]

NEIL, JOHN, a grocer, was admitted as a burgess of Kirkcaldy, Fife, on 23 November 1793. [KBR]

NEIL, WILLIAM, in Kinghorn, Fife, of the Excise yacht <u>Royal George,</u> testament, 23 March 1809, Comm. St Andrews. [NRS]. [NRS.B3.7.5]

NESS, THOMAS, former apprentice to skipper Thomas Shanks, was admitted to the Pittenweem Sea Box Society on 9 January 1797

NICOLL, ANDREW, a labourer, son of Andrew Nicoll, was admitted as a burgess of Kirkcaldy, Fife, on 21 October 1795. [KBR]

NICOLL, DAVID, agent in Leven for the Commercial Bank of Scotland in 1849. [POD]

NICOL, ROBERT, a grocer, was admitted as a burgess of Cupar, Fife, on 24 November 1802. [CuBR]

NICOL, ROBERT, a merchant in Cupar, died 23 November 1851, father of William Nicol in Spritzkop, Sudbury, Albany district, later in Oakwell, Grahamstown, Cape of Good Hope, South Africa. [NRS.S/H] [NRS.SC20.34.32.100/110]

NICOL, WILLIAM, eldest son of Reverend James Nicol in Leslie, Fife, died in Auckland, New Zealand, on 2 December 1855. [AJ.5647]

NICOLSON, JAMES, a boatman in Burntisland, Fife, testament, 15 August 1805, Comm. St Andrews. [NRS]

NICOLSON, ROBERT, a butcher, was admitted as a burgess of Cupar, Fife, on 13 September 1803. [CuBR]

NICHOLSON, WILLIAM, born 1749, died in Macao, China, in 1801. [Burntisland gravestone, Fife].26]

NOREY, JOHN, the Kng's boatman in Crail, Fife, was buried there on 29 November 1798. [SBC]

NORMAND, JAMES, a sailor in Dysart, Fife, testament, 8 December 1812, Comm. St Andrews. [NRS]

NORMAND, JAMES, born 10 January 1827 in Dysart, Fife, son of James Normand a linen manufacturer, settled in New York in 1850, a linen merchant, died in Edinburgh on 26 May 1882. [ANY]

NORMAND, JOHN, in Bank Street, Cupar, Fife, father of William Normand in New York in 1873. [NRS.SC20.40]

NORRIE, JAMES, a weaver, was admitted as a burgess of Crail, Fife, in 1792. [CBR]

NORRIE, ROBERT, a mariner in Crail, Fife, was buried there on 4 February 1798. [NRS.B10.5.1.80][SBC.23]

OGG, HENDRIE, a watchmaker, was admitted as a burgess of Dunfermline on 8 December 1809. [DM]

OGILVIE, CHRISTINA MURRAY, born 1833, wife of John White, died at Teviot Junction, New Zealand, on 25 September 1869. [Ferry Port on Craig grave.]

OLIPHANT, D., master of the Margaret of Kirkcaldy trading between Leith and Quebec in 1820, between Greenock and Quebec in 1821. [NRS.E504.22.90; E504.15.135]

OLIPHANT, PHILIP, agent in Anstruther, Fife, for the Eastern Bank in 1849. [POD]

OLIPHANT, WILLIAM, a weaver, was admitted as a burgess of Kirkcaldy, Fife, on 29 July 1802. [KBR]

OSWALD, HENRY, was admitted as a burgess of Kirkcaldy, Fife, on 19 September 1792. [KBR]

OSWALD, JAMES TOWNSEND, of Dunikier, Fife, was admitted as a burgess and guilds-brother of Dunfermline on 25 June 1798. [DM]

OSWALD, JAMES, born 1830, died aboard the Marco Botsares in the Black Sea on 30 June 1859, buried in Constantinople, Turkey. [Boarhills gravestone, Fife]

OSWALD, ROBERT C. B., born 1784, son of J. T. Oswald of Dunnikier, a Lieutenant Colonel of the Greek Light Infantry, died in 1848. [Kirkcaldy gravestone, Fife]

PAGAN, WILLIAM, agent in Cupar, Fife, for the British Linen Company in 1849. [POD]

PAGE, GEORGE, son of George Page a wright burgess, was admitted as a burgess of Dunfermline on 26 April 1798. [DM]

PAGE, HENRY, from Kirkcaldy, Fife, settled in New York, a sasine, 1858. [NRS.RS.Kirkcaldy.11.62]

PANTON, Mr, a merchant, was admitted as a burgess of Cupar, Fife, on 3 October 1804. [CuBR]

PARKER, MATHEW, a watchmaker, son of John Parker a smith burgess, was admitted as a burgess of Dunfermline on 8 February 1788. [DM]

PATERSON, ANDREW, son-in-law of Thomas Anderson the deacon of the bakers in Dunfermline, was admitted as a burgess of Dunfermline on 13 April 1803. [DM]

PATTERSON, CHARLES, master of the Christian of Kirkcaldy bound via Greenock for Kirkcaldy, Fife, in 1813. [NRS.E504.15.100]

PATERSON, HENRY, a candlemaker, was admitted as a burgess of Kirkcaldy, Fife, on 21 November 1795. [KBR]

PATERSON, JAMES, a weaver in Dunfermline, Fife, was found guilty of sedition in Perth on 22 September 1798, and sentenced to five years transportation to the colonies. [AJ.2647]

PATERSON, JAMES, a baker from Torryburn, Fife, son-in-law of Andrew Donald a burgess, was admitted as a burgess of Dunfermline on 21 June 1809. [DM]

PATTERSON, JAMES, born 1835, a shipmaster who died in Rangoon, Burma, on 19 December 1874. [Rosyth gravestone, Fife]

PATTERSON, JOHN, born 1838 in Fife, a farmer and a butcher, with his wife, son and daughters, settled in Saltcoats, Assiniboia, North West Territories, Manitoba, Canada, by 22 May 1888. [BPP.Emi.9/185]

PATERSON, R. B., son of Robert Paterson, [1811-1897], and his wife Margaret Low, [1812-1851], settled in St John, Canada. [Portmoak gravestone, Fife]

PATERSON, ROBERT, born 1745, a skipper, died on 30 July 1829. [St Andrews gravestone, Fife]

PATERSON, ROBERT, born 1779, son of Robert Paterson and his wife Rosetta Maitland, died on Great Courland Estate, Tobago, on 23 July 1803. [St Andrews gravestone, Fife]

PATERSON, WILLIAM, son of William Paterson in St Andrews, Fife, was apprenticed to James Swan, a barber in Edinburgh, for six years, on 27 March 1800. [ERA]

PATTON, ALEXANDER, born 13 December 1779 in Auchtermuchty, Fife, a cooper who settled in New York in 22 June 1801. [SG.32.3]

PATTON, JAMES, a weaver, son-in-law of James Johnston a weaver burgess, was admitted as a burgess of Dunfermline on 24 June 1798. [DM]

PATTON, JOHN, a weaver, son-in-law of John Bayne a weaver burgess, was admitted as a burgess of Dunfermline on 26 July 1791. [DM]

PATON, ALEXANDER, born 26 November 1786, a surgeon in Bombay, India, died on 26 April 1852. [Torryburn gravestone, Fife]

PATON, THOMAS, born 1806 in Freuchie, Fife, son of David Paton, settled in New York as a merchant in 1826, died in Dobbs Ferry, N.Y., on 19 June 1874. [ANY]

PATON, THOMAS, father of David Paton, born 1862, died in Texas on 21 February 1886. [Balgonie gravestone, Fife]

PATRICK, JOHN, a smith, was admitted as a burgess of Kirkcaldy, Fife, on 23 August 1802. [KBR]

PAUL, Reverend WILLIAM, from Edinburgh, was admitted as a burgess and guilds-brother of Dunfermline on 30 June 1791. [DM]

PAUL, WILLIAM, a grocer, was admitted as a burgess of Cupar, Fife, on 3 October 1804. [CuBR]

PEACOCK, DAVID, son-in-law of Henry Smieton, was admitted as a burgess of Dunfermline on 24 September 1801. [DM]

PEACOCK, WILLIAM, a tobacconist from Leith, was admitted as a burgess and guilds-brother of Dunfermline on 13 September 1793. [DM]

PEARSON, ALEXANDER, son of Robert Pearson a merchant, was admitted as a burgess of Dunfermline on 8 May 1790. [DM]

PEARSON, JAMES, from Dysart, Fife, a mariner aboard the Governor Halket of London, testament, 1820, Comm. St Andrews. [NRS]

PEARSON, PATRICK, son of Robert Pearson a merchant, was admitted as a burgess of Dunfermline on 8 May 1790. [DM]

PEARSON, ROBERT, a baker, was admitted as a burgess and guilds-brother of Cupar, Fife, on 14 November 1798. [CuBR]

PEAT, ISABELL, in Pickering, Canada West, letters to the Mitchell family in Cupar, Fife, letters 1835-1842. [SAUL.ms37515]

PEAT, WILLIAM, the Salt Officer in Inverkeithing, Fife, son-in-law of baillie David Rankine, was admitted as a burgess of Dunfermline on 7 July 1791. [DM]

PEATTIE, JAMES, a baker, was admitted as a burgess of Crail, Fife, in 1805. [CBR]

PEATTIE, JOHN, a coal seller, was admitted as a burgess of Crail, Fife, in 1792. [CBR]

PEATIE, THOMAS, born 1827, son of Thomas Peatie and his wife Mary Cairns, died in Saldhana, Africa, on 7 April 1845. [St Andrews gravestone, Fife]

PEDDIE, JOHN SMART, born 1 February 1816, son of James Peddie, a surgeon in the Royal Navy who sailed aboard HMS Terror on Franklin's Arctic Expedition in 1845. [Inverkeithing gravestone, Fife]

PEEBLES, ANDREW, son of William Peebles a merchant guilds-brother, was admitted as a burgess of Dunfermline on 27 February 1799. [DM]

PEEBLES, THOMAS, a slater, son-in-law of George Walker a wright burgess, was admitted as a burgess of Dunfermline on 16 January 1798. [DM]

PEIRSON, JOHN, born 1789, son of John and Margaret Peirson, a Lieutenant of the 3rd Native Infantry Regiment, died in Cannanore in Madras, India, on 18 February 1812. [Kettle gravestone, Fife]

PENMAN, ROBERT, a watchmaker, former apprentice of John Turnbull a watchmaker, was admitted as a burgess of Dunfermline on 26 October 1789. [DM]

PENNY, DAVID, a tailor, son of John Penny a weaver burgess, was admitted as a burgess of Dunfermline on 9 October 1796. [DM]

PENNY, JOHN, a weaver, son of John Penny a weaver burgess, was admitted as a burgess of Dunfermline on 9 October 1796. [DM]

PHILP, ANDREW, son of Andrew Philp a weaver burgess, was admitted as a burgess of Dunfermline on 9 October 1796. [DM]

PHILP, BELLA, born 1846, daughter of David Philp and his wife Anne Lowe, wife of John Martin, died in Brisbane, Queensland, Australia, on 26 November 1869. [Aberdour gravestone, Fife]

PHILP, CHRISTINA, born 1844, daughter of David Philp and his wife Anne Lowe, wife of Alexander Kelly, died in Brisbane, Queensland, Australia, on 23 March 1888. [Aberdour gravestone, Fife]

PHILP, GEORGE, son of James Philp a weaver burgess, was admitted as a burgess of Dunfermline on 18 September 1792. [DM]

PHILP, JOHN, son of George Philp a butcher burgess, was admitted as a burgess of Dunfermline on 11 August 1796. [DM]

PHILP, JOHN, a wright, was admitted as a burgess of Cupar, Fife, on 10 August 1798 [CuBR]

PHILP, JOHN, son of Thomas Philp a wright, was admitted as a burgess of Dunfermline on 8 August 1801. [DM]

PHILP, ROBERT, a merchant, was admitted as a burgess of Kirkcaldy, Fife, on 29 September 1792. [KBR]

PHILP, ROBERT HAIG, born 1827, son of Andrew Philp and his wife Magdalene Haig, died in Queensland, Australia, on 13 November 1863. [St Andrews gravestone, Fife]

PHILP, WILLIAM, in Canada, son of Robert Philp a brewer in Cupar, Fife, a deed, 1836. [NRS.B13.8.2/71]

PHILIP, DAVID, in Randerston, was admitted as a burgess of Crail, Fife, in 1806. [CBR]

PHILLIPS, JOHN, born 1834, a Corporal of the 74th Regiment, died in Hong Kong on 7 August 1878. [Aberdour gravestone, Fife]

PITCAIRN, JOSEPH, born 1 November 1764 in Carnbee, Fife, son of Reverend James Pitcairn and his wife Janet McCormick, a merchant in New York, US Vice Consul in Paris in 1795, and in Hamburg in 1798, married Lady Pamela Fitzgerald in 1800, a partner in the firm Pitcairn, Brodie and Company in Hamburg, died in New York on 18 June 1844. [EEC.21059][F.5.189][ACK]

PITCAIRN, ROBERT, born 1737, a tavernkeeper in Newburgh, Fife, settled in Spanish Town, Jamaica, before 1780, died on 22 July 1799. [NRS.GD1.675.113] [Spanish Town gravestone]

PITTENDREICH, DAVID, born 1798, son of Robert Pittendreich and his wife Catherine Gay, died off the coast of Africa in 1833. [Cupar gravestone, Fife]

PLAYFAIR, GEORGE, born 1782, Inspector General of Hospitals in Bengal, India, husband of Jessie Ross, died on 26 June 1846. [St Andrews gravestone, Fife]

PLAYFAIR, GEORGE WILLIAM, born 1827, son of William Davidson Playfair, a Colonel in Madras, India, died in Edinburgh on 26 November 1876. [St Andrews gravestone, Fife]

PLAYFAIR, JAMES, born 1818, son of William Davidson Playfair, died in Calcutta, India, on 6 April 1465. [St Andrews gravestone, Fife]

PLAYFAIR, JAMES OCTAVIUS, born 1839, son of George Playfair, died in Buenos Ayres, Argentina, on 19 August 1864. [St Andrews gravestone, Fife]

PLAYFAIR, ROBERT HALDANE, born 1836, son of William Davidson Playfair, died in Buenos Ayres, Argentina, on 3 June 1865. [St Andrews gravestone, Fife]

PLAYFAIR, WILLIAM DAVIDSON, born 1784, a Lieutenant Colonel in the Service of the East Inia Company in Bengal, India, died on 31 January 1852. [St Andrews gravestone, Fife]

PLAYFAIR, WILLIAM DALGLEISH, born 1822, son of Sir Hugh Lyon Playfair, a Lieutenant of the Indian Army, died at Sobraon, Punjab, India, on 16 February 1846. [St Andrews gravestone, Fife]

PLAYFAIR, WILLIAM, born 1831, son of William Davidson Playfair, a Major General in Bengal, India, died in Surrey, England, on 1 November 1891. [St Andrews gravestone, Fife]

PORTER, THOMAS, a sailor in Burntisland, Fife, testament, 31 July 1801, Comm. St Andrews. [NRS]

PRATT, ALISON, born 1787, died in Philadelphia, Pennsylvania, on 10 June 1878, widow of Ninian Lockhart. [Abbotshall gravestone, Kirkcaldy, Fife]

PRATT, ROBERT, a manufacturer in Linktown, Fife, was admitted as a burgess of Kirkcaldy, Fife, on 19 February 1791. [KBR]

PRATT, ROBERT, was admitted as a burgess of Cupar, Fife, on 3 October 1809. [CuBR]

PRESTON, Sir CHARLES, of Valleyfield, Fife, PHILP, ROBERT, a merchant, was admitted as a burgess of Kirkcaldy, Fife, on 29 September 1792. [KBR]

PRIMROSE, JOHN, born 1776, a skipper, died in 1813. [Tulliallan gravestone, Fife]

PRIMROSE, PETER, minister in Dalgetty, Fife, was admitted as a burgess and guilds-brother of Dunfermline on 30 June 1791. [DM]

PRINGLE, Reverend FRANCIS, born 1747 in Fife, died in New York on 2 November 1833. [AJ.44990]

PRINGLE, JAMES, and his wife Marion, were parents of Robert McRobert Pringle, born 1853, died in New Plymouth, New Zealand, on 3 November 1881. [Aberdour gravestone, Fife]

PRINGLE, Sir JOHN, a farmer in Carlowrie, Fife, was admitted as a burgess of Dunfermline on 23 February 1797. [DM]

PURVES, ALEXANDER, married Miss Campbell, eldest daughter of James Campbell, in Burntisland, Fife, on 30 November 1819. [SM.85]

PYE, WILLIAM, born 1830 in Dunfermline, Fife, died in South Africa on 8 September 1875. [St George gravestone, Port Elizabeth, Cape of Good Hope, South Africa]

RAE, ANN BELL, born 1844, died in Dow City, Iowa, on 20 June 1888. [Kettle gravestone, Fife]

RAE, HENRY, a carrier, was admitted as a burgess of Kirkcaldy, Fife, on 14 June 1802. [KBR]

RAE, ISABELLA, born 1855, daughter of Thomas Rae and his wife Janet born 1740 in Leven, Fife, died in Dow City, Iowa, in March 1888. [Kettle gravestone, Fife]

RAINNIE, ROBERT, son of William Rainnie a weaver burgess, was admitted as a burgess of Dunfermline on 7 August 1797. [DM]

RAINNIE, ROBERT, son of William Rainnie a weaver burgess, was admitted as a burgess of Dunfermline on 5 July 1797. [DM]

RAIT, DAVID, born 1782 in Fife, died in St Andrews, New Brunswick, on 8 May 1838. [STA.12.5.1838]

RAIT, ROBERT, in St Andrews, Fife, father of Helen Rait, who married David Walker, a mason, at 19 Bethune Street, New York, on 12 June 1872. [S.9030]

RAMSAY, DAVID, born 1740 in Leven, Fife, served in the Royal Navy from 1756 to 1765, then settled in Canada as a fur trader, died around 1810 probably in Quebec. [DCB]

RAMSAY, ALEXANDER, a messenger, was admitted as a burgess of Cupar, Fife, in 1811. [CuBR]

RAMSAY, DAVID, , was admitted as a burgess of Crail, Fife, in 1805. [CBR]

RAMSAY, MICHAEL, was apprenticed to John Malcolm a skipper in Kirkcaldy, Fife, in 1799.

RAMSAY, WILLIAM, a spirit dealer in Dunfermline, Fife, and his wife Janet Muir, a Process of Divorce in 1792. [NRS.CC8.6.49]

RANALDSON, JOHN, of Blairhall, was admitted as a burgess and guildsbrother of Dunfermline on 13 April 1791. [DM]

RANKINE, ANDREW, a schoolmaster, and his wife Joanna Currie, parents of Dr David Rankine, born 1866, a medical missionary in China from 1895 until his death in I-Chang on 4 July 1899, husband of Agnes R. Lillie in Crail, Fife. [Auchterderran gravestone, Fife] [FFP.8.7.1899]

RANKINE, THOMAS, born 1803 in Kincardine-on-Forth, Fife, emigrated to Canada in 1824, a biscuit manufacturer in St John's, New Brunswick. [SG]

RANKIN, THOMAS, in Smithfield, Rhode Island, nephew and heir of James Rankin a mason in Auchtermuchty, Fife, who died 12 October 1860. [NRS.S/H]

REDDIE, ALEXANDER, a skipper in Limekilns, Fife, testament, 1829, Comm. Edinburgh. [NRS]

REDDIE, JAMES, a wright, was admitted as a burgess of Dunfermline on 2 September 1802. [DM]

REDDIE, JOHN, a Captain in the Service of the East India Company, died on 31 October 1826. [Dysart gravestone, Fife]

REEKIE, Mrs ISABELLA, daughter of Reverend David Ross in Burntisland, Fife, wife of J R Reekie in Quebec, died in Burntisland, Fife, on 3 July 1859. [GM.ns.2.9.199]

REEVE, THOMAS CAMPBELL TWISS, born 1813, son of Thomas Reeve and his wife Helen Campbell, died in India on 25 January 1840. [Cupar gravestone, Fife]

REID, ALEXANDER, born 6 September 1820 in Dunfermline, Fife, in Demerara later in Rome, died there on 29 March 1886. [Protestant Cemetery, Rome]

REID, ANDREW, son of John Reid a weaver burgess, was admitted as a burgess of Dunfermline on 4 July 1797. [DM]

REID, ANDREW, born 1789, son of William Reid, in the Service of the East India Company, died in Chittagong, Bengal, India, on 16 March 1822. [Creich gravestone, Fife]

REID, DAVID, born 1764, a fisherman in Cellardyke, Fife, husband of Margaret Boytar, died on 14 July 1830. [Kilrenny gravestone, Fife]

REID, DAVID, a grocer, was admitted as a burgess and guilds-brother of Cupar, Fife, on 10 October 1808. [CuBR]

REID, DUNCAN, was admitted as a burgess and guilds-brother of Cupar, Fife, in 1810. [CuBR]

REID, JAMES, a minister in Beath, was admitted as a burgess and guilds-brother of Dunfermline on 30 June 1791. [DM]

REID, JOHN, son of John Reid a weaver burgess, was admitted as a burgess of Dunfermline on 18 September 1795. [DM]

REID, JOHN, a skipper in Limekilns, Fife, died in 1803. [Rosyth gravestone, Fife]

REID, JOHN, a skipper in Anstruther Easter, Fife, son of John Reid a cordiner there, a sasine in 1782. [NRS.RS.Fife.425]; husband of Janet Thomson, born 1716, died 1783, died in 1805.[Anstruther Easter gravestone]

REID, WILLIAM, son of John Reid, was admitted as a burgess of Dunfermline on 4 July 1797. [DM]

REID, WILLIAM, in the Service of the East India Company, father of William Reid, born 1821, died 22 April 1825. [Creich gravestone, Fife]

REID, Sir WILLIAM, born 25 April 1791, son of Reverend James Reid in Kinglassie, Fife, the Governor of Malta, died in January 1859. [SGS]

RENWICK, Major EDWARD, son of Henry and Jane Renwick, died in Santander, Spain, on 12 January 1836. [St Andrews gravestone, Fife]

RICHARD, JAMES WALTER, born 1844, a banker in Hoblee, died in Bombay, India, on 12 July 1881. [St Andrews gravestone, Fife]

RICHARD, MELVILLE, son of William Richard and his wife Catherine Bell, master of the Jane of Glasgow, died at Black River, Jamaica, on 26 July 1817. [St Andrews gravestone, Fife]

RICHARDSON, JOHN, son of Andrew Richardson a burgess, was admitted as a burgess of Dunfermline on 26 September 1804. [DM]

RICK, HENRY, son of Charles Rick a weaver burgess, was admitted as a burgess of Dunfermline on 4 July 1797. [DM]

RIDDELL, DAVID, son of Andrew Riddell a coppersmith burgess, was admitted as a burgess of Dunfermline on 18 May 1792. [DM]

RIDDLEY, JOHN, a horse-hirer, was admitted as a burgess of Dunfermline on 27 April 1792. [DM]

RINTOUL, JOHN, son-in-law of Peter Westwood a burgess, was admitted as a burgess of Dunfermline on 28 February 1810. [DM]

RITCHIE, ALEXANDER, a skipper in Burntisland, Fife, testament, 26 October 1808, Comm. St Andrews. [NRS]

RITCHIE, ANDREW, a grocer, son-in-law of Thomas Morrison a shoemaker burgess, was admitted as a burgess of Dunfermline on 12 December 1809. [DM]

RITCHIE, JOHN, a master in the Royal Navy, testament, 1809, Comm. St Andrews, Fife. [NRS]

RITCHIE, JOHN, born 1795, master of the Caledonia of Dundee, died in Elsinore, Denmark, on 18 June 1842. [St Andrews gravestone, Fife]

ROB, JAMES, the tacksman of Coustoun, Fife, was admitted as a burgess of Dunfermline on 14 April 1797. [DM]

ROBERTSON, Reverend ANDREW, was admitted as a burgess and guilds-brother of Dunfermline on 30 June 1791. [DM]

ROBERTSON, ANDREW, a manufacturer from Glasgow, was admitted as a burgess and guilds-brother of Dunfermline on 6 June 1792. [DM]

ROBERTSON, GEORGE, son of George Robertson a weaver burgess, was admitted as a burgess of Dunfermline on 2 March 1792. [DM]

ROBERTSON, GEORGE, a weaver, was admitted as a burgess of Cupar, Fife, on 26 September 1795 [CuBR]

ROBERTSON, GEORGE ADAM LYON, born 19 December 1832 in Lindores, Fife, son of James Robertson and his wife Janet Edmiston, died in South Yarra, Melbourne, Victoria, Australia, on 24 March 1882. [Abdie gravestone, Fife]

ROBERTSON, JAMES, a minister, was admitted as a burgess and guilds-brother of Dunfermline on 6 June 1792. [DM]

ROBERTSON, JAMES, a weaver, son-in-law of Peter Ireland a wright burgess, was admitted as a burgess of Dunfermline on 25 October 1797. [DM]

ROBERTSON, JAMES, a baker, was admitted as a burgess of Kirkcaldy, Fife, on 2 February 1798. [KBR]

ROBERTSON, JAMES, born 1796 in Fife, a merchant in Charleston, South Carolina, was naturalised there on 5 April 1823. [NARA.M1183.1]

ROBERTSON, JAMES, in New York, a sasine, 1826. [NRS.Dysart.Fife, 2.112]

ROBERTSON, JAMES, born 5 February 1835 in Lindores, son of James Robertson and his wife Janet Edmiston, died in South Yarra, Melbourne, Victoria, Australia, on 20 June 1893. [Abdie gravestone, Fife]

ROBERTSON, JOHN, a weaver, son-in-law of William Anderson a weaver burgess, was admitted as a burgess of Dunfermline on 4 July 1793. [DM]

ROBERTSON, JOHN, a bookseller, was admitted as a burgess of Kirkcaldy, Fife, on 9 July 1801. [KBR]

ROBERTSON, JOHN, born 1834, eldest son of Thomas Robertson in Colinsburgh, Fife, a sergeant of the 42nd Highland Regiment, [the Black Watch], died at Camp Cheerat, East India, on 8 September 1867. [FJ]

ROBERTSON, METHVEN, in Millbury, Worcester, USA, nephew and heir of Margaret Methven, widow of Robert Whyte in Leslie, Fife, 1856. [NRS.S/H]

ROBERTSON, PETER, an innkeeper, was admitted as a burgess of Cupar, Fife, on 25 November 1795. [CuBR]

ROBERTSON, ROBERT, born 1722, formerly a master mariner in the Royal Navy, later a merchant in Kirkcaldy, died on 24 March 1796, husband of Margaret Bachop. [Kirkcaldy gravestone, Fife]

ROBERTSON, ROBERT, son of David Robertson a baker burgess, was admitted as a burgess of Dunfermline on 4 July 1797. [DM]

ROBERTSON, SAMUEL, from New York, drowned in the wreck of the brig Petrel of Stockton off Boarhills, Fife, on 30 November 1839. [Boarhills gravestone, Fife]

ROBERTSON, WILLIAM, a wright, son of Thomas Robertson, was admitted as a burgess of Cupar, Fife, on 4 October 1796. [CuBR]

ROBERTSON, WILLIAM, son-in-law of Andrew Ingles a mason burgess, was admitted as a burgess of Dunfermline on 4 April 1797. [DM]

ROBERTSON, WILLIAM, a sloop-master in Dubbyside, Fife, testament, 1817, Comm. St Andrews. [NRS]

ROBSON, WILLIAM, a mariner who was buried in Crail on 26 August 1799. [SBC.28]

RODGER, AGNES BERRY, wife of John Johnston a farmer in Chatham, Canada, grand-daughter and heir of Andrew Rodger, a weaver and merchant in St Monance, who died 19 February 1819, also, heir to her great grandfather David Rodger a merchant in St Monance, Fife, 1851. [NRS.S/H]

RODGER, DAVID, born 1766, a mariner in Kilrenny, Fife, husband of Elizabeth Watson, died on 30 December 1811. [Kilrenny gravestone]

RODGER, JAMES, a skipper in St Andrews, Fife, testament, 1807, Comm. St Andrews. [NRS]

ROGER, JAMES, born 1767, minister at Dunbog for 44 years, died 29 November 1849, husband of Jane Haldane, died 18 April 1825, parents of Reverend Charles Rogers, born 18 April 1825, died in Edinburgh on 17 September 1890. [Dunbog gravestone, Fife]

RODGER, ROBERT, a baker, was admitted as a burgess of Kirkcaldy, Fife, on 21 June 1799. [KBR]

RODGER, WILLIAM, a merchant, was admitted as a burgess of Kirkcaldy, Fife, on 27 July 1801. [KBR]

ROLLAND, ANDREW, son of Andrew Rolland a labourer burgess, was admitted as a burgess of Dunfermline on 5 July 1797. [DM]

ROLLAND, MICHAEL, a weaver, was admitted as a burgess of Kirkcaldy, Fife, on 22 September 1792. [KBR]

ROLLAND, ROBERT, a weaver, son-in-law of John Ingles a weaver burgess, was admitted as a burgess of Dunfermline on 7 July 1791. [DM]

ROLLO, FRANCIS, born 1843, son of Alexander Rollo and his wife Elizabeth Duncan, was drowned at St Petersburg, Russia, on 28 June 1863. [Balmerino gravestone, Fife]

ROLLO, JOHN, a weaver, was admitted as a burgess of Cupar, Fife, on 28 September 1795. [CuBR]

ROSE, JOHN, factor for the Earl of Elgin, was admitted as a burgess and guilds-brother of Dunfermline on 4 September 1793. [DM]

ROSS, HELEN, wife of James Watson, a ship's carpenter in America, heir to her father David Ross a wright in Anstruther, Fife, 1839. [NRS.S/H]

ROSS, JAMES, born 1754, tenant of Stravithie Cottow, died 7 April 1830, husband of [1] Janet Studd who died on 16 June 1789, and [2] Janet Brown, [1763-1831]. [Dunino gravestone, Fife]

ROSS, JOHN, a smith in Crossford, Fife, formerly an apprentice to Thomas Thomson a smith, was admitted as a burgess of Dunfermline on 25 May 1810. [DM]

ROXBURGH, ANDREW, son of John Roxburgh a beadle, was admitted as a burgess of Dunfermline on 31 July 1790. [DM]

ROXBURGH, JANET, born 1785, wife of William Ellis of Netherton, from Dunfermline, Fife, to New York in 1857, died at Bayside, Long Island, on 18 August 1865. [PJ]

ROXBURGH, JOHN, son of Andrew Roxburgh a weaver burgess, was admitted as a burgess of Dunfermline on 23 September 1806. [DM]

ROXBURGH, THOMAS, son of John Roxburgh a beadle, was admitted as a burgess of Dunfermline on 4 August 1787. [DM]

ROY, ALEXANDER, born 10 October 1843, son of Alexander Roy and his wife Elizabeth Keeler, a cabinetmaker who died in Lithgow, New South Wales, Australia, on 4 October 1893. [Dunfermline gravestone, Fife]

ROY, JAMES, born in Fife, died in Augusta, Georgia, on 25 July 1818. [Colonial Museum and Savana Advertiser, 4.8.1818]

RUSSELL, DAVID, son-in-law of James Main a burgess, was admitted as a burgess of Dunfermline on 26 September 1804. [DM]

RUSSELL, DAVID, second son of David Russell and his wife Mary Black in St Andrews, died on Mesopotamia Estate, Jamaica, on 24 April 1867. [St Andrews gravestone, Fife]

RUSSEL, GEORGE, son of Robert Russel in Tailabout, was admitted as a burgess of Cupar, Fife, on 18 September 1809. [CuBR]

RUSSELL, HENRY, son of Henry Russell a merchant, was admitted as a burgess of Dunfermline on 27 March 1810. [DM]

RUSSELL, JAMES, a mariner in Philadelphia, Pennsylvania, a sasine, 1791. [NRS.RS.Fife.2943]

RUSSELL, JAMES, son of Henry Russell a merchant, was admitted as a burgess of Dunfermline on 4 August 1803. [DM]

RUSSELL, JOHN, son of John Main a wright, was admitted as a burgess of Dunfermline on 4 August 1803. [DM]

RUSSELL, JOHN, son of Henry Russell a merchant, was admitted as a burgess of Dunfermline on 4 August 1803. [DM]

RUSSELL, ROBERT, son of Henry Russell a merchant, was admitted as a burgess of Dunfermline on 27 March 1810. [DM]

RUSSEL, ROBERT, son of Robert Russel in Tailabout, was admitted as a burgess of Cupar, Fife, on 18 September 1809. [CuBR]

RUSSELL, ROBERT, son of David Russell and his wife Mary Black, died in Jamaica on 5 August 1867. [St Andrews gravestone, Fife]

RUSSELL, WILLIAM, a sailor in Dysart, Fife, testament, 1816, Comm. St Andrews. [NRS]

RUSSELL, Lieutenant Colonel of the 7th Native Infantry Regiment in the Service of the East India Company, died 10 July 1839. [Pittenweem gravestone, Fife]

RUTHERFORD, DAVID, born 1812 in Kirkcaldy, Fife, died at 49 Horatio Street, New York, on 27 August 1871. [S.8807]

RUTHERFORD, D. G., agent in Dunfermline, Fife, for the Commercial Bank of Scotland in 1849. [POD]

RUTHERFORD, EBENEZER, a merchant, was admitted as a burgess of Kirkcaldy, Fife, on 14 June 1802. [KBR]

RUTHERFORD, JOHN, a merchant, was admitted as a burgess of Kirkcaldy, Fife, on 1 February 1797. [KBR]

RUTHERFORD, LUMSDEN, a skipper in Dysart, Fife testament, 10 March 1803, Comm. St Andrews. [NRS]

RUTHERFORD, ROBERT, a merchant, was admitted as a burgess of Kirkcaldy, Fife, on 21 September 1797. [KBR]

RUTHERFORD, THOMAS, born 1766 in Kirkcaldy, Fife, son of Thomas Rutherford and Janet Meldrum, educated at Glasgow University, emigrated to Virginia in 1784, settled in Richmond, Va., married Sallie Winston in 1790, died in 1852. [BAF][TSA]

ST CLAIR, ARCHIBALD, 'long resident in California', died in Newport, Fife, on 14 August 1874. [Forgan gravestone, Fife]

SALMON, DAVID, master of the Hope of Anstruther, Fife, trading between St Petersburg, Russia, and Dundee in 1818. [NRS.E504.11.21]

SALMON, DAVID, a skipper in East Wemyss, Fife, testament, 1819, Comm. St Andrews. [NRS]

SALMOND, JOHN BROWN, born 9 October 1843, died at Point de Galle, Ceylon, on 29 September 1867. [Dunnikier gravestone, Fife]

SAMPSON, GEORGE LESLIE, born 2 April 1798 in Kirkcaldy, Fife, son of George Sampson and his wife Euphemia Leslie, emigrated to America in 1816, an iron founder in Richmond, Virginia, later in New York, died at 122 Columbia Street, Brooklyn, N.Y., on 2 January 1866. [ANY]

SAMPSON, JOHN, a skipper in Leith, son-in-law of bailie Thomas Wardlaw, was admitted as a burgess of Dunfermline, on 26 May 1796. [DM]

SANDILANDS, ROBERT, born 1790, son of George Sandilands of Nuthill, Fife, was apprenticed to John Tod, admitted to the Society of Writers on 26 May 1818, husband of Mary Style in 1829, was the assistant judge at Nassau, New Providence, the Bahamas, died on 20 May 1872. [WS]

SANDS, PETER, son-in-law of John Davidson a weaver burgess, was admitted as a burgess of Dunfermline, on 4 July 1797. [DM]

SANG, DAVID, born 1800, husband of Helen Brodie, died in New York on 15 October 1842. [St Andrews gravestone, Fife]

SCOTLAND, GEORGE, son of Henry Scotland a burgess, was admitted as a burgess of Dunfermline, on 25 March 1805. [DM]

SCOTLAND, HENRY, son of Henry Scotland a burgess, was admitted as a burgess of Dunfermline, on 23 May 1797. [DM]

SCOTT, ANDREW, an innkeeper, was admitted as a burgess of Cupar, Fife, on 19 April 1796. [CuBR]

SCOTT, ANDREW, a hairdresser, was admitted as a burgess of Cupar, Fife, on 16 April 1801. [CuBR]

SCOTT, DAVID, a weaver, son of Robert Scott, was admitted as a burgess of Cupar, Fife, on 8 October 1799. [CuBR]

SCOTT, ELIZABETH DOW, born 1824, daughter of William Scott and his wife Elizabeth Bell, died in Melbourne, Victoria, Australia, in 1916. [Ferry Port on Craig gravestone, Fife]

SCOTT, HENRY, from Cupar, Fife, emigrated via Belfast aboard the Perseverance bound for New York in 1811. [NWI]

SCOTT, JAMES, a weaver, was admitted as a burgess of Kirkcaldy, Fife, on 22 September 1792. [KBR]

SCOTT, JAMES, a shoemaker, was admitted as a burgess of Crail, Fife, in 1807. [CBR]

SCOTT, JOHN, son of John Scott, a schoolmaster, [1750-1813], and his wife Jane French, [1750-1816], died in America. [Monimail gravestone, Fife]

SCOTT, JOHN, [1831-1911], and his wife Ann Bruce, [1827-1910], parents of Annie Scott or Gerrard who died in North Dakota on 15 June 1903. [Aberdour gravestone, Fife]

SCOTT, MARGARET, married John Craig in Tranent, East Lothian, in 1804, he later joined the Durham Militia and abandoned her. In 1815 she found him working as a baker in Auchtermuchty, Fife, she was awarded a decreet of adherence by the court. [NRS.CC8.6.120]

SCOTT, ROBERT, was admitted as a burgess and guilds-brother of Cupar, Fife, in October 1810. [CuBR]

SCOTT, ROBERT, born 1831, son of William Scott and his wife Elizabeth Bell, died in Cape Town, Cape of Good Hope, South Africa, in 1890/ [Ferry-port-on-Craig gravestone, Fife]

SCOTT, PHILIP, a skipper in Pittenweem, Fife, on 9 July 1787, [NRS.B3.7.5]; in 1803, [NRS.B60.8.1]; testament, 7 March 1805, Comm. StAndrews.[NRS]

SCOTT, ROBERT, a manufacturer and flax spinner in Cupar, Fife, trading with Archangel, Russia, between 1826 and 1837. [NRS.CS96.785]

SCOTT, ROBERT, born 1831, son of William Scott and his wife Elizabeth Bell, died in Cape Town, Cape of Good Hope, South Africa, in 1890. [Ferry Port on Craig gravestone, Fife]

SCOTT, THOMAS, a mason, was admitted as a burgess of Kirkcaldy, Fife, on 25 June 1802. [KBR]

SCOTT, WALTER, born 1772, son of John Scott in Letham, Fife, a partner in the merchant company Scott and Clerk in Camden, South Carolina, died in August 1798. [EA.3648.383]

SETON, WILLIAM, born 24 April 1746, son of John Seton and his wife Elizabeth, in Parbroath, Fife, emigrated to America in 1758, married Rebecca Curzon in Baltimore, Maryland, in 1767, a merchant and a banker, a Loyalist, died on 9 June 1798. [SOP]

SHANKS, MARY, second daughter of Archibald Shanks in the State of New York, died in Cupar, Fife, in October 1819. [S.144.19]

SHANKS, THOMAS, a skipper in Pittenweem, Fife, master and manager of the Pittenweem Sea Box Society on 14 January 1793. [NRS.B3.7.5]

SHEPHERD, ALEXANDER, born 1843, son of James Shepherd and his wife Cecilia Wilson, died in Havannah, Cuba, on 11 July 1858. [Balmerino gravestone, Fife]

SHEPHERD, DAVID, son of William Shepherd, [1792-1832], in Dunfermline, emigrated to New Orleans, Louisiana, before 1847. [Dunfermline gravestone, Fife]

SHEPHERD, JOHN, a wheelwright, was admitted as a burgess of Kirkcaldy, Fife, on 15 June 1791. [KBR]

SHEPHERD, ROBERT, born 1810, died in Calcutta, India, on 10 September 1839. [Burntisland gravestone, Fife]

SHEPHERD, THOMAS, was admitted as a burgess and guilds-brother of Cupar, Fife, on 4 October 1809. [CuBR]

SHIELDS, HENRY, born 1778 in Fife, son of Henry Shields a farmer in Coaltown of Balmull, a grocer in Charleston, S.C., was naturalised in South Carolina on 6 October 1813. [NARA.M1183.1]

SHOOLBRED, GEORGE, born 1745, died in May 1814, husband of Anne Ramsay, born 1749, died in April 1795. [Dunbog gravestone, Fife]

SHOOLBRED, JOHN, a tailor in Chamber Street, Dunfermline, was admitted as a burgess of Dunfermline, on 13 March 1810. [DM]

SIM, ROBERT, a labourer, son of John Sim in Buckbin, was admitted as a burgess of Dunfermline, on 4 July 1797. [DM]

SIMONS, Mrs MARGARET A., bon 19 May 1804 in Fife, wife of Dr Thomas Simons, died in Charleston, South Carolina, on 17 October 1837. [Old Scots gravestone, Charleston]

SYMSON, ANDREW, a weaver, son of Robert Symson a wright burgess, was admitted as a burgess of Dunfermline, on 16 August 1793. [DM]

SIMPSON, DAVID, a shoemaker, was admitted as a burgess of Crail in 1807. [CBR]

SIMSON, HENRY BRUCE, of the Bengal Civil Service, second son of George Simson of Pitcorthie, Fife, married Madge Vincent, daughter of Lieutenant General Vincent of the Bengal Army, in Poonah, Bengal, India, on 14 April 1857. [FJ]

SYMSON, JAMES, son of Robert Symson a wright burgess, was admitted as a burgess of Dunfermline, on 22 September 1797. [DM]

SIMSON, JAMES, born 1821, son of Robert Simson and his wife Elizabeth Carstairs, died in Brim Brim, Victoria, Australia, on 15 August 1858. [Anstruther West gravestone, Fife]

SIMSON, JOHN, a merchant, was admitted as a burgess of Cupar, Fife, on 1 December 1801. [CuBR]

SIMPSON, JOHN, born 1800 in Fife, third son of George Simpson, died in Calcutta, India, on 19 September 1820. [South Park gravestone, Calcutta]

SIMPSON, JOHN, son of James Simpson, [1770-1852], and his wife Christian Whyte, [1777-1841], died in New Orleans, Louisiana, on 16 October 1843. [Kirkcaldy gravestone, Fife]

SIMPSON, MARY, widow of Principal McCormick of St Andrews University, died in Kilconquhar Manse, Fife, on 5 September 1822. [SM.90.632]

SIMPSON, ROBERT, a tailor, was admitted as a burgess of Kirkcaldy, Fife, on 14 February 1797. [KBR]

SIMPSON, Colonel, born in Fife, an officer of the Royal Imperial Marines, died in Trieste on 3 July 1820. [SM.86.287]

SINCLAIR, ALEXANDER, from Culross, Fife, Commander of HMS Fancy, inventory, 1812, Comm. Dunblane. [NRS]

SINCLAIR, JAMES, a weaver, son of Joseph Sinclair at the bleachfield a weaver burgess, was admitted as a burgess of Dunfermline, on 11 September 1791. [DM]

SINCLAIR, ROBERT, son of Joseph Sinclair a weaver burgess, was admitted as a burgess of Dunfermline, on 23 September 1802 [DM]

SIVEWRIGHT, JOHN HENRY, born 1847, third son of C. K. Sivewright in Burntisland, Fife, died in Orange Valley, Falmouth, Jamaica, on 23 August 1865. [Falmouth gravestone, Jamaica]

SKINNER, JAMES, son of George Skinner and his wife Jean Laing, died in Madras, India, on 26 September 1846. [St Andrews gravestone, Fife]

SKINNER, WILLIAM, a baker, son of William Skinner, was admitted as a burgess of Kirkcaldy, Fife, on 13 September 1794. [KBR]

SKINNER, WILLIAM, born 10 April 1839, died in St Louis, USA, on 23 August 1869. [Bendochy gravestone, Kirkcaldy, Fife]

SKIRVING, ROBERT, a merchant, was admitted as a burgess of Kirkcaldy, Fife, on 3 August 1801. [KBR]

SLIGHT, Reverend PATRICK, was admitted as a burgess and guilds-brother of Dunfermline, on 6 June 1792. [DM]

SMALL, DAVID, a merchant, was admitted as a burgess of Crail, Fife, in 1792. [CBR]

SMART, JOHN, a merchant, was admitted as a burgess of Cupar, Fife, on 3 December 1801. [CuBR]

SMART, ROBERT, was admitted as a burgess of Cupar, Fife, on 4 October 1809. [CuBR]

SMART, THOMAS, a weaver, son of Peter Smart a weaver burgess, was admitted as a burgess of Dunfermline, on 4 July 1797. [DM]

SMIETON, HENRY, son-in-law of Robert Chrystie a tailor burgess, was admitted as a burgess of Dunfermline, on 1 August 1792. [DM]

SMIETON, JAMES, a weaver, son-in-law of Alexander Hart a weaver burgess, was admitted as a burgess of Dunfermline, on 16 September 1791. [DM]

SMITH, ARCHIBALD, a mason in Gauldry, Fife, father of Archibald Smith, born 1858, died in South Africa, on 12 December 1894. [PJ]

SMITH, DALRYMPLE, a tailor, was admitted as a burgess of Kirkcaldy, Fife, on 4 April 1792. [KBR]

SMITH, DAVID, born 1732, a minister in St Andrews, Fife, in 1764, settled in Londonderry, Nova Scotia, in 1771, a Presbyterian minister there from 1771 until his death in 1795. [HPC]

SMITH, DAVID, born 1796, son of Robert Smith and his wife Janet Henderson, a merchant in New Orleans, Louisiana, died in Perth on 27 December 1882. [Logie gravestone, Fife]

SMITH, GEORGE, a saddler, was admitted as a burgess of Kirkcaldy, Fife, on 21 February 1797. [KBR]

SMITH, JAMES, a teacher, was admitted as a burgess and guilds-brother of Dunfermline, on 22 September 1791. [DM]

SMITH, JAMES, a tailor from Edinburgh, was admitted as a burgess and guilds-brother of Dunfermline, on 26 September 1791. [DM]

SMITH, JAMES, second son of John Smith in Largo, Fife, died in Savannah, Georgia, on 25 October 1817. [S.51.18]

SMITH, JAMES, born 1838, son of Peter Smith and his wife Christina Swinton, died in Auckland, New Zealand, on 1 November 1872. [Largo gravestone, Fife]

SMITH, JOHN, son of John Smith a saddler burgess, was admitted as a burgess of Dunfermline, on 20 August 1802. [DM]

SMITH, JOHN, born 1793, son of David Smith and Euphame Ramsay, died in Jamaica in 1820. [Dunnikeir gravestone, Fife]

SMITH, JOHN, born 1832, daughter of John and Helen Smith, died in Bangalore, Mysore, India, on 13 November 1894. [Saline gravestone, Fife]

SMITH, JOHN, born 1840, son of William D. Smith and his wife Janet Morrison, died in Nickerie, Surinam, on 16 May 1872. [Burntisland gravestone, Fife]

SMITH, JOHN J., and his wife Isabella Walker, parents of Thomas Walker Smith, born 1852, died in Moulmein, Burma, on 5 February 1879. [St Andrews gravestone, Fife]

SMITH, MARGARET, born 1839, daughter of John and Helen Smith, died in Bangalore, Mysore, India, on 8 July 1889. [Saline gravestone, Fife]

SMITH, PETER, a flaxdresser from Leven, Fife, was admitted as a burgess of Dunfermline, on 5 May 1793. [DM]

SMITH, PETER, in Halifax, Nova Scotia, son and heir of Peter Smith, a miller at Lundin Mill, Fife, died 3 September 1871. [NRS.S/H]

SMITH, ROBERT, born 1798, son of David Smith and his wife Euphame Murray, died in Calcutta, India, on 28 September 1844. [Dunnikier gravestone, Fife]

SMITH, ROBERT, born 1837, son of Peter Smith and his wife Christina Swinton, died in Auckland, New Zealand, on 30 August 1882. [Largo gravestone, Fife]

SMITH, Dr THOMAS, born 1763 in Largo, Fife, '57 years in the West Indies, survivor of the Carib Wars', died on St Vincent on 3 January 1840. [FH.3.1.1840]

SMITH, WILLIAM, a tinplate-worker from Edinburgh, was admitted as a burgess and guilds-brother of Dunfermline, on 22 March 1794. [DM]

SMITH, WILLIAM, a merchant, was admitted as a burgess of Kirkcaldy, Fife, on 21 February 1797. [KBR]

SORLIE, WILLIAM, born 1756, a skipper, died on 16 May 1803. [Tulliallan gravestone, Fife]

SPARK, Captain, master of the Chieftain of Kirkcaldy, from Cromarty with passengers bound for Quebec in 1835. [QM.4.8.1835]

SPEARS, CATHERINE, born 1809, daughter of Robert Spears of Kininmont and his wife Margaret Millie, died in Paris, France, on 21 May 1827. [Cupar gravestone, Fife]

SPEARS, JAMES, born 1740 in Fife, died in Charleston, South Carolina, on 24 January 1808. [Old Scots gravestone, Charleston]

SPEARS, THOMAS, born 5 May 1807 in Kirkcaldy, son of Robert Spears of Kininmont and his wife Margaret Millie, died in Calcutta, India, on 22 December 1845. [Scotch Burial Ground gravestone, Calcutta][Cupar gravestone]

SPEARS, THOMAS, born 1814, son of Thomas Spears and his wife Margaret Roy, died in Rangoon, Burma, on 14 February 1868. [Kirkcaldy gravestone]

SPENCE, ALEXANDER, a wright, was admitted as a burgess of Dunfermline, on 18 May 1810. [DM]

SPENCE, ANDREW BISHOP, probably from Dunfermline, an accountant in Philadelphia, Pennsylvania, a deed, 1819. [NRS.RD5.175.635]

SPENCE, ANDREW GREIG, second son of George Spence in Dunfermline, Fife, settled in New Jersey, died in New York on 16 June 1853. [EEC.22460]

SPENCE, GEORGE, a manufacturer, was admitted as a burgess of Dunfermline, on 13 April 1797. [DM]

SPENS, JAMES, born 1737 in Fife, died on 24 January 1805. [Old Scots gravestone, Charleston, South Carolina.

SPENCE, JAMES, a manufacturer, was admitted as a burgess of Dunfermline, on 4 July 1797. [DM]

SPITTAL, GEORGE, son-in-law of John Wilson, was admitted as a burgess of Dunfermline, on 28 October 1791. [DM]

STAIG, JAMES, a land labourer, was admitted as a burgess of Crail, Fife, in 1794. [CBR]

STALKER, DANIEL, son of Daniel Stalker a burgess, was admitted as a burgess of Dunfermline, on 26 March 1806. [DM]

STALKER, JAMES, a weaver, son-in-law of Daniel McEwan a weaver burgess, was admitted as a burgess of Dunfermline, on 23 March 1792. [DM]

STALKER, JOHN, a carter, son-in-law of James Birrell a gardener in Haddington, East Lothian, was admitted as a burgess of Dunfermline, on 3 December 1796. [DM]

STALKER, WILLIAM, jr., a skipper, was admitted as a burgess of Crail, Fife, in 1805. [CBR]

STARK, ROBERT, a writer in Cupar, Fife, was admitted as a burgess and guildsbrother of Dunfermline, on 14 November 1791. [DM]

STARK, ROBERT, Captain of the Dunfermline Volunteers, was admitted as a burgess of Dunfermline, on 6 June 1798. [DM]

STEDMAN, ANDREW, a weaver, son of Robert Stedman a weaver, was admitted as a burgess of Dunfermline, on 4 April 1797. [DM]

STEEDMAN, JAMES, son of Robert Steedman a weaver burgess, was admitted as a burgess of Dunfermline, on 24 September 1802. [DM]

STEDMAN, JOHN, a weaver, son of William Stedman a weaver burgess was admitted as a burgess of Dunfermline, on 4 July 1797. [DM]

STEDMAN, PETER, son of George Stedman, was admitted as a burgess of Dunfermline, on 5 May 1796. [DM]

STEEDMAN, ALEXANDER, a sailor in Aberdour, Fife, husband of Catherine Wemyss in 1794. [NRS.S/H]

STEEDMAN, JAMES, son of Robert Steedman a weaver burgess, was admitted as a burgess of Dunfermline, on 24 September 1802. [DM]

STEEL, JOHN, eldest son of Mrs Steel in Cupar, Fife, died in Westmoreland, Jamaica, on 27 August 1857. [FJ]

STEEN, ROBERT, in Loanside, was admitted as a burgess of Dunfermline, on 5 May 1796. [DM]

STENHOUSE, ADAM, son of Adam Stenhouse a burgess, was admitted as a burgess of Dunfermline, on 21 March 1805. [DM]

STENHOUSE, DAVID, a Lieutenant of the Dunfermline Volunteers, was admitted as a burgess and guilds-brother of Dunfermline, on 5 June 1797. [DM]

STENHOUSE, DAVID, son of Adam Stenhouse a brewer burgess, was admitted as a burgess of Dunfermline, on 11 August 1802. [DM]

STENHOUSE, JOHN, a weaver, son of George Stenhouse a weaver burgess, was admitted as a burgess of Dunfermline, on 24 June 1793. [DM]

STENHOUSE, JOHN, a Second Lieutenant of the Dunfermline Volunteers, was admitted as a burgess and guilds-brother of Dunfermline, on 4 June 1801. [DM]

STENHOUSE, JOHN, son-in-law of Thomas Anderson of Headwell, was admitted as a burgess of Dunfermline, on 1 April 1808. [DM]

STENHOUSE, MOWBRAY, son of William Stenhouse a baker in Dunfermline, Fife, was apprenticed to Robert Laing, a saddler in Edinburgh, for six years, in 1792. [ERA]

STENHOUSE, ROBERT, son of John Stenhouse a brewer burgess, was admitted as a burgess of Dunfermline, on 11 March 1791. [DM]

STEVENSON, WILLIAM, son of Andrew Stevenson a weaver burgess, was admitted as a burgess of Dunfermline, on 27 August 1791. [DM]

STEWART, HELEN, in St Andrews, Fife, heir to her father James Stewart a merchant in Mexico, later in Wellhall, Hamilton, Lanarkshire, 1851. [NRS.S/H]

STEWART, JAMES, born 1757 in Fife, to America in 1778 as a soldier of the 74th Regiment, fought at the Battle of Castine, Maine, died in St Patrick's parish, Charlotte County, New Brunswick, on 14 December 1835. [NBC.19 December 1835]

STEWART, JAMES AFFLECK, son of Robert and Ann Stewart, a Captain of the 11th Hussars, died in Brantford, Canada West, on 15 May 1867. [Forgan gravestone, Fife]

STEWART, JOHN, was admitted as a burgess of Cupar, Fife, in 1811]. [CuBR]

STEWART, ROBERT, born 1752 in Fife, died in Calcutta, India, on 11 March 1811. [North Park gravestone, Calcutta]

STEWART, ROBERT, born 1817, son of Alexander Stewart and his wife died on Isle de France, [Mauritius], on 19 January 1845. [Burntisland gravestone, Fife]

STEWART, SAMUEL, born 1813, son of Alexander Stewart and his wife Christine Scott, died on a voyage bound for Bombay, India, on 12 April 1866. [Burntisland gravestone, Fife]

STEWART, WILLIAM, born 1768, from Inverkeithing, Fife, died in Stamford, Upper Canada, on 3 July 1838. [GM.ns.10.343][AJ.4728]

STEWART, WILLIAM, a candlemaker, was admitted as a burgess of Kirkcaldy, Fife, on 18 October 1798. [KBR]

STIRLING, ALEXANDER, son of Alexander Stirling a weaver burgess, was admitted as a burgess of Dunfermline, on 13 August 1796. [DM]

STIRLING, ANDREW, born 1818, son of John Stirling of Eldershaw and his wife Elizabeth Willing, died in Western Australia, on 5 November 1844. [St Andrews gravestone, Fife]

STIRLING, JAMES, son of Alexander Stirling a weaver burgess, was admitted as a burgess of Dunfermline, on 4 July 1797. [DM]

STIRLING, JOHN, born 1836, son of John Stirling of Eldershaw and his wife Elizabeth Willing, died at Inkerman, Crimea, Russia, in 1854. [St Andrews gravestone, Fife]

STOBIE, DAVID, a land labourer, was admitted as a burgess of Crail, Fife, in 1805. [CBR]

STOBIE, GEORGE, son of Thomas Stobie, [1752-1841], and his wife Margaret Condie, [1774-1852], died in Ebobicok, Western Canada, on 15 October 1855. [Portmoak gravestone, Fife]

STRACHAN, WILLIAM, a manufacturer, son-in-law of David Black a manufacturer burgess, was admitted as a burgess of Dunfermline, on 4 July 1797. [DM]

STRANG, ALEXANDER, born 1771, son of Thomas Strang and his wife Margery Bruce, a skip. [Kilrenny gravestone]per who died on 30 December 1835

STRONG, JOHN, 'an old sailor' in Pittenweem, Fife, on 21 March 1798. [NRS.B3.7.5]

STRUTHERS, ESTHER C. W., daughter of Reverend James Struthers in Edinburgh, and grand-daughter of Robert Briggs, MD, University of St Andrews, married Reverend George Burns, DD, a minister in St John, New Brunswick, in St Andrews, Fife, on 6 August 1827. [NBC.15.9.1827]

STRUTHERS, JOHN, a wright, was admitted as a burgess of Kirkcaldy, Fife, on 18 February 1803. [KBR]

STUART, HUGH, a writer from Edinburgh, was admitted as a burgess of Dunfermline, on 26 September 1791. [DM]

STUART, JOHN, son of John Stuart a weaver burgess, was admitted as a burgess of Dunfermline, on 7 August 1795. [DM]

SWAN, ANDREW, a currier, was admitted as a burgess of Kirkcaldy, Fife, on 15 March 1791. [KBR]

SWAN, ANDREW, grandson of Andrew Swan in Kennaway, Fife, settled at the Cape of Good Hope, South Africa, before 1846. [NRS.S/H]

SWAN, JAMES, son of George Swan a tailor burgess, was admitted as a burgess of Dunfermline, on 4 July 1797. [DM]

SWAN, JAMES, born 1837, son of James Swan and his wife Jean McRitchie, died in Melbourne, Victoria, Australia, on 17 April 1855. [Cupar gravestone, Fife]

SYME, DAVID, a wright, son of David Syme a wright burgess, was admitted as a burgess of Dunfermline, on 11 September 1792. [DM]

SYME, GEORGE, born 1764, died in Osnaburgh, [Dairsie], in 1834. [Dairsie gravestone, Fife]

SYME, WILLIAM, a gardener, son of William Syme, was admitted as a burgess of Dunfermline, on 5 July 1797. [DM]

TAIT, WILLIAM, an Advocate, was admitted as a burgess and guildsbrother of Dunfermline, on 13 April 1797. [DM]

TAIT, WILLIAM, from Kilconquhar, Fife, died in Philadelphia, Pennsylvania, on 18 February 1867. [S.7385]

TAYLOR, ANDREW, agent in Cupar, Fife, for the Clydesdale Bank in 1849. [POD]

TAYLOR, JOHN, born 1767 in Fife, a mariner who was naturalised in South Carolina on 18 March 1799. [NARA.M1183.1]

TAYLOR, JOHN, a grocer, was admitted as a burgess of Kirkcaldy, Fife, on 18 November 1793. [KBR]

TAYLOR, JOHN, born 1788, son of John Taylor, a Colonel in the Service of the East India Company in Bengal, India, died in St Andrews on 26 July 1841. [St Andrews gravestone, Fife]

TAYLOR, ROBERT, former apprentice to J. Stenhouse a baker burgess, was admitted as a burgess of Dunfermline, on 22 June 1801. [DM]

TAYLOR, ROBERT, with his wife Elisabeth Henderson, and their family, emigrated from Auchtermuchty, Fife, to Canada around 1832. [SG.39.2/8]

TAYLOR, THOMAS, a shoemaker, was admitted as a burgess of Crail, Fife, in 1800. [CBR]

TAYLOR, Captain THOMAS, born 1799, died in Bahia, Brazil, in 1850. [Anstruther Easter gravestone, Fife]

TAYLOR, WILLIAM, a shoemaker, was admitted as a burgess of Crail, Fife, in 1799. [CBR]

TEMPLEMAN, THOMAS, son of Thomas Templeman a weaver burgess, was admitted as a burgess of Dunfermline, on 8 August 1796. [DM]

TENNANT, WILLIAM, born 1789 in Fife, died at St John, New Brunswick, on 14 January 1831. [CG.19.1.1831]

THOM, GEORGE, a skipper in Charlestown, Fife, testament, 16 April 1814, Comm. St Andrews. [NRS]

THOMS, JOHN HENDRY, born 1842, son of George Thoms, [1801-1857], a merchant, and his wife Elizabeth Watt Hendry, [1819-1892], died in San Francisco, California, on 25 November 1883. [Forgan gravestone, Fife]

THOMSON, ALEXANDER, a weaver, son of Henry Thomson a burgess, was admitted as a burgess of Dunfermline, on 20 June 1793. [DM]

THOMPSON, ALEXANDER, born 1810 in Kirkcaldy, Fife, died in India on 16 March 1840. [Scotch Burial Ground gravestone, Calcutta, India]

THOMSON, ANDREW, minister of Balmerino, Fife, was admitted as a burgess and guilds-brother of Dunfermline, on 27 October 1790. [DM]

THOMSON, ANDREW, a smith, son-in-law of David Martin a grocer, was admitted as a burgess of Dunfermline, on 22 December 1809. [DM]

THOMSON, ANDREW, son of Andrew Thomson of Kinloch, Fife, was admitted to the Society of Writers to the Signet on 2 June 1809, died in Saratoga, New York, in August 1831. [WS]

THOMSON, ANDREW, born 1789, son of John Thomson of Prior Letham, Fife, was admitted to the Society of Writers to the Signet on 23 June 1820, who died in Florida on 14 July 1841. [WS]

THOMSON DAVID, born 1813, a classical teacher in the Seminary in Dundee, died 23 May 1852. [Dunbog gravestone, Fife]

THOMSON, GEORGE, son-in-law of James Blaik a tailor burgess, was admitted as a burgess of Dunfermline, on 4 July 1806. [DM]

THOMSON, GEORGE, a contractor, son-in-law of Henry Scotland a burgess, was admitted as a burgess of Dunfermline, on 8 December 1809. [DM]

THOMSON, GEORGE EBENEZER, born 1839, son of George Thomson and his wife Josephine Watt, died in Shanghai, China, in 1864. [St Andrews gravestone, Fife]

THOMSON, JAMES, son of James Thomson a weaver burgess, was admitted as a burgess of Dunfermline, on 14 September 1792. [DM]

THOMSON, JAMES, a wright, a former apprentice to Thomas Bonnar a wright burgess, was admitted as a burgess of Dunfermline, on 21 August 1802. [DM]

THOMSON, JAMES, son-in-law of Thomas Colville, was admitted as a burgess of Dunfermline, on 4 August 1803. [DM]

THOMSON, JAMES, born 1823, son of David Thomson and his wife Ann Spens, died at Fitzroy Town Hall, Melbourne, Victoria, Australia. [St Andrews gravestone, Fife]

THOMSON, JOHN, a tailor, was admitted as a burgess of Dunfermline, on 2 October 1801. [DM]

THOMSON, JOHN, a mariner in Crail, Fife, testament, 1819, Comm. St Andrews. [NRS]

THOMSON, JOHN, born 7 January 1819 in St Andrews, Fife, a student at St Andrews University, later a minister in England, New England, New Brunswick, and New York by 1851, returned to Scotland in 1875, died 1 March 1893. [ANY]

THOMSON, JOHN, messenger at arms, St Andrews, Fife, 1849. [POD]

THOMSON, JOHN THOMAS, born 1836, son of George Thomson and his wife Josephine Watt, died in Shanghai, China, in 1864. [St Andrews gravestone, Fife]

THOMSON, JOSEPH, born 19 June 1789, a skipper who died at sea on 13 July 1827. [Tulliallan gravestone, Fife]

THOMSON, PETER, son of John Thomson in Burntisland, Fife, died in Kingston, Jamaica, in 1803. [GM.72.374]

THOMSON, PETER, a baker in Kirkcaldy, Fife, father of William Thomson, who died in Poughkeepsie, New York, on 26 September 1874. [S.9744]

THOMSON, ROBERT, born 1731, a skipper, died on 1 January 1815. [Aberdour gravestone, Fife]

THOMSON, WILLIAM, son of William Thomson a smith in Easter Gellits, Fife, was admitted as a burgess of Dunfermline, on 25 September 1793. [DM]

THOMSON, WILLIAM, a mariner in Crail in 1800. [SBC.30]

THOMSON, WILLIAM, a merchant in Cupar, Fife, 1822. [NRS.SC20.4.31]

THOMSON, Lieutenant Colonel WILLIAM ADAM ANSTRUTHER, born 4 December 1822, husband of Isabella Steel, died in Calcutta, India, on 3 August 1865. [Kilconquhar gravestone, Fife]

THOMSON, WILLIAM HENRY, born 1840, son of George Thomson and his wife Josephine Watt, died in Victoria, Australia, in 1871. [St Andrews gravestone, Fife]

THOMSON, WILLIAM, son of Peter Thomson a baker in Kirkcaldy, Fife, died in Poughkeepsie, New York, on 26 September 1874. [S.9744]

TODD, GEORGE, born 1808, son of David Todd and his wife Christine Fair, died in Bengal, India, on 22 July 1876. [Cupar gravestone, Fife]

TODD, HENRY, second son of Richard Todd in Balcormie, Fife, died in Boston, Massachusetts, on 25 December 1852. [FH]

TODD, JOHN, a grocer, was admitted as a burgess of Kirkcaldy, Fife, on 9 July 1801. [KBR]

TOD, JOHN, a brewer, son of Robert Tod a farmer in Chapelwell, was admitted as a burgess of Dunfermline, on 7 September 1808. [DM]

TODD, JOHN, born 1807 in Anstruther, Fife, died in Brooklyn, New York, in 1877. [S.10506] [EFR]

TOD, JOHN, born 1828, eldest son of Captain Robert Tod in Kirkcaldy, Fife, was drowned at Kati Kati, Bay of Plenty, New Zealand, on 29 April 1885. [S.13091]

TOD, ROBERT, tenant in Leckerston, son of David Tod a tenant in Blairathie, was admitted as a burgess of Dunfermline, on 10 March 1804. [DM]

TOD, ROBERT, son of Robert Tod tenant in Leckesrston, was admitted as a burgess of Dunfermline, on 4 April 1804. [DM]

TOD, ROBERT, a merchant, was admitted as a burgess of Cupar, Fife, in 1811. [CuBR]

TOSH, RICHARD, son of Andrew Tosh a writer in Kirkcaldy, Fife, a writer, was admitted as a burgess of Kirkcaldy, Fife, on 29 September 1796. [KBR]; a messenger there, was admitted as a Notary Public on 21 December 1799. [NRS.SC20.50.27.1221]

TOSH, THOMAS, born 1794, son of Thomas Tosh and his wife Sophia Henderson, died in Calcutta, India, on 24 November 1859. [Carnbee gravestone, Fife]

TRAILL, WILLIAM, a messenger at arms, Kirkcaldy, Fife, 1849. [POD]

TULLOS, JAMES, a weaver, was admitted as a burgess of Cupar, Fife, on 29 September 1795. [CuBR]

TULLIS, ROBERT, a stationer, was admitted as a burgess of Cupar, Fife, in 1802. [CuBR]

TULLIS, ROBERT WILSON, from Pittenweem, Fife, married Annie Thompson Greig, daughter of David Greig, grand-daughter of

Alexander Reddie a merchant in Dunfermline, Fife, in New York on 22 July 1871. [S.8751]

TURCAN, WILLIAM, born 1826, son of George Turcan and his wife Agnes Mercer, died in Rio de Janeiro, Brazil, on 2 March 1852. [Tulliallan gravestone, Fife]

TURNBULL, ANDREW, son of David Turnbull a merchant burgess, was admitted as a burgess of Dunfermline, on 26 June 1798. [DM]

TURNBULL, DAVID, son of David Turnbull, [1720-1788], and his wife Janet Whyte, [1731-1784], died in Jamaica. [Dunfermline gravestone, Fife]

TURNBULL, DAVID, a shoemaker, son of James Turnbull a burgess, was admitted as a burgess of Dunfermline, on 5 July 1797. [DM]

TURNBULL, GEORGE, a tailor, son of James Turnbull a burgess, was admitted as a burgess of Dunfermline, on 5 July 1797. [DM]

TURNBULL, JAMES, a weaver, son of James Turnbull, , was admitted as a burgess of Dunfermline, on 4 July 1797. [DM]

TURNBULL, JAMES, son of Robert Turnbull a burgess and guilds-brother, was admitted as a burgess and guilds-brother of Dunfermline, on 14 December 1798. [DM]

TURNBULL, ROBERT, a day labourer in Crossford, Fife, son-in-law of Patrick Wilson late tenant in Kestock, was admitted as a burgess of Dunfermline, on 21 December 1792. [DM]

TURNBULL, ROBERT, son of David Turnbull, was admitted as a burgess of Dunfermline, on 26 June 1798. [DM]

TURNER, JAMES, a grocer, was admitted as a burgess and guilds-brother of Cupar, Fife, on 9 October 1808. [CuBR]

URE, JOHN, a day labourer in Dowlock, son-in-law of Alexander Black a burgess, was admitted as a burgess of Dunfermline, on 16 September 1795. [DM]

URQUHART, JOHN, born 1770, died 2 June 1866, husband of Ann Scott, born 1772, died 12 February 1831. [Dunbog gravestone, Fife]

WADDELL, ALEXANDER, a builder in Burntisland, Fife, father of George C. W. Waddell, born 1869, died in Denver City, Colorado, on 8 January 1899. [S.17343]

WADDEL, JAMES, jr., was admitted as a burgess of Cupar, Fife, in 1807. [CuBR]

WALKER, ALEXANDER, son of Livingston Walker, [1734-1810], and his wife Mary Ballingall, [1730-1808], a shipbuilder in Grenada before 1810. [Dunino gravestone, Fife]

WALKER, ALEXANDER, son of Samuel Walker, [1797-1870], and his wife Elspeth Oswald, [1799-1874], died in Australia aged 47. [St Andrews gravestone, Fife]

WALKER, ANDREW, a shoemaker, was admitted as a burgess of Cupar, Fife, on 2 October 1810. [CuBR]

WALKER, ANDREW, born 1819, son of Andrew Walker and his wife Isobel Landale, died in Buninyong, Victoria, Australia, in August 1887. [Cupar gravestone, Fife]

WALKER, ARCHIBALD, a writer in Edinburgh, son of David Walker a merchant in Strathmiglo, Fife, was admitted as a Notary Public on 21 December 1799. [NRS.SP2.36.297]

WALKER, DAVID, a saddler from Cupar, Fife, died in Jamaica on 2 December 1838. [FH.27.6.1839]

WALKER, DAVID, late in Westmoreland, Jamaica, died in Leslie, Fife, on 26 July 1841. [AJ.4883]

WALKER, ELIZABETH, born 1817, daughter, wife of James L. Main, of William Walker in Luthrie, Fife, died at Little Falls, Minneapolis, on 1 December 1889. [PJ]

WALKER, ISOBEL, born 4 September 1771, daughter of Reverend William Walker and his wife Margaret Manderston in Collessie, Fife, married Paul Samuels MD, in Jamaica, died there on 9 February 1853. [F.5.135]

WALKER, JAMES, a flax-dresser, son-in-law of James Wilson the town clerk, was admitted as a burgess of Dunfermline, on 17 August 1792. [DM]

WALKER, JAMES, son of George Walker a wright burgess, was admitted as a burgess of Dunfermline, on 16 September 17975 [DM]

WALKER, JAMES, was admitted as a burgess of Crail, Fife, in 1800. [CBR]

WALKER, JAMES, a writer, was admitted as a burgess and guildsbrother of Cupar, Fife, on 6 October 1809. [CuBR]

WALKER, JAMES, son of John Walker, died in Lisbon, Portugal, on 4 December 1841. [St Andrews gravestone, Fife]

WALKER, JOHN, a merchant, was admitted as a burgess of Kirkcaldy, Fife, on 22 February 1794. [KBR]

WALKER, JOHN, in Blebo Mill, Fife, was admitted as a burgess of Cupar, Fife, on 6 October 1809. [CuBR]

WALKER, MARGARET, daughter of John Walker a leather merchant in St Andrews, died in New York on 30 August 1849. [St Andrews gravestone] [SG.1857]

WALKER, Mrs MARGARET, widow of John Walker, died in New York in August 1875. [St Andrews gravestone]

WALKER, NEIL, born in Leven, Fife, married Barbara Murray in Leven on 13 January 1821, emigrated to USA in 1844, settled in Frye Village, Andover, Massachusetts. [PJ.4.3.1871]

WALKER, PARTHINIA, daughter of John Walker, and widow of John Carmichael, died in New York in 1855. [St Andrews gravestone, Fife]

WALKER, ROBERT, born 24 January 1772 in Cupar, Fife, died in South Carolina on 30 July 1833. [Old Scots gravestone, Charleston]

WALKER, WALTER, agent in St Andrews, Fife, for the Clydesdale Bank in 1849. [POD]

WALKER, WILLIAM, born 1768, son of Reverend William Walker and his wife Margaret Manderston in Collessie, Fife, an attorney who died in Jamaica in 1799. [F.5.135]

WALKER, WILLIAM, was admitted as a burgess of Cupar, Fife, on 4 October 1809. [CuBR]

WALKER, WILLIAM, born 1810, second son of Andrew Walker, a leather merchant, and his wife Isobel Landale, in Cupar, died in Williamsburgh, New York, on 15 September 1853. [FH] [Cupar gravestone, Fife]

WALLACE, ANDREW, born 1737, a skipper, died on 26 October 1812. [St Andrews gravestone, Fife] [NRS.B65.18.1-90]

WALLACE, ANDREW, son of Andrew Wallace a farmer in Balgreen, Fife, died at Whitehills, Oakland County, Michigan, on 30 December 1842. [FH.9.3.1842]

WALLACE, ARCHIBALD, a writer from St Andrews, Fife, died in Quebec on 21 June 1832. [FH.23.8.1832]

WALLACE, DAVID, a baker, was admitted as a burgess of Crail, Fife, in 1807. [CBR]

WALLACE, DAVID, born 21 August 1791 in Pittenweem, husband of Helen...., late resident of Calcutta, India, died in Pittenweem on 17 December 1839. [Pittenweem gravestone, Fife]

WALLACE, DAVID, son of David Wallace of Balmeadowside and his wife Margaret Meldrum, died in Copmanhurst on the Clarence River, New South Wales, Australia, on 19 November 1845. [Creich gravestone, Fife]

WALLACE, ROBERT, son of Laurence Wallace and his wife Cecilia Taylor, died in New Zealand on 3 February 1845. [St Andrews gravestone, Fife]

WALLACE, THOMAS, born 1794, son of William and Esther Wallace, died on the Amazon, Brazil, on 12 October 1863. [St Andrews gravestone, Fife]

WALLS, JAMES, a mason, was admitted as a burgess of Dunfermline, on 27 November 1809. [DM]

WALLS, JOHN, in Pitliver, Fife, son-in-law of Robert Hutton tenant in Urquhart, was admitted as a burgess of Dunfermline, on 24 April 1793. [DM]

WALLS, MARGARET, born 1817 in Beath, Fife, wife of Alexander Scott, died in Toronto, Ontario, on 1 September 1887. [FFP]

WALLS, WILLIAM, son of John Walls in Pitliver, Fife, was admitted as a burgess of Dunfermline, on 29 June 1793. [DM]

WANN, JOHN, born 1838, son of Alexander Wann and his wife Janet Johnston, died in Calcutta, India, on 7 November 1859. [Balmerino gravestone, Fife]

WARDLAW, DAVID, ashoemaker, son of James Wardlaw a shoemaker burgess, was admitted as a burgess of Dunfermline, on 4 July 1797. [DM]

WARDLAW, JAMES, son of James Wardlaw a weaver burgess, was admitted as a burgess of Dunfermline, on 21 September 1793. [DM]

WARDLAW, JOHN, a skipper in Inverkeithing, Fife, son and heir of Henry Wardlaw a wright in Limekilns, Fife, in 1798. [NRS.S/H]

WARDLAW, JOHN, son-in-law of Adam Low the former Provost, was admitted as a burgess of Dunfermline, on 2 April 1803. [DM]

WARDLAW, MARION A., died in Toronto, Ontario, on 12 January 1855. [FJ]

WARDLAW, ROBERT, a farmer in Myrehall, son of Robert Wardlaw tenant in Killernie a burgess, was admitted as a burgess of Dunfermline, on 23 November 1796. [DM]

WARDLAW, THOMAS, tenant in Killerney, son of Robert Wardlaw a tenant there, was admitted as a burgess of Dunfermline, on 19 July 1799. [DM]

WATSON, ALEXANDER, born 1795 in Fife, a planter who was naturalised in South Carolina on 17 October 1825. [NARA.M1183.1]

WATSON, DAVID, born 1820, a shipmaster in Anstruther, Fife, husband of Anne Sharp, died when bound for St George Sound, Western Australia, on 27 November 1870. [Kilrenny gravestone, Fife]

WATSON, JAMES, a fisherman, was admitted as a burgess of Crail, FIfe, in 1794. [CBR]

WATSON, JAMES, a weaver, was admitted as a burgess of Cupar, Fife, on 28 September 1801. [CuBR]

WATSON, JAMES, a shoemaker, was admitted as a burgess of Cupar, Fife, on 28 September 1801. [CuBR]

WATSON, JAMES, born 1782 in Fife, a mariner who was naturalised in South Carolina on 16 March 1807. [NARA.M1183.1]

WATSON, JOHN, a wright, was admitted as a burgess of Cupar, Fife, on 4 October 1808. [CuBR]

WATSON, PATRICK, a sailor in St Andrews, Fife, in 1797. [NRS.S/H]

WATSON, ROBERT, a skipper in Pittenweem, master and manager of the Pittenweem Sea Box Society on 13 January 1794. [NRS.B3.7.5]

WATSON, ROBERT, son of Andrew Watson and his wife Ann Hutton, died in St Vincent, British West Indies, in 1803. [St Andrews gravestone]

WATSON, ROBERT, born 1849, son of David Watson and his wife Anne Sharp in Anstruther, died in Adelaide, South Australia, on 7 April 1869. [Kilrenny gravestone, Fife]

WATSON, THOMAS, son of Alexander Watson and his wife Agnes Key, died in India on 13 August 1802. [St Andrews gravestone, Fife]

WATSON, THOMAS, born 1765, a mariner in Cellardyke, Fife, died on 17 December 1831. [Kilrenny gravestone, Fife]

WATSON, THOMAS, a skipper in Crail in 1793. [NRS.B10.14.641]

WATT, JAMES, in Auchtertool, Fife, son-in-law of Alexander Hutton a shoemaker burgess, was admitted as a burgess of Dunfermline, on 25 September 1795. [DM]

WATT, JAMES, master of the Renown of Kirkcaldy from Leith bound for Quebec and Montreal in 1817 and in 1819. [NRS.E504.22.76, 84]

WATT, JAMES, born 1838, son of George Watt and his wife Helen Meikle, died in Kansas on 29 March 1884. [Dunfermline gravestone, Fife]

WEBSTER, JANET, eldest daughter of Andrew Webster at Scoonie Bridge, Leven, Fife, married Robert Yule from New Orleans, Louisiana, in Edinburgh on 21 July 1873. [EC.27707]

WEBSTER, ROBERT FARQUHAR, born 24 September 1826 in Balgarvie, Fife, died in Algiers, Algeria, on 25 February 1889. [Cupar gravestone, Fife]

WELSH, CHARLES, a baker, was admitted as a burgess of Cupar, Fife, on 21 October 1795. [CuBR]

WELSH, JOHN, born 1827, son of Walter Welsh, died in Mobile, Alabama, on 8 April 1860. [Auchtertool gravestone]

WELCH, ROBERT, a manufacturer, son of Andrew Welch, was admitted as a burgess of Cupar, Fife, on 16 October 1804. [CuBR]

WELSH, THOMAS, born 1770 in Dysart, Fife, died in Charleston, South Carolina, on 12 August 1796. [Old Scots gravestone, Charleston]

WEMYSS, JOHN, a merchant, was admitted as a burgess of Kirkcaldy, Fife, on 23 November 1793. [KBR]

WEMYSS, ROBERT, born 1796, Commander of Bombay Castle in India, died in Edinburgh on 19 February 1860. [St Andrews gravestone, Fife]

WEMYSS, WILLIAM, of Cuttlehill, was admitted as a burgess and a guildsbrother of Dunfermline, on 3 January 1795. [DM]

WEST, JAMES, born 11 June 1791, son of John West in Kirkcaldy, Fife, emigrated to America in 1815, settled in Wood County, West Virginia, died in Fox township, Ohio. [OVG.125]

WEST, Captain JAMES, in Burntisland, Fife, father of John West, 1858, who died in Sourabaya, in the East Indies, in 1876. [FFP.10.2.1877]

WESTON, ROBERT, son of Thomas Weston a wright burgess, was admitted as a burgess of Dunfermline, on 4 July 1797. [DM]

WESTWATER, GEORGE, master of the Mollie of Anstruther in 1793, 1802. [NRS.SC20.36.16; SC20.33.15]

WESTWOOD, CATHERINE, third daughter of Hugh Westwood in Torryburn, Fife, married Robert Thomson, in Portland, Maine, on 10 March 1870. [DP]

WESTWOOD, J., from Torryburn, Fife, a merchant in New York in 1796. [NRS.CS17.1.15/403]

WESTWOOD, P., from Torryburn, Fife, a merchant in New York in 1796. [NRS.CS17.1.15/403]

WESTWOOD, PETER, a merchant, was admitted as a burgess of Crail, Fife, in 1792. [CBR]

WESTWOOD, ROBERT, son of Peter Westwood a weaver burgess, was admitted as a burgess of Dunfermline, on 7 October 1799. [DM]

WESTWOOD, ROBERT, son of William Westwood a weaver burgess, was admitted as a burgess of Dunfermline, on 17 August 1802. [DM]

WHYTE, ALEXANDER, a wheelwright, son-in-law of James Anderson a smith burgess, was admitted as a burgess of Dunfermline, on 30 December 1808. [DM]

WHITE, ANDREW, born 1769, died 15 May 1841, father of Thomas White in Petersburg, Virginia. [Abbotshall gravestone, Kirkcaldy]

WHYTE, ANDREW, a wright, was admitted as a burgess of Kirkcaldy, Fife, on 14 April 1791. [KBR]

WHYTE, JAMES, a merchant, son of William Whyte, was admitted as a burgess of Kirkcaldy, Fife, on 17 January 1793. [KBR]

WHYTE, JAMES, Supervisor of the Excise in Dunfermline, was admitted as a burgess and guilds-brother of Dunfermline, on 17 July 1804. [DM]

WHYTE, JAMES, born 1777 in Kirkcaldy, Fife, via Liverpool bound for Mississippi to be a merchant, was naturalised in New York on 6 January 1819. [NY Court of Common Pleas] [NRS.CS17.1.25/45]

WHITE, JOHN, born 1800 in Abercrombie, Fife, '50 years in Montreal', died there on 14 December 1885. [PJ]

WHITE, JOHN W., born 1820 in Dunfermline, Fife, a merchant in Brooklyn, New York, died in Plainfield, New Jersey, on 30 May 1890. [FFP]

WHYTE, ROBERT, a merchant, son of William Whyte, was admitted as a burgess of Kirkcaldy, Fife, on 17 January 1793. [KBR]

WHITE, ROBERT, a weaver, son of John White, was admitted as a burgess of Cupar, Fife, on 30 September 1795. [CuBR]

WHITE, THOMAS, son of Andrew White, [1769-1841], settled in Petersburg, Virginia. [Kirkcaldy gravestone, Fife]

WHITE, WILLIAM, a slater, was admitted as a burgess of Cupar, Fife, on 4 October 1808. [CuBR]

WHYTE, WILLIAM, born 1766, a skipper, died on 31 March 1838. [Anstruther Easter gravestone]

WILKIE, ANDREW, died in Melbourne, Victoria, Australia, in July 1863. [Cults gravestone]

WILKIE, JAMES, a gardener, was admitted as a burgess of Dunfermline, on 29 December 1791. [DM]

WILKIE, JAMES, born 1788 in Fife, died in Halifax, Nova Scotia, on 21 August 1832. [AR.25.8.1832]

WILKIE, JOHN, a Captain of the 49th Regiment of Bengal Native Infantry, died in Dinapur, India, on 10 August 1824. [Cults gravestone, Fife]

WILKIE, JOHN, MD, Inspector General of Hospitals, died in Nynee-Tal, Bengal, India, on 23 May 1870. [Cults gravestone, Fife]

WILKIE, THOMAS, born 1825 in Strathmiglo, Fife, a stonemason, son of Thomas Wilkie, [died 1827], and his wife Margaret Kay, [died 1859], emigrated to USA in 1884, settled in Eau Claire, Wisconsin, died there on 29 June 1899. [PJ]

WILKIE, THOMAS, born 1849 in Strathmiglo, Fife, son of Thomas Wilkie, was killed in Eau Claire, Wisconsin, on 7 January 1884. [PJ]

WILLIAMSON, ALEXANDER, a skipper, was admitted as a burgess of Kirkcaldy, Fife, on 4 October 1794. [KBR]

WILLIAMSON, ALEXANDER, born 1845, son of George Williamson in Kirkcaldy, Fife, died in Hamburg, Germany, on 1 May 1878. [FH]

WILLIAMSON, ANDREW, a weaver, was admitted as a burgess of Cupar, Fife, on 26 September 1795. [CuBR]

WILLIAMSON, DAVID, an Advocate, was admitted as a burgess and guilds-brother of Dunfermline, on 26 September 1796. [DM]

WILLIAMSON, Reverend DAVID, born in Fife, for 30 years pastor of the Associate congregation in Whitehaven, died in New York on 13 May 1821. [EA]

WILLIAMSON, DAVID, born 1818, from Clunie, Newburgh, Fife, died in Port Albert, South Australia, on 26 August 1884. [S.128851]

WILLIAMSON, J., messenger at arms, Auchtermuchty, Fife, 1849. [POD]

WILLIAMSON, JAMES, son of Andrew Williamson a shoemaker burgess, was admitted as a burgess of Dunfermline, on 26 February 1793. [DM]

WILLIAMSON, JAMES, a meal-seller, was admitted as a burgess of Kirkcaldy, Fife, on 7 October 1796. [KBR]

WILLIAMSON, JAMES, jr, a grocer, was admitted as a burgess of Kirkcaldy, Fife, on 14 June 1802. [KBR]

WILLIAMSON, JAMES S., born in Cowdenbeath, Fife, married Annie E. Todd, daughter of Samuel A. Todd, in St Louis, Missouri, in January 1883. [PJ.10.2.1883]

WILLIAMSON, MARGARET, born 1831, wife of Daniel Stewart, died in Acapulco, Mexico, on 3 September 1853. [Abbotshall gravestone, Kirkcaldy, Fife]

WILLIAMSON, ROBERT, son of John Williamson a shoemaker burgess, was admitted as a burgess of Dunfermline, on 2 February 1790. [DM]

WILLIAMSON, THOMAS, a mariner and owner of the Balcomie of Kinghorn, Fife, testament, 26 October 1803, Comm. St Andrews. [NRS]

WILLIAMSON, THOMAS, son of William Williamson a saddler, was admitted as a burgess of Dunfermline, on 1 December 1809. [DM]

WILLIAMSON, WILLIAM, a saddler from Edinburgh, was admitted as a burgess of Dunfermline, on 27 June 1794. [DM]

WILLIAMSON, Captain, master of the Minerva of Anstruther from Greenock bound for Quebec on 10 April 1820. [NRS.E504.15.129]

WILLIS, GEORGE, son of Thomas Willis in Kirkcaldy, Fife, died in Jamaica on 16 December 1824. [EA]

WILLIS, THOMAS, a merchant, was admitted as a burgess of Kirkcaldy, Fife, on 13 September 1794. [KBR]

WILSON, ADAM, son of Provost John Wilson, was admitted as a burgess of Dunfermline, on 9 April 1790. [DM]

WILSON, ADAM, son of Thomas Wilson a weaver burgess, was admitted as a burgess of Dunfermline, on 3 August 1791. [DM]

WILSON, ADAM, a writer in Edinburgh, son of John Wilson a mason burgess, was admitted as a burgess of Dunfermline, on 28 October 1791. [DM]

WILSON, ALEXANDER, jr., a vintner, was admitted as a burgess of Kirkcaldy, Fife, on 7 August 1792. [KBR]

WILSON, ALEXANDER, a tobacconist, was admitted as a burgess of Kirkcaldy, Fife, on 18 January 1793. [KBR]

WILSON, ANDREW, born 1820, son of James Wilson and his wife Elizabeth Whyte, died in Demerara on 19 April 1856. [Newburgh gravestone, Fife]

WILSON, ANN, eldest daughter of Thomas Wilson a carpenter in St Monance, Fife, married Thomas Dodds of HM Naval Yard, in Victoria, Vancouver, Canada, on 20 November 1866. [FA]

WILSON, DAVID, a mason, son of William Wilson a slater burgess, was admitted as a burgess of Dunfermline, on 4 July 1797. [DM]

WILSON, DAVID, born 1794, son of David Wilson and his wife Margaret Duncan, died in Calcutta, India, in 1815. [Carnbee gravestone, Fife]

WILSON, DAVID, a painter, was admitted as a burgess of Kirkcaldy, Fife, on 23 July 1802. [KBR]

WILSON, GEORGE, son of George Wilson a farmer in Lundin, Fife, a burgess, was admitted as a burgess of Dunfermline, on 23 November 1797. [DM]

WILSON, GEORGE, a currier, was admitted as a burgess of Crail, Fife, in 1800. [CBR]

WILSON, GEORGE, a slater in Torryburn, Fife, was admitted as a burgess of Dunfermline, on 15 May 1810. [DM]

WILSON, JAMES, a member of the Pittenweem Sea Box Society in 1791. [NLS.B3.7.5]

WILSON, JAMES, was admitted as a burgess of Cupar, Fife, on 26 September 1795. [CuBR]

WILSON, JAMES, was admitted as a burgess of Cupar, Fife, on 4 October 1809. [CuBR]

WILSON, JAMES, a smith, was admitted as a burgess of Dunfermline, on 3 January 1810. [DM]

WILSON, JAMES, born 1822, from Lesliehead, Burntisland, Fife, died in London, Ontario, on 2 May 1898. [PJ]

WILSON, JAMES, born 1828, son of James Wilson and his wife Elizabeth Whyte, died in Australia in 1848. [Newburgh gravestone, Fife]

WILSON, Dr JAMES ATKINSON, born 1829, son of John Wilson and his wife Janet McLachlan in Dunfermline, died in Old Calabar, West Africa, on 4 April 1851. [FJ.908][W.124][Dunfermline gravestone, Fife]

WILSON, JOHN, a vintner was admitted as a burgess of Dunfermline, on 15 September 1791. [DM]

WILSON, JOHN, son of Thomas Wilson a weaver burgess, was admitted as a burgess of Dunfermline, on 5 July 1797. [DM]

WILSON, JOHN, son-in-law of David Sime a wright burgess, was admitted as a burgess of Dunfermline, on 9 November 1797. [DM]

WILSON, JOHN, son of Patrick Wilson a burgess, was admitted as a burgess of Dunfermline, on 3 August 1803. [DM]

WILSON, JOHN, jr., son of John Wilson sr., was admitted as a burgess of Dunfermline, on 27 September 1804. [DM]

WILSON, JOHN, son of David Wilson a burgess, was admitted as a burgess of Dunfermline, on 20 March 1805. [DM]

WILSON, JOHN, son-in-law of John Ingls a burgess, was admitted as a burgess of Dunfermline, on 26 March 1805. [DM]

WILSON, JOHN, a smith, was admitted as a burgess of Cupar, Fife, in 1806. [CuBR]

WILSON, JOSEPH, son of John Wilson in Nether Mill, Fife, was admitted as a burgess of Dunfermline, on 20 March 1810. [DM]

WILSON, RICHARD, son-in-law of John Brunton a farmer in Pitdinne a burgess, was admitted as a burgess of Dunfermline, on 6 August 1803. [DM]

WILSON, ROBERT, a weaver, son-in-law of Alexander Gibb a wright burgess, was admitted as a burgess of Dunfermline, on 14 August 1792. [DM]

WILSON, ROBERT, son of George Wilson a farmer in Lundin, Fife, was admitted as a burgess of Dunfermline, on 23 November 1797. [DM]

WILSON, ROBERT, born 2 April 1736, an apprentice under Dr Martin Eccles of the Royal College of Physicians in Edinburgh, a surgeon apothecary in Burntisland, Fife, emigrated via London to South Carolina as an indentured servant in 1753, married Ann Chisholm in Charleston, S.C. on 8 April 1759, died on 26 August 1815. [BLG.2978] [LGR] [SA]

WILSON, ROBERT, a wright, was admitted as a burgess of Kirkcaldy, Fife, on 9 February 1792. [KBR]

WILSON, ROBERT, born 1801, son of Alexander Wilson and his wife Helen Kellock, died in Bombay, India, on 20 January 1859. [Burntisland gravestone, Fife]

WILSON, ROBERT, born 1846, third son of David Wilson from Cowdenbeath, Fife, died in Brooklyn, New York, in 1909. [DJ.6.11.1909]

WILSON, THOMAS, born 1779, son of Dr Charles Wilson and his wife Elizabeth Stark, a Lieutenant General in the Service of the East India Company, died in Wales in April 1856. [St Andrews gravestone, Fife]

WILSON, THOMAS, born 1802, son of Alexander Wilson and his wife Helen Kellock, died in Melbourne, Victoria, Australia, in 1852. [Burntisland gravestone, Fife]

WILSON, THOMAS, a mason from Fife, settled on Prince Edward Island, Canada, a letter 1818. [NLS.acc.6981]

WILSON, WILLIAM, son of John Wilson, was admitted as a burgess of Dunfermline, on 10 July 1804. [DM]

WILSON, WILLIAM, born 1811, son of Alexander Wilson and his wife Helen Kellock, died in Bombay, India, on 7 February 1852. [Burntisland gravestone, Fife]

WISHART, ANDREW, in Dunbar, Pennsylvania, heir to his grandfather William Sutherland, a carter in Burntisland, Fife who died in January 1846, re property in Largs, Ayrshire. [NRS.S/H]

WISHART, DAVID, a weaver, son-in-law of David Ferguson a weaver burgess, was admitted as a burgess of Dunfermline, on 23 August 1791. [DM]

WISHART, WILLIAM, a sailor in Crail, Fife, son and heir of Robert Wishart there, in 1790. [NRS.S/H]

WISHART, WILLIAM, a sailor in Burntisland, Fife, testament, 22 May 1805, Comm. St Andrews. [NRS]

WOOD, JOHN, agent in Colinsburgh, Fife, for the Commercial Bank of Scotland in 1849. [POD]

WOOD, WILLIAM, born 1766, a fisherman in Cellardyke, Fife, died on 23 February 1820. [Kilrenny gravestone, Fife]

WOTHERSPOON, WILLIAM, in Charlestown, North Queensferry, Fife, letters, 1801. [NRS.GD1.517.243]

WRIGHT, ANDREW, born 1835, son of Duncan Wright and his wife Helen Baird, died in New York on 1 February 1873. [Tulliallan gravestone, Fife]

WRIGHT, DAVID, son of Charles Wright tenant in Foodie, Fife, a writer in St Andrews, was admitted as a Notary Public. [NRS.NP2.34.225]

WRIGHT, GEORGE TOD, born 1823, son of Reverend George Wright and his wife Mary Blundell, in the Service of the East India Company in the Straits Settlements, Malaya, died on 5 January 1883. [St Andrews gravestone, Fife]

WRIGHT, JAMES MCINTYRE, a shoemaker in Cupar, Fife, married Christian Walker in Edinburgh, emigrated to Canada in 1801, settled at English River, Quebec, in 1802. [CP]

WRIGHT, ROBERT, from Limekilns, Fife, a carpenter in America, testament, 1829, Edinburgh. [NRS.SC70.1.352]

WYLLIE, ANDREW, a perfumer and hatmaker, was admitted as a burgess of Kirkcaldy, Fife, on 18 November 1793. [KBR]

YELTON, JOHN, a merchant in Kincardine-on-Forth, trading with Gothenburg, Sweden, between 1798 and 1809. [NRS.CS96.58]

YOUNG, DAVID, an innkeeper, was admitted as a burgess of Crail, Fife, in 1800. [CBR]

YOUNG, DAVID, and his wife Barbara Forgan, were parents of John Young, born 1851, a banker in Melbourne, Victoria, Australia, died 1 November 1879. [St Andrews gravestone, Fife]

YOUNG, GEORGE, born 1804, son of Nathaniel Young a shipmaster, died in St Petersburg, Russia, on 3 October 1844. [Ferry Port on Craig gravestone, Fife]

YOUNG, Captain GEORGE, master of the brig Gowrie of Dundee, died in Acapulco, Mexico, on 30 October 1852, husband of Mary Oswald. [Kingsbarns gravestone, Fife]

YOUNG, JOHN, born 1843, fourth son of John Young in Anstruther, Fife, died in Moville, USA, on 17 September 1873. [EFR]

YOUNG, MARGARET, relict of Alexander Cruickshank schoolmaster in Forgan, Fife, testament, December 1799, Comm. Brechin. [NRS]

YOUNG, PETER, son of John Young and his wife Helen Walls, died in Honduras on 18 December 1808. [Burntisland gravestone, Fife]

YOUNG, THOMAS, a sailor in Kinghorn, Fife, husband of Margaret Baxter in 1792. [NRS.S/H]

YOUNG, THOMAS, a skipper in Kinghorn, Fife, husband of Marion Bowman, testament, 1795, Comm. Edinburgh. [NRS]

YOUNGER, ANDREW, born 1820, son of John Younger and his wife Margaret Horne, died in Buenos Ayres, Argentina, on 26 December 1844. [St Monance gravestone, Fife]

YOUNGER, JAMES, born 1844 in Ceres, Fife, a shipbuilder who settled in Philadelphia, Pennsylvania, in 1872, died there on 27 April 1894. [FH.16.5.1894]

YOUNGER, JOHN, a baker, servant o Peter Anderson a baker in Dunfermline, was admitted as a burgess of Dunfermline, Fife, on 20 February 1798. [DM]

YOUNGER, THOMAS, a sailor in Leven, Fife, in 1796. [NRS.S/H]

YOUNGER, THOMAS, from Leven, Fife, a Lieutenant of the Royal Navy, testament, 1819, Comm. St Andrews. [NRS]

YULE, DAVID, a manufacturer at the Bridgend of Ceres, Fife, was admitted as a burgess of Cupar, Fife, on 1 August 1809. [CuBR]

www.ingramcontent.com/pod-product-compliance
Lightning Source LLC
Chambersburg PA
CBHW052059230426
43662CB00036B/1698